Co-operative Membership and Globalization

Co-operative Membership and Globalization

New Directions in Research and Practice

Edited by Brett Fairbairn
and Nora Russell

Centre for the Study of Co-operatives
University of Saskatchewan

Copyright © 2004 The Individual Authors Contained Herein
Collection copyright © 2004 Centre for the Study of Co-operatives
University of Saskatchewan

All rights reserved. No part of this publication may be reproduced in any form or by any means without the prior written permission of the publisher. In the case of photocopying or other forms of reprographic reproduction, please consult Access Copyright, the Canadian Copyright Licensing Agency, at 1–800–893–5777.

Cover design by Brian Smith, Articulate Eye
Editing, layout, and interior design by Nora Russell
Translation, noted on chapter openings, by Nancy Senior and Wayne Hudson

LIBRARY AND ARCHIVES CANADA CATALOGUING IN PUBLICATION

Co-operative membership and globalization : new directions in research and practice / edited by Brett Fairbairn and Nora Russell.

Includes bibliographical references.

ISBN 0–88880–491–1

1. Cooperative societies—Canada. 2. Cooperation—Canada.
I. Fairbairn, Brett, 1959– II. Russell, Nora III. University of Saskatchewan. Centre for the Study of Co-operatives.

HD3448.C6564 2004   334'.0971   C2004–904971–2

Printed and bound in Canada by Houghton Boston, Saskatoon
04 05 06 07 08 / 5 4 3 2 1

Centre for the Study of Co-operatives
101 Diefenbaker Place
University of Saskatchewan
Saskatoon SK Canada S7N 5B8
Phone: (306) 966–8509 / Fax: (306) 966–8517
E-mail: coop.studies@usask.ca
Website: http://www.usaskstudies.coop

Contents

PART ONE
Globalization, Social Cohesion, and Membership

WILLIAM D. COLEMAN
Globalization and Co-operatives 3

BRETT FAIRBAIRN
Cohesion, Adhesion, and Identities in Co-operatives 18

BENOÎT LÉVESQUE, PATRICK DE BORTOLI,
AND JEAN-PIERRE GIRARD
Social Cohesion and Deliberative Democracy:
A Challenge for Co-operatives in Building
the Common Good 51

PART TWO
New Directions in Research and Practice

Issues

KAREN PHILP
The Challenges of Co-operative Membership,
Social Cohesion, and Globalization 65

CHRIS McCARVILLE
Membership and Public Relations: An Examination
of Arctic Co-operatives Limited 74

ANDREA HARRIS
Co-operative Social Responsibility:
A Natural Advantage? 84

BILL TURNER
    Co-operative Membership: Issues and Challenges — 102

THEORY

MICHAEL GERTLER
    Co-operative Membership
    as a Complex and Dynamic Social Process — 113

LOU HAMMOND KETILSON
    Revisiting the Role of Values and Principles:
    Do They Act to Include or Exclude? — 132

ISOBEL M. FINDLAY
    Remapping Co-operative Studies:
    Re-Imagining Postcolonial Co-operative Futures — 145

MURRAY FULTON AND JULIE GIBBINGS
    Cognitive Processes
    and Co-operative Business Strategy — 165

LESLIE BROWN
    Innovations in Co-operative Marketing
    and Communications — 179

CRISTINE DE CLERCY
    Leadership and Representational Diversity:
    Theory, Operationalization, and Measurement — 195

WARREN WEIR AND WANDA WUTTUNEE
    Respectful Research in Aboriginal Communities
    and Institutions in Canada — 207

CASES

DANIEL CÔTÉ
    The Issues and Challenges Facing a Co-operative
    in Search of New Cohesion: The Case of Agropur — 240

MARIO CARRIER
    Forestry Co-operatives in Québec:
    Social Cohesion and Economic Ties   258

JEAN-PIERRE GIRARD AND PATRICK DE BORTOLI
    The Solidarity Co-operative in Québec
    and Social Cohesion: Measuring and
    Understanding the Impact   269

PART THREE
                                                       APPLICATION

BRETT FAIRBAIRN
    Setting New Directions   283

ABOUT THE AUTHORS   311

*The Centre for the Study of Co-operatives
gratefully acknowledges the award from
the Social Sciences and Humanities Research Council of Canada,
which provided the funding for the project
upon which this book is based.*

PART ONE

GLOBALIZATION, SOCIAL COHESION, AND MEMBERSHIP

Five scholars examine the broad concepts of globalization, social cohesion, identities, and the role of deliberative democracy in building the common good.

WILLIAM D. COLEMAN

GLOBALIZATION AND CO-OPERATIVES

THIS PAPER offers some thoughts on two of the core concepts at issue in any current study of co-operatives: globalization and identity. The research project that is the subject of this book[1] is examining the "impact of globalization on membership identities and practices in selected communities." In order to address this relationship well, I introduce one further concept into the mix: autonomy. Certainly, when I think about co-operatives and why they are created and sustained in communities, it is related in some ways to a concern about social autonomy. I suggest that an examination of these three concepts and their relationships with one another might provide some background thinking that will help us better understand some of the challenges faced by co-operatives in Canada today.

GLOBALIZATION

Globalization is typical of many concepts in the social sciences in that it carries considerable ideological baggage. Its meaning differs depending on whether one is talking to José Bové, the French farmer who attacked a McDonald's outlet in southern France and led others to burn fields seeded with genetically modified crops; to Tony Blair, the British prime minister, who sees globalization as something inevitable and with high potential for the British people and British corporations; to the governments of Zimbabwe or Zambia, which see globalization as a process that marginalizes and impoverishes their people; to the executives of Monsanto Corporation, who look to sell their product innovations in agricultural biotechnology in every market in the world; or to Jan Aart Scholte, a political scientist at the University of Warwick in the UK, who has written an academic textbook on the concept.[2]

Many people, when they hear mention of globalization, think of the José Bovés of this world and why they were attacking McDonald's outlets or burning fields of GM crops in western European countries. Social scientists, however, cannot leave the topic there. We cannot start from the point of view that globalization is what José Bové says it is. We have to look at what he says critically. There is an additional complication.

Not only does the term globalization carry considerable ideological baggage, but it is also a term at the centre of an increasingly developing body of social theory that is challenging other theories and ways of understanding the world in which we live. So, like many other concepts in our social science disciplines—corporatism, autonomy, democracy, human rights—globalization is both a theoretical tool and a term that has varied meanings among individuals and organizations that we study. In referring to it and using it in our research, accordingly, we walk on treacherous ground.

Going back to José Bové and his charred fields for a moment, as a social scientist, I *am* interested in what he says about globalization. When he speaks about attacking globalization by burning these fields, he means a range of things. He is attacking US capitalism, which he sees as the principal motor of globalization; he is attacking Monsanto Corporation, as a typical transnational corporation (TNC) interested in profit at the expense of smaller people everywhere, and small farmers in France in particular; he is attacking a concept of intellectual property increasingly enshrined in domestic and international intellectual property regimes; he is attacking "science," an apparently objective set of disciplines that works hand in hand, in his view, with TNCs; he is attacking an approach to eating and food that empties out long-standing traditions of food preparation and quality at the expense of an agriculture based on industrial techniques of plant production and animal husbandry sustained by a world-wide set of other

TNCs associated with the chemical industry. In short, even for M. Bové, globalization is a complex, layered concept, featuring economic, political, cultural, and knowledge components.

In his essays on the methodology of the social sciences—essays that still form a central core to social science thinking on theoretical development—Max Weber argues convincingly that our concepts in the social sciences are built on the meanings of those concepts held by individual persons.[3] So, when social scientists begin to think about whether a concept called globalization might be helpful in understanding certain kinds of events, conflicts, and debates in the social world, they necessarily listen to José Bové, but not just to him. They listen also to Monsanto, the farmers in Zimbabwe, the scientists on the Canadian Biotechnology Advisory Council as well as, of course, to other social scientists who have a similar suspicion to their own: social theories built around globalization as a concept might help us improve our understanding of the world in which we currently live. Perhaps even more interesting, Martin Albrow, a British sociologist, adds one other point to consider when he writes: "Globalization theory puts on the agenda a recasting of the whole range of sociological concepts which were forged for the period of nation-state sociology."[4]

Many social scientists have engaged in this careful process of reflection when it comes to globalization. After examining the competing definitions of globalization, the political scientist Jan Aart Scholte suggests that globalization involves "the growth of 'supraterritorial relations' among people."[5] Supraterritorial refers to relations that are somehow "above" territory, that is they are relatively unconstrained by one's physical location. John Tomlinson, a sociologist, characterizes this "empirical condition" of supraterritoriality as one of "complex connectivity," a set of "connections that now bind our practices, our experiences and our political, economic and environmental fates together across the modern world."[6] Associated with this change in the character of social relationships for both authors is "deterritorialization." The relative importance of physical location as a basis for building social relationships is declining as supraterritorial ties grow in significance. In this respect, globalization is bringing far-reaching changes to the nature of social space: social space is less and less defined by the physical location in which we live.

Following Held et al., we can begin to assess the scope of these changes by looking at three properties of supraterritorial relations.[7] First, we can observe shifts in *extensity*, the degree to which cultural, political, and economic activities are stretching across new frontiers, creating a global space. For example, if we are interested in the globalization of the agrifood industry, and note that trade in processed foods is engaged in by a larger number of countries and at higher levels than it was twenty years ago, we can argue that the exchange of foods is becoming more extensive over time. Second, we can assess *intensity*, changes in the magnitude and regularity of interconnectedness. Continuing with our agrifood example, if we observe that more imported foods are now featuring in the daily meals of people in these countries and that they are displacing locally produced foods, then we can argue that the exchange of foods is becoming more intensive. Third, Held and his colleagues draw our attention to the property of *velocity*, changes in the speed of global interactions and processes. If, thanks to improvements in communications technology and in transportation, fresh and processed foods are distributed more quickly around the world, so much so that they are consumed in foreign countries at virtually the same time that they are consumed where they are harvested and processed, we can say that the velocity of agrifood trade is increasing.

Together these three properties contribute to a fourth—*enmeshment*, changes in the interdependence of the global and the local. Suppose we look at an apple grower in the Okanagan Valley in British Columbia. If apples from both Chile and South Africa are found increasingly in BC grocery stores in the winter and spring, while they were not present twenty years ago, and if they appear in sufficient quantity at prices such that they displace local apples, we can say that local consumers and apple growers are more enmeshed in global economic processes today than they were two decades ago. What happens in this small, beautiful valley is more closely linked to what is happening globally in the agrifood industry. This enmeshment goes both ways. If some farmers in this valley were to become concerned about the increased presence of foreign produce and burn down some supermarkets in protest, then we can be almost certain that this local act will have global effects. Its meaning will be transmitted across the globe, perhaps emboldening other farmers concerned about the globalization of food production, while perhaps worrying agribusiness corporations profiting from this business.

Contrary, then, to what might have happened in the past, globalization is not just a matter of the rich and the famous travelling the globe. Rather, it involves changes to the lives of more people in more walks of life, living in an even more diverse range of local communities. Robertson offers the concept of "global unicity" for understanding how these changes are linked to one another.[8] Unicity comes first from a global context of trading rules, of international regimes including those related to the environment, of cultural transmission, and of corporate activities that has an ever-increasing impact on how individuals and groups relate to one another in their local settings. Second, it arises from the creation of global frames of reference, often referred to as *globality,* within which social actors increasingly understand who they are and how they should orient their activities. More people than ever before think of the world as one place. Accordingly, even acts of resistance, whether these be attempts to prevent massive depopulation of agricultural areas or to secure the traditional family in a strong religious community, are taken with an eye to what is happening globally. Demonstrations by farmers about agricultural policies, for example, are now more often targeted on what is happening during negotiations for an Agreement on Agriculture at the World Trade Organization (WTO) and co-ordinated with the protests of their counterparts with similar concerns in other parts of the globe. In the same vein, religious fundamentalists make effective use of current communications technologies to broadcast widely their message about resisting secularization, thereby seeking to build alliances with other religious communities with similar concerns around the globe.

When social scientists talk about globalization, therefore, they are referring to a complex phenomenon that occurs in many aspects of our lives. I have spoken above about agrifood business, using the example of the distribution of fresh fruit. There are examples in other domains. In the areas of banking and finance, an area of frequent activity by co-operatives, foreign exchange markets now reach fully around the globe (more extensive) and involve trades of about a trillion dollars per day (more intensive). These trades take place almost instantly, thanks to computers (higher velocity), and affect the lives of people in many localities (prices of imported and exported goods go up and down depending on the exchange rate). In the social realm, migration to Canada now draws from all parts of the globe, not just Europe (more extensive); we have been admitting between 200,000 and 250,000 immigrants per year since the 1980s (more intensive); people can get here more quickly by airplane than in the past (higher velocity), and many of our cities are becoming much more culturally diverse (more enmeshment of the local and the global). In politics, the rules of the international trade regime at the WTO now bind the activities of 130 states, including China (more extensive); these rules affect systematically a large range of policies, even to the point that they influence how policymakers think about and design domestic policies (more intensive). Meetings on the interpretation and implementation of these rules go on almost constantly (higher velocity), and the economic fates of a larger number of workers and firms are affected by them (greater enmeshment of local production with global rules).

Just as important, these various dimensions of globalization are often linked. Fresh fruits are more easily distributed across the globe because global rules on trade and intellectual property make it more difficult for countries to block their entry. Religious fundamentalists in one part of the world are able to work with those in other parts of the world because migration has brought a greater diversity of religions to a larger number of places. Foreign exchange markets are so active because so many more firms are trading goods and services, and many more people are travelling to more and more areas of the world. Tourism has become an industry serving the ordinary people in many countries, not just the rich and the elite as in the past. Accordingly, what happens in the local places in which we live is affected to a larger extent by global events. Conversely, local events can have a global impact.

Identity

One of the common questions faced by researchers interested in co-operatives is whether globalization is undermining the kinds of identities that have traditionally supported co-operative formation and maintenance. What do we mean when we speak of "identity"? For individuals or communities, it involves a process of construction of the self, of who they are. It involves giving the self some meaning based on a social attribute or a set of social attributes that are given priority over other sources of meaning.[9] These attributes might be nationality, ethnicity, occupation, sexual orientation, gender, religion, local place of residence, and so on. Individuals and groups give their actions *meaning* by reference to a symbolic identification with one or more of these attributes. So if someone comes up to you and asks, "Why are you a member of this co-operative?" you might answer, "I am a farmer," or "I am a member of this parish," or "I work here." These identities are invariably constructed depending on the social and cultural context in which people live.

In order to think about the relationship between identity and globalization, I begin with the work of the sociologist Manuel Castells, who distinguishes three forms of identity building, each with a different origin.[10]

1. *Legitimizing Identity.* This identity refers to a system of meaning that is introduced and cultivated by the dominant institutions of society. Such an identity generates a *civil society,* a set of institutions and organizations that reproduce that identity. Being "Canadian" refers to this kind of identity. There is a set of institutions ranging from our Parliament and our flag to perhaps our health-care system, our annoyingly vigorous federal-provincial conflicts, our service clubs, and our voluntary associations that reinforce the idea of being Canadian.

2. *Resistance Identity.* Some actors may be in positions or living in conditions that are devalued or stigmatized by the logic of the dominant institutions in society. Accordingly, they try to build trenches of resistance and survival on the basis of principles different from those permeating the given society. Some Indigenous peoples, for example, have formed resistance identities in Canada. Their experience in the country, whether living on impoverished reserves or being sent to residential schools, has led them to construct a different meaning system, and they resist being called Canadian because that term implies assimilation and acculturation to them.

3. *Project Identity.* Some individuals try to build a new identity that redefines their position in society, and they use this act to challenge some fundamental components of social structure. Think, for example, of the suffragette movement at the turn of the century, when women were seeking the right to vote in national and provincial elections. In this process, they constructed a new identity for themselves and represented themselves as full members of society—as "persons"—even though the law at the time did not recognize them as such. In redefining their identity to include being persons like men, and being the political equal to men, these women were changing their place in Canadian society, and what is more, changing that society as well.

In the period prior to the present globalizing era, what Castells refers to as the legitimizing identity tended overwhelmingly to come through the nation-state. The nation-state had sufficient authority and sovereignty that it could define such critical things as the boundary between the private and the public, that it could intervene in the economy in ways to promote full employment or in society to ensure that health-care services were provided universally. It could call for the singing of the national anthem or the flying of the flag, or provide support to culture.

Accordingly, when persons and organizations sought to define a new identity and to promote for themselves a new position in society or to create a new social structure, their project identity was constructed within the context of the nation-state. After all, if we think back to Marx's plans for the labour movement, which had such a project, it was to found what he called a "dictatorship of the proletariat." The workers' movement's first objective was to gain control of the nation-state. Similarly, when the suffragettes were seeking to define a new place in society for women based on political equality with men, it was again an institution of the nation-state—the electoral system—that was their target.

Now let us turn to the present globalizing era. Without necessarily going into detail at this point, the redefinitions of space and time brought on by globalizing processes have had a decided impact on the nation-state as we know it. Suffice it to say that most states no longer have the capacity or the sovereignty to make as many of the crucial decisions on their own that affect the lives of their citizens that they once were able to do. The nation-state is no longer in nearly as strong a position to provide that legitimizing identity noted above. It no longer is as dominant a force in providing the umbrella for the trade unions, the voluntary associations, the co-operatives, the cultural groups, and the interest groups that constitute what we call civil society. Power has leached out into the global sphere.

Accordingly, globalizing processes are changing the social, territorial, and cultural reproduction of group identity.[11] As people move from the rural areas or Aboriginal reservations to the cities, or from one part of the world to another, they regroup in their new locations and reconstruct their own personal narratives, their own histories. As the anthropologist Appadurai notes, their identities become more slippery, less localized. In general, groups are no longer as tightly territorialized, spatially bounded, historically unselfconscious, or culturally homogeneous as in the past.[12]

Under these conditions, what happens then to those in our societies who are unsatisfied with their situation, who wish to build an identity that redefines their place in society, and who wish to transform the overall social structure? Those individuals who wish to build a project identity, as Castells calls it, no longer feel content with focussing on the nation-state and working within national civil society. So where can they turn? What becomes more likely is that they will turn to communities where they feel a sense of solidarity and support to search for meaning and to build a resistance identity. What we now call "identity politics" is the search for relevant communities and the building of those communities for resisting change, particularly for resisting the effects of globalization. Where people turn to build these communities is much more fluid; it might be the localities in which they live, or it might involve new social spaces involving transnational connections; or it might involve some combination of the two.

Autonomy

With this understanding of globalization in mind and some hypotheses about the impact of globalization on identity building, a crucial component of co-operative formation, we can now turn to focus more specifically on co-operatives. In doing so, however, I introduce a third concept or idea, and one that is central to co-operative practices, that of social autonomy. Autonomy is another concept that has a controversial and debated place in the social sciences and humanities. It is also one often characterized as being particularly Western, or European, in origin. I do not want to dwell on these debates here. Rather, I would like to assess what autonomy might mean in a country like Canada.

David Held, the political philosopher, offers us a liberal understanding—he sees autonomy as the capacity of individuals to shape the conditions under which they live.[13] Social autonomy thus exists when this capacity is available to individuals rather broadly across a society. Held identifies a series of conditions necessary for the existence of autonomy, ranging from being physically healthy, to being educated, and to enjoying basic political and civil rights. In this understanding, autonomy is present in Canadian society, albeit somewhat unevenly.

Others take a stronger position. Cornelius Castoriadis, a French philosopher of Greek origin, argues that even in a formally democratic society like Canada, heteronomy (being unselfconsciously subject to the power of another) can prevail over autonomy.[14] What is important in his view is that a society have a place for politics, public spaces where citizens are freely able to ask themselves, "Are the rules and the laws under which we exist the right ones?" "Are they just?" "Could they be better?" For Castoriadis, therefore, autonomy exists when a society is more reflexive, more able to look at itself critically, and where its members are free, have access to public spaces, and possess the resources, the understanding, and the education needed to interrogate their society and its laws.

What is also clear about autonomy in this sense is that it involves an act of the imagination. Castoriadis terms it the "radical imagination."[15] Individuals and groups are able to imagine different futures, different ways of living, different arrangements in their own lives. They are able to take an idea, talk about it, imagine how it might work in practice, and then take action to see if they can get it to work.

A reading of the histories of co-operatives in many fields suggests that these organizations were often assertions of autonomy in this sense. Whether it be farmers seeing markets for storing or transporting grain or for buying milk being destroyed through monopoly or oligopoly power, or rural communities unable to gain access to investment capital because of the disinterest of large banks, the individuals affected imagined a different set of arrangements and a more promising future. They chose to act together; they sought to create these arrangements and that imagined future.

The key questions for many studying globalization, then, are the following: In the presence of globalizing processes, is autonomy in this strong meaning more or less likely to obtain? Do these processes detract from the opportunities for identity construction that would permit the working together, the imagining together, and the social commitment that are inherent to the co-operative instinct? These are difficult questions. Their difficulty is such that team-based, interdisciplinary research is necessary for their investigation. At this point, I can offer only some preliminary thoughts on the answers. There would seem to be aspects of globalization that might lead to pessimism and others that support some optimism.

Let me begin with the pessimistic side. Globalizing processes in the economy have clearly brought on an acceleration of the advance of capitalism into virtually all aspects of our own economic lives in Canada. They have also linked our economic situations more closely to advances of capitalism into almost all parts of the world. This linkage between the local and the global can have profound, highly unpredictable effects in our daily lives. Why, for example, should the devaluation of Thailand's currency, the baht, in 1997, a country with which Canada trades very little if at all, trigger in the following months a 15 percent decline in the value of the Canadian dollar against the US currency? Such a rapid change in the value of our currency can have profound effects in the daily lives of millions of Canadians. And when these economic processes are supported by an increasingly global consensus among political and economic elites in favour of neoliberalism—the idea that markets work best when left alone—fatalism can often result. Citizens get the sense that there is something inevitable or unchangeable to such economic processes; they are so global, so strong, so dominant, that it is fruitless to challenge them.

When this advancing global capitalism has the effect of ever-increasing production of greenhouse gases in eastern Canada, the US, and in many other countries, and these begin to destabilize weather patterns to the extent in the Canadian prairies that some ask whether traditional economic activities such as the growing of grain have a future, pessimism is difficult to resist. Again, the processes seem so large, so global, so out of the control of individual persons like you and me, they seem to invite heteronomy and resignation. By extending the reach of events across a global space, structures such as global capitalism and processes such as global climate change would seem to shrink, if not remove completely, opportunities for autonomy.

When it comes to co-operatives, the impact of globalizing processes on identity formation might also be relevant. I suggested above that these processes destabilize long-standing identities based on place of work, on community ties, on religion, and even on nationality. The neoliberal ideology of globalism favours an idea of rugged individualism and entrepreneurship that represents community-based co-operation as less entrepreneurial or as outmoded. The pressure towards individualism also often has a highly gendered impact, increasing the divide between women and men in some social settings. Finally, it adds to the long-standing devaluation of communal processes inherent in many First Nations communities.

Where might there be grounds for optimism? If we draw a little on our knowledge of history, one might argue that the forces of monopoly or oligopoly capitalism faced by farmers in western Canada at the turn of the twentieth century may have appeared just as strong, just as unchallengeable, just as inevitable as the globalizing economic forces appear to us today. And yet those farmers took action. Or if we think of the poor rural communities in Québec, where credit was nonexistent and capital was held in the cities by rather foreign, English-speaking banks in Montréal, poverty might also have seemed permanent and inevitable. And yet again, Alphonse Desjardins, using the ideas set out by Friedrich Raiffeisen in Germany, persisted with his ideas of caisses populaires tied to every parish. Relatively speaking, the economic forces may not appear any more dominant to us today than they did to our ancestors a century ago.

Remember, as well, that Castoriadis's notion of autonomy puts a great emphasis on imagination and on finding social spaces where discussion, debate, and deliberation can give life to that imagination. Arjun Appadurai, an anthropologist who has written extensively on cultures and globalizing processes, makes the argument that these processes also create new opportunities for social imagination.[16] The very linkages between global processes and local life that seem to produce the weight of economic inevitability, also open up vistas for the imagination that were not available before for many people. Appadurai argues that it creates a basis for "emancipatory politics."[17]

Take, for example, Indigenous peoples. Advances in transportation, information, and communications technologies have permitted the development in many Aboriginal communities of relationships not previously possible. These include relationships with other Aboriginal communities and First Nations in Canada, and with Aboriginal peoples in other parts of the world, whether in Central and South America, northern Europe, Russia, Southeast Asia, or Africa. Building on these relationships, some members of Aboriginal communities have added an international identity as Indigenous peoples that now sits alongside their local identity as Cree or Haudenausaunee and so on. They are talking about "rights" that they might have as "Indigenous peoples" and are doing so in transnational policy spaces, whether at the UN or through linked web sites.

Some believe, therefore, that the possibility for new forms of translocal and transnational relationships that are created through globalizing processes provides a basis for the kind of co-operation that might be needed to counter global capitalism and to challenge some of its most destructive social effects. These relationships might provide the basis for new types of identity construction, and perhaps new forms of co-operation. If we consider the possibility that feelings of resignation, views about the irreversibility of some of globalization's effects, beliefs that we have reached the end of history and the triumph of modernity—if we can remember that all of these perceptions are themselves creations or representations of the world favoured by the powerful—then we can be a little less pessimistic. And if Appadurai is right that globalizing processes have created new vistas for the social imagination, not only here in Canada but also in most other parts of the globe, then local acts of imagination and assertions of autonomy might prove to be stronger and more possible than we think.

To my understanding, the establishment of co-operatives and the will to sustain them in the face of many obstacles are very much local acts of imagination and autonomy. Further research is needed on how these new forms based on co-operation and how these acts of imagination might be possible under globalizing conditions. Perhaps then researchers can make suggestions about what changes to laws and public policies are needed to ensure that these actions and practices are welcomed and sustainable over time. For these reasons, then, research on the relationship between globalization and the sustainability and potential growth of co-operatives promises to be an important contribution to understanding one of the most important questions of our time: What is the relationship between globalization and autonomy?

ENDNOTES

1. Co-operative Membership and Globalization: Creating Social Cohesion through Market Relations, a study funded by the Social Sciences and Humanities Research Council of Canada, and based at the Centre for the Study of Co-operatives at the University of Saskatchewan.
2. Jan Aart Scholte, *Globalization: A Critical Introduction* (Hound Mills, Basingstoke: Palgrave, 2000).
3. Max Weber, *The Methodology of the Social Sciences* (New York: The Free Press, 1949).
4. Martin Albrow, "Travelling beyond Local Cultures," in *The Globalization Reader*, eds. Frank J. Lechner and John Boli (Oxford: Blackwell, 2000), p. 118.
5. Scholte, p. 46.
6. John Tomlinson, *Globalization and Culture* (Chicago: University of Chicago Press, 1999), p. 2.
7. David Held, Anthony McGrew, David Goldblatt, and Jonathan Perraton, *Global Transformations* (Stanford: Stanford University Press, 1999).
8. Roland Robertson, *Globalization: Social Theory and Global Culture* (London: Sage, 1992), p. 26.
9. Manuel Castells, *The Power of Identity* (Oxford: Blackwell, 1997), p. 6.
10. Ibid., pp. 6–12.
11. Arjun Appadurai, *Modernity at Large: Cultural Dimensions of Globalization* (Minneapolis, MN: University of Minnesota Press, 1996), pp. 48–49.
12. Ibid.

13. David Held, *Democracy and the Global Order* (Stanford: Stanford University Press, 1995).
14. Cornelius Castoriadis, *Philosophy, Politics, Autonomy: Essays in Political Philosophy* (New York: Oxford University Press, 1991), p. 146.
15. Ibid., pp. 146, 162.
16. Appadurai, chapter 2, and "Grassroots Globalization and the Research Imagination," *Public Culture* 12, no. 1 (2000): p. 6.
17. Ibid., "Grassroots."

BRETT FAIRBAIRN

COHESION, ADHESION, AND IDENTITIES IN CO-OPERATIVES

INTRODUCTION

I*F PEOPLE ARE TRULY CONCERNED* about the negative aspects of globalization—loss of local control, the power of transnational corporations—then they should be attracted to local alternatives, local ownership, and community-based institutions. That thought was on my mind recently as I conducted interviews with managers, leaders, staff, and members in local retail co-operatives across western Canada. There is a proportion of co-op members who are clearly motivated by what some refer to as ideology or philosophy, who see co-operatives as a kind of crusade for community and for local control. These people's attitude to corporate globalization is not in doubt. But my initial impression is that, for the great majority, involvement with a local co-operative represents a diffuse bundle of characteristics, some of them quite practical or prosaic in nature. This should not be surprising. "Co-ops arise from need," say the leaders in the co-operative movement, a deceptively simple statement that covers some very complicated ideas. One thing "need" denotes is that co-ops generally provide immediate, practical, and often material services. In a fundamental way, a retail co-op is and must be *about* retailing—an agricultural co-op is about agriculture; a housing co-op is about housing; a credit union is about banking. They are not, on the surface, *about* being co-ops, are not *about* democracy or participation. After all, how many citizens (at least of the nonintelligentsia class) sit down and say, "What our town needs is more democracy: let's form a co-op!" To understand these institutions requires that one meet them on their terms, and begin with (in the case of my recent interviews) understanding their retailing, their merchandising, their marketing and promotions. To know a co-op, you must know its business.

But there is a remarkable subtext to co-operative enterprises. It became clear to me as I listened to people talk—people who had been employees of a co-op for just three weeks and others who had been members and leaders for more than fifty years—that there is a co-op difference, beneath the surface, that few people have the vocabulary to describe. Certainly the mid-twentieth-century rhetoric of the co-operative movement—the philosophy and ideology that some refer to—does a poor job of expressing the difference because it is so abstract in its idealism. I talked to staff members who had only a vague idea of what a co-op was and of how to compare their own organization to others. And yet they knew and could communicate that it was a good place to work, a place where individuals could develop themselves and go far—to the limits of their ambition and potential. A successful local co-op is these things because it is stable and diversified. It is stable and diversified because its "head office," so to speak, is in the local community. It is not likely to be bought out by a competitor; it has a range and diversity of tasks to be done, decisions that must be made locally. It can be flexible, innovative, and entrepreneurial, because it does not receive its orders from a far-away corporate head office. It is all of these things *because it is locally owned and voluntarily controlled by local people*—in other words, because of its ownership structure as a co-operative.[1]

The character of being a co-operative shapes the experience and the identities of staff and members, even when they lack the language to put the co-operative difference into words.

Do people *know*, even without words, what different kinds of institutions mean to the health and vibrancy of their communities? I suspect many do, to a certain extent. At root, this is a question of social cohesion. In some way, co-op members know they have a connection to their co-op, they have a connection to their communities, and their co-op and their community have connections to each other. It's like a triangle of interactions and affective bonds that solidifies their concept of who and where they are. But this cohesive sense does not trump all other influences in their lives. Members daily make trade-offs, choose to patronize their co-operative and a competitor, and in effect, do a social-economic calculus in their heads. *Will I patronize the co-op if it costs a few cents more? A few dollars? Tens of dollars? How do I weight the future value of a possible patronage refund, versus the present value of the sale offered by the competitor? Do I like shopping in a well-designed, well-maintained local store, or would I prefer the bare-bones warehouse style of the urban big-box outlet?* There is a perception, and a fear, that price is the only thing that matters to people. If this is true, then perhaps WAL-MART must triumph, and we have our answer to how concerned people really are about corporate globalization. But whatever people say, we have considerable evidence that behaviour does not follow price alone. Local pride, local identity, competitive prices but not necessarily the lowest ones, have a chance. Cohesion has a chance, and maybe more than just a chance.

The purpose of this essay is to provide some partial answers to three questions. First, what is the concept of social cohesion that has been discussed in recent years by Canadian policymakers and academics? Second, how does thinking about social cohesion contribute to an understanding of co-operatives—of their internal processes and their roles in communities? Finally, what does an understanding of co-operatives say, in turn, about discussions of social cohesion? Posing the questions in this way is an effort to engage theory with practice—to ground highly abstract discussions in a specific sector where organizations experience and "do" social cohesion; to see how their experience suggests adapting or changing the theory; and to see what practical observations or proposals result from the exercise. For people in co-operatives and in policymaking positions, this is an opportunity for *praxis*, the mutual fitting together of theory and experience, or what some would call reflective practice.

Words make a difference. Especially in today's world, the use of words is strategic. Certain words evoke assumptions, activate complexes of related ideas in our minds, or imply concepts that guide our thinking. The use of certain words and the avoidance of others may be significant.

In relation to co-operatives, it is common to say that co-operatives serve "the community." Often co-operative supporters will point out that co-ops have both "social" and "economic" aspects. Some have said that "co-operatives are people," while others have stressed that "co-operatives are businesses." All of these statements (and others) are true. Introducing a new term such as social cohesion is an opportunity to make connections between what co-ops do and what policymakers are interested in. At the same time, using a new term offers a chance to forego old debates and look at co-operatives in new ways.

I want to argue, below, that co-operative business success in an era of globalization depends on co-ops pursuing and implementing ideas of *linkage, transparency,* and *cognition.* Though these terms are themselves somewhat new, the ideas behind them are essential to co-operatives and similar organizations. I will also argue that the idea of social cohesion has something to do with how co-operatives can implement these ideas and succeed in business; and finally, that understanding co-operatives can lead to understanding social cohesion in new ways. First, it is important to define, as best we can, social cohesion itself.

SOCIAL COHESION

The term social cohesion will be unfamiliar to many people, though it has come into common use in recent years in federal policy circles and among researchers in Canada. On a large scale—and many who have used the term are thinking on a large scale—social cohesion is about the cohesion of society itself: what holds together an entire society and enables it to function as a unit. Typically, cohesion at this level is seen as depending on broadly shared values and a common sense of national identity. Social cohesion, so conceived, is diffuse, but its effects are visible on a macro scale. Others study social cohesion on a micro scale, as a phenomenon connected with what social-science researchers call social capital. In this view, individual people form relationships, trust one another, co-operate, and in so doing, give rise to social cohesion. The following discussion begins with

Canadian perspectives on the term, then broadens into a wider examination of the international context and origins.

A useful recent discussion by economist Jeff Dayton-Johnson of Dalhousie University helps sort out some possible distinctions among these terms. Dayton-Johnson suggests that we can best think of *social capital* as an individual asset, rather like human capital. Individuals can invest in their human capital by acquiring training, skills, and experience. They can also invest in social capital by devoting time and energy to building relationships and reputations. The investment they make today in social capital helps give them a claim to the future returns resulting from co-operating in those relationships.[2] By contrast, Dayton-Johnson suggests we should regard *social cohesion* as a society-level characteristic that is inherent in populations, not individuals. Social cohesion is a kind of historical aggregate that results from individuals experiencing and perceiving each other's past investments in social capital. Dayton-Johnson also relates these two terms to the more familiar one of *community*, which he describes as a kind of state where information and social standards support co-operation. Community, in his view, is a stronger condition than individual calculation of benefit (social capital) or an abstract aggregation of individual decisions (social cohesion). While not all researchers follow Dayton-Johnson's usage, his synthesis is a good starting point for relating the new term social cohesion to other, more familiar terms.

The preceding discussion provides one useful definition of the terms, but equally important is to understand the context of the debate. *Why* do we see discussion of social cohesion now, and what is its importance? In 1998, Jane Jenson, writing for the Canadian Policy Research Networks (CPRN), argued that "concerns about social cohesion are a product of our times," a result of "serious social and political strains" created by neoliberal policies such as free trade, deregulation, downsizing of the state, and so on.[3] Jenson traces the widespread use of the term social cohesion to policy discussions in the Organization for Economic Co-operation and Development (OECD) and the European Union (EU). Reviewing the literature and use of the term, she suggests a definition of social cohesion as "shared values and commitment to a community." Jenson's language is reminiscent of the much-cited formulation of Judith Maxwell, who guides the CPRN:

"Social cohesion involves building shared values and communities of interpretation, reducing disparities in wealth and income, and generally enabling people to have a sense that they are engaged in a common enterprise, facing shared challenges, and that they are members of the same community."[4]

One can (as Benoît Lévesque, Patrick De Bortoli, and Jean-Pierre Girard do elsewhere in this volume) analyse the history of European thought during the emergence of modern society—in particular, the emergence of the discipline of sociology and its schools—in terms of ideas about what integrates a society under modern conditions. The OECD's concern, described by Jenson, is then one historical instance of a long-standing worry about the impact of modernity and economic development on social stability. Jenson, too, traces the antecedents of the term, at least in (her exclusive focus) European and North American thinking. According to Jenson, since the nineteenth century, "each moment of rapid social change in which diversity threatened to overwhelm commonalities and restructuring menaced past political compromises" occasioned "explicit discussions of social cohesion."[5] She locates the term particularly in political sociology, citing authorities such as Émile Durkheim, Alexis de Tocqueville, and Talcott Parsons. For example, fear of fragmentation in nineteenth-century French society led to Durkheim's sociology, and to the political doctrine of solidarism (or interclass harmony) based upon it. In France, solidarism and attendant social, political, and economic policies were a foundation of the long-lasting Third Republic (1876–1940).[6] The search to define a modern form of social cohesion, then, is a search for a concept that, like solidarism, can underpin a new, long-term framework of national policies. To discuss social cohesion in relation to Canada implies a search for a new Canadian policy framework, a vision or a consensus that integrates and provides legitimacy.

This European-centred, intellectual, historical view of the term also helps explain why it is a subject of discussion now, at this moment in history. The neoliberal policies to which Jenson refers cast into doubt the nation-state and the welfare state, which were (in large part) the twentieth-century West's answers to the challenge of social integration. If these institutions, upon which we relied for most of a century, are now shaky, then what other institutions can create cohesion? At the same time, we could ask how traditional societies—Aboriginal societies in Canada, for example—understood social cohesion. The latter exercise might lead us to root social cohesion in spirituality and relationship with the land, in stories and language, in respect for Elders and humility in one's own role. Beginning with a traditional understanding of social cohesion would certainly highlight the dilemma of modern European and Western societies: if these are the roots of social cohesion, how can it exist after they have been disturbed? Perhaps we can re-read the idea of social cohesion as a search for centredness and balance in imbalanced, unstable, modern (and postmodern) societies. This implies that one answer to the social-cohesion challenge may be to restore some of the things modern societies have lost—such as spirituality, relationship to the land, sacred stories, and so on—if this is possible.

As Jenson notes, the idea of social cohesion is used in different ways by different people. To help distinguish important aspects of social cohesion, she maps five dimensions of the concept: belonging/isolation; inclusion (or integration)/exclusion; participation/noninvolvement; recognition/rejection; and legitimacy/illegitimacy.[7] Perhaps one could sum up by saying that social cohesion involves belonging, inclusion, participation, recognition, and legitimacy. While the first three of these concepts are intuitively fairly clear and (as Jenson notes) well studied at least in certain respects, her last two dimensions are less familiar. "Recognition" implies explicit public acceptance of groups that might otherwise be marginalized; in other words, it may not be enough merely that people feel they belong, are included, and participate. It may further be necessary that their belonging, etc., is publicly acknowledged or celebrated. "Legitimacy" appears to be used by Jenson as an attribute of necessary social-political institutions. She writes, "Social cohesion depends at least in part on maintaining the legitimacy of those public and private institutions that act as mediators and maintain the spaces within which mediation can occur. Social cohesion can be threatened by rising tides of cynicism or negativity that question the representativity of intermediary institutions, for example, or [by] sectarian forms of public discourse."[8]

In reviewing academic and policy literature that touches on dimensions of social cohesion, Jenson identifies several large bodies of thought and practice. One of these is the discussion, especially in Québec, of économie sociale, or social economy. In Québec, the idea of the social economy serves as a focal point for both academic research and public policy. As defined by the October 1996 socio-economic summit (a conference of community and policy representatives convened by the government), the social economy is a sector of economic activity based on associations embodying solidarity, autonomy, and citizenship. These values are embodied in five principles: (1) service to members of the community; (2) autonomous management; (3) democratic decision making; (4) the primacy of persons and work over capital and profits; and (5) participation, empowerment, and individual or collective accountability.[9] As Jenson observes, this school of thought stresses the importance of the economic basis of inclusion and participation. An underlying idea is that full citizenship and democracy require economic inclusion; that creating jobs for people is essential to social cohesion.[10]

Jenson also devotes considerable space to discussing current ideas of social capital as advanced by Robert Putnam and others, though she seems concerned to view such ideas critically and to question their importance and application. Briefly, Putnam argued that networks of relationships among people in communities constitute a kind of capital in the community, a resource that can be tapped for any number of new projects in the same way that financial capital is a fluid medium that can be invested into any kind of endeavour. In particular, Putnam highlighted the importance of *trust*. Relationships that develop trust over time permit those involved to go into action more quickly and easily when they perceive that something needs doing. In economic terms, the development of trust lowers the transaction costs for collective action thereafter.[11] Jenson's questions about social capital seem principally to relate to the idea that it could replace institutional or governmental action; she also poses questions about whether it is necessarily fair or inclusive.

Behind Jenson's skepticism seems to lie a particular orientation: that the national level is important (and localities are suspect because they might undermine national-level cohesion); that federal policies and governmental institutions are important (we can't rely just on values and social capital); that community and cohesion are themselves suspicious (because they might mean violating rights of individuals). While Jenson phrases her criticisms as questions of the concept of social cohesion, she is also questioning locality, values, community, social capital, and their advocates. Both implicitly and to a degree explicitly, she is defending or advocating a culture of individual rights grounded in national institutions as a corrective or alternative to community, values, and social capital. Most urgently, however, Jenson repeatedly raises the issue of marginalization/exclusion. If social cohesion is to be meaningful, it must involve integrating those who are otherwise excluded, such as the poor, the jobless, those who suffer discrimination, and so on. One gets the sense that Jenson is wary of "feel-good" forms of social cohesion that may avoid tough social, economic, and political issues, and thereby serve, in the end, to reinforce a complacent status quo for the well off. (Rather like solidarism in late nineteenth and early twentieth-century France, one might say.)

The kind of doubts voiced by Jenson were made more explicit by Paul Bernard in a piece published in 1999, also by the CPRN. Bernard warned of social cohesion being employed as a "quasi-concept" that could lead to us addressing the shortcomings of neoliberalism through "a dose of compassion and a return to values rather than a correction of social inequalities and an institutional mediation of interests."[12] What social cohesion leaves out, according to Bernard, is equality, the inclusion and empowerment of the marginalized. Bernard, like Jenson, therefore argues "that what is important for social cohesion is less the sharing of common values than the presence of public institutions capable of adequately managing social conflicts."[13] There are really two claims here that may in some ways need to be separated: first, that equality is important; second, that state action or institutional arrangements are the best way to guarantee it. Therefore, any interpretation of social cohesion that distracts from the importance of state or institutional action is unhelpful.

A glance at the European usage of the term social cohesion indicates that similar debates have occurred there, and in fact are central to the origins of the term. One of the earliest prominent uses was at a 1995 forum in Denmark sponsored by the United Nations Educational, Scientific, and Cultural Organization (UNESCO), the results of which were later distributed in a policy paper.[14] At that point, social cohesion was already used as a phrase related to social justice; social cohesion was presented as the opposite of social exclusion. The argument at that time was about a need to "go from a logic of economic growth to a logic of social development," reducing the short-term "dictatorship of economism" in order to draw attention to other, long-term aspects of quality of life. To accomplish this was seen in 1995 to involve changing people's ways of life and re-examining cognitive structures, redefining the role of the state, "mending the social fabric," and giving new meaning to democracy. Subsequently in October 1997, a Council of Europe summit of heads of state and government identified social cohesion as "one of the foremost needs of the wider Europe and an essential complement to the promotion of human rights and dignity"; this was followed by the creation of a European Committee for Social Cohesion.[15] The committee adopted a new Strategy for Social Cohesion on 12 May 2000 in which it did not define the term, but it did propose "setting up mechanisms and institutions which will prevent the factors of division (such as an excessive gap between rich and poor or the multiple forms of discrimination) from becoming so acute as to endanger social harmony." The strategy also prominently listed "the importance of decent and adequately remunerated employment," combating poverty and social exclusion, social security, policy for families, and working with civil society bodies, "in particular trade unions, employers' representatives and NGOs."[16] Newsletters and reports from various countries seem to indicate that the term was being used in a fashion roughly comparable to "social justice," but perhaps less confrontational: reported social-cohesion initiatives dealt with subjects such as discrimination, low wages, unjust dismissal, and so forth.[17] The usage of the term in Europe resembles the CPRN's usage, then, in its conscious effort to maintain an emphasis on justice and equality as integral parts of social cohesion.

To return to Jenson, she does lay out elements for a research agenda in that she defines some of the unanswered or contested questions about social cohesion, including the following:[18]

- what fosters social cohesion? Is all participation equal? Do people have to share in paid employment for social cohesion to exist, or is "any form of participation ... sufficient to generate feelings of belonging"? Also, is it true that

"shared values" are what create cohesion?—what about the role of institutions?
- can a country accumulate social capital? If social capital collects in local places, does this necessarily make provinces, regions, or the country more cohesive? Might social capital in particular communities lead them to exclude others? This is in effect a question of the interrelationships among different levels or kinds of social cohesion.
- finally: cohesion of what, and for whom? "Can citizens' identities be both varied and multiple, without threatening social cohesion, or is adherence to a single national vision necessary?" And what about inequality and discrimination?—cohesive communities of the past were often highly inequitable.
- what are the connections between the "micro" processes that create cohesion among small assortments of people—perhaps assortments as small and ephemeral as those who view the same art—and the "macro" cohesion of all of society, which seems to be a key concern of sociological theorists and policymakers?

The operationalization of the concept of social cohesion is, indeed, the key challenge. Where do we find social cohesion in the behaviour and choices of individuals, in the decisions and activities of organizations and institutions at the local level? Is it a trivial or an insightful use of the term when a magazine writer raises the possibility that we can find social cohesion in the reactions of people coming to a gallery to view a painting? Does the common viewing of a painting by people who see it as a great work of art create social cohesion among the viewers, as one writer claimed in *Oxford Today* recently?[19] Is this simply a devaluation of the term, or has the author identified one of the innumerable, small-scale processes by which social cohesion is built? If viewing art can create social cohesion, then likely the architecture of a community building, the familiar logo of an organization, and common attachment or membership will do so as well. Many organizations may function to create some kind of social cohesion, and it would be surprising if co-operatives were not among them.

COHESION IN CO-OPERATIVES

Leaders in and analysts of the co-operative sector have not often spoken of cohesion as an issue. However, they have frequently referred to some related concepts: the concept of *community* as a characteristic within co-operatives as well as a setting within which co-operatives are rooted; the idea of *member loyalty;* and the idea of *homogeneity or heterogeneity* of members as an important factor in organizations. Cohesion—in the senses of member cohesion as well as wider social cohesion between the co-operative's membership and others in their community—is relevant to these common concerns of co-operatives.

In an important study, one of the first explicitly to consider the role of co-operatives in relation to social cohesion, Marie-Claire Malo, Benoît Lévesque, and three co-authors studied the regional reorganization of financial co-operatives in Québec and New Brunswick in the context of globalization.[20] They determined that the caisses populaires were not simply merging, but also developing new relationships with external institutions, new forms of connection to their territories, and new internal structures. They characterize the resulting caisses, whether formed through mergers or re-engineering, as new co-operatives. The researchers paid particular attention to five aspects of these organizations: their connection to local place, the accessibility of their financial services, the employability of employees displaced by changes, democratic functioning, and their connections to networks of community-economic-development institutions. They concluded that the caisses were creating new territories for themselves that were doubly defined by market potential and member affinities. Within these territories they demonstrated a new localist emphasis, in that the co-operatives were developing further ties with local communities, keeping service points open for accessibility to member-customers, while centralizing or sharing specialized backroom functions.[21] They remained universal, local financial-services institutions in that they continued to serve small economic actors (small communities, small businesses, less-well-off individuals) despite the pressure on their levels of profitability. At the same time, governance and management were more professionalized and consistent with norms established by the wider federation of caisses populaires. Given the centralization of some functions and the professionalization of management, the main distinguishing features of the co-operatives were found to reside in their charitable granting programs, their patronage refunds, and their collective investments in communities. The authors identified challenges for the co-operatives, including the need to go beyond compromise solutions and pursue greater innovation, and the need to commit themselves to new forms of social cohesion more suited to the contemporary age than the environment of the old French Canadian Catholic parish in which they grew up.

As Malo, Lévesque, and the co-authors make clear, co-operatives must adapt and innovate in an era of globalization, both renewing and reinventing their co-operative character. Everything must change so that what matters can stay the same. In such a process, language is important. The principles and ideas of decades ago are not likely to be adequate guides to success, and yet accumulated experience and understanding can't be thrown out the window, either. Co-operatives need ways to focus on what is essential in the midst of change. The underlying reality is that to be successful, co-operatives have to serve their members; they have to be understood by their members; and they have to be thinking organizations that can adapt coherently to changing circumstances. We can use the concepts of *linkage, transparency,* and *cognition* to describe these essential strategic elements in co-operative business success.[22] Cohesion has a role to play in each of them.

LINKAGE WITH MEMBERS

Co-operatives are sustained by their members. But why do members invest capital, time, and loyalty in their relationship with a co-operative? While there are a variety of answers to this question, in general the key one is *because they trust that doing so will be in their own interest, as well as the interest of other members.* Co-operatives earn this trust when members perceive them to be dedicated to serving the members' needs, not the needs of the organization or of any other group. Members support co-ops because co-ops are dedicated to making members better off. This dedication is reinforced by other aspects of the co-operative relationship, including shared values and member identification with the co-operative's purposes (about which, more below).

Another way of putting this is that the members trust the co-operative when they perceive it as an effective agent for themselves. The co-operative is a kind of combination, representation, or projection of the individual economies and interests of its members. There are two significant parts to this agency relationship. First, the co-operative must actually be an efficient agent for what its members want and need; if it is not, it will, in the long run, be unable to earn members' trust and support. But second, the members must *perceive* that the co-op is an efficient agent. Perception, in this case, is everything. A co-operative that is a faithful agent of its members, but is not known or perceived to be so, will gain no advantage from the relationship. It is the perception, created by communication and experience, that creates trust.

The dedication of co-operatives to serving members has been expressed in many forms. "Not for profit, not for charity, but for service to the members" is an old motto of the credit-union movement. But the concept of *service* to members is a broad one, which may not encompass any different relationship from the normal business-customer kind. While a service orientation is a good starting point, we can be more specific: co-operatives undertake those activities that *promote the economic success or well-being* of their members. What distinguishes them from other forms of enterprise is that they exist not to maximize or optimize their own profits or welfare, but rather those of their members. This interlocking of the co-op's interest and the members' interests is part of what we can call the *economic linkage* between the co-op and its members.

Co-operative Economic Linkage
- the co-operative's activities *promote the economic success* or well-being of the member's household or income
- there is a *close connection* between the success of the co-op and of the member; if one does well, the other shares in the success
- the co-op's products and services are tailored to *specific member needs*
- member choices and behaviour are tailored to what is needed for the co-op to succeed

The traditional co-operative practice of paying patronage refunds —although it is only one form of economic linkage—can be understood as a common example of this linked relationship. Patronage refunds are, among other things, a mechanism for ensuring that *members share necessarily in the economic success of the co-op*. In other words, it cannot prosper without them prospering, too. The member can trust that the co-op will not profit off the members' backs, because any surplus is returned to the members in proportion to their business. Where close relationships exist between co-ops and their members, the reverse also tends to be the case: the better off the members become, the better the co-op does. Again, in the classic case of a consumer co-operative, when the members are better off, they have more disposable income to spend; and if they are loyal to the co-op, the co-op will benefit in volume and efficiency from the members spending more. Such linkages create incentives or rewards for the co-op to serve the members and for the members to patronize the co-op. Incentives and rewards are one aspect of linkage, and the loyalty/patronage refund mechanism is one of the most common ways in which linkage has been institutionalized in co-ops. There can be many others.

Linkage is not only about a service orientation, distribution of surplus, or incentives. A further aspect is that co-ops' business operations and members' business or household decisions can become closely co-ordinated with one another, leading to a situation where each provides exactly the *kind* of service, product, or patronage that the other can best use. In such a close, integrated relationship, the economy of the member and the economy of the co-op fit together like hand and glove. Neither could attain a better fit out of any other partner, because each has tailored its behaviour to suit the other's needs. This tailoring is not an accident, but is the result of structure, strategy, and evolution over time to achieve results that are achievable in no other way.

The business goals of co-operatives are best realized when member economies and the co-operative's economy become linked in the ways described here. Such a strategy embodies economic cohesion among the members, and between the members and the co-operative. *Social cohesion contributes to co-operative success because it makes it easier for members to trust each other and the co-operative, and to make the* necessary economic commitments. But at the same time, co-operative success contributes to social cohesion because—recalling Dayton-Johnson's use of the term—social cohesion is an aggregate of experiences. Where members see themselves having benefited from co-operation, and see other members benefiting as well, this is social cohesion in Dayton-Johnson's sense.

TRANSPARENCY

Members support co-ops because they <u>trust</u> that doing so will be in their own interest as well as the interest of other members. The discussion of linkage, above, related to why and how the co-op is devoted to meeting member needs. The second part of trust, however, is that the co-op must not only promote member well-being: it must also be *seen* to do so—seen clearly, repeatedly, and over time to be making members better off. This question of how members see their co-operative and its activity is the question of *transparency*. While transparency, at one level, has to do with reporting and communications, it goes far beyond the superficial use of information and has implications for the conduct of co-operative business and for the legal, organizational, and technical structuring of co-operative activities. A co-operative is made transparent not only by good communications but by structures and operations that members can see are designed around their own needs.

Transparency is in fact critical to the long-term survival of co-operatives. It is all too easy for members to begin to take their co-operatives for granted, to lose sight of where they would be if the co-operative no longer existed. The longer a co-operative exists, the easier it is for members to forget why it was created. Transparency, as both an organizing principle and a communications approach, is fundamental to reproducing co-operative membership and loyalty from generation to generation (and even within a generation). Transparency requires that members understand not only their co-operative, but also the industry or sector of which it is a part, so that they can see clearly what their co-operative does for them. This is the root of member loyalty.

The trust that members have in their co-operative is a source of economic success and co-operative advantage. Trust means greater member loyalty, which assists the co-operative to be more successful.

In more formal language, trust lowers contract, monitoring, and agency costs, effectively reducing the barriers between the business and its customers. Any business that creates trust among its customers will be able to perform more efficiently as a result, but co-operatives have some special advantages in this regard. The fact that they are member owned and controlled and do not exist to create profits for any group outside the membership means they can more easily be trusted by their members.[23] This potential co-operative advantage is made real to the extent that the co-operative succeeds in making itself transparent to its members.

The more a co-operative requires of its members—in time, loyalty, capital, and so on—the more transparent it must be to them to justify the level of commitment. Put another way, one method for co-ops to get more from their memberships, to enjoy greater loyalty, to raise capital, or to have higher participation and better leadership, is to make themselves more transparent.

Transparency in Co-operatives

- members are *well informed*—frequently and through multiple channels—about business, service, and financial results
- members understand the *industry or sector* of which their co-op is part; they can see "through" their co-op to markets, forces, and social and economic trends beyond
- members see the different clusters or "pillars" of activity *within* their co-op, the incentives or cross-subsidizations that are built in, and accept the appropriateness of these
- members understand the different *interests or stakeholders* in their co-op

Transparency, as I am using the term, entails at least three different kinds of things. Maintaining the visual metaphor, I refer to these as *seeing the co-operative, seeing into the co-operative,* and *seeing through the co-operative.* Each of these types of seeing is a kind of perception or understanding, or perhaps merely an impression, on the part of members, which they gain in a variety of ways and not only through formal communications.

By seeing the co-operative I mean members have a bird's-eye overview of its historical identity, its contemporary mission, and the various members and stakeholders of whom it is composed. Appreciating the *different* interests of these member and stakeholder groups may be especially important, because latent conflicts among these interests may directly affect how much the members actually trust the co-operative. If, for example, old and young members are thought to have different interests, but both are served by the same co-op, both groups of members may be less enthusiastic in their support —unless they *understand,* on some level, what the different interests are and how both may be satisfied. This is a question of the singular or plural identity of the co-operative and its membership, about which I will say more below, under Cognition.

Seeing into the co-operative entails two pieces, one of which is governance—what many people mean, solely, by transparency. Members need to have adequate knowledge of the governance structures of the co-operative, both to know how they could become involved but also, more importantly, to know why and how far they can trust those structures. The second and related piece is that they have to see "into" the co-operative's business. They have to have knowledge of what lines of business or activities it is in, how these perform and what their challenges are, who benefits, and how much. If members suspect there are hidden cross-subsidizations that benefit others, their commitment to the co-op will likely be less.

Seeing through the co-operative means having an appropriate level of understanding of the wider industry, its challenges and trends. Without such an understanding, members are unlikely to have a real idea why they need the co-operative, what it is good for, and what its limits are. Again, members do not require the detailed knowledge of a marketing expert, but they do need the level of understanding appropriate for the kinds of decisions members make. If, for example, the perception is that WAL-MART dominates the industry, then members need to have some opinion about why WAL-MART is successful and what it means.

Undoubtedly more could be done in terms of formal member education—consumer or member education, newsletters, public meetings and presentations, web sites, courses, and so on—but these are not the main means by which members glean information about the co-op, its inner workings, and its environment. People pick up their impressions from subtle cues, from image and advertising, from word of mouth and interactions, from merchandising and signage on shelves, and many other sources. Instead of concentrating on texts—newsletters, speeches: the tools of the past—co-operatives may have to become much more sophisticated in considering what messages actually reach their members, and from what sources.[24] A store design is a message. How staff act is a message. A patronage refund or other incentive conveys important information. All of this and more makes up the way the co-op presents itself to members. This presentation can be more or less transparent. A number of co-ops in different sectors have discovered that the message *we're a big, complicated business and you should trust us, just because* does not go over well.

COGNITION

Linkage is about serving members; transparency is about making it clear that members are served. The third aspect of the co-operative relationship with members has to do with how the relationship changes over time—because no co-operative relationship stays the same for long. Co-operative relationships must change constantly as the business or service sector and the membership change. The concepts of linkage and transparency may help guide co-operatives to select *what kinds* of change are most appropriate from among the known options. But by themselves, these concepts do not say much about *how* co-operatives change, nor how they identify the options for change in the first place. In today's world, co-operatives have to aim not only to create a structure (or relationship), but even more so, they have to plan for how they will change over time.

Change can happen *to* an organization, as an unconscious process, but this is not always desirable. Change should be undertaken by an organization as a *thinking* or cognitive process, involving imagination, discovery, systematic investigation, and pragmatic choice among well-understood options. This thought process should presumably involve more than just the individual mind of the CEO. Thinking, learning, imagining, and investigating are functions that need to be shared, and to some extent diffused, in a successful organization. They are to a considerable degree functions *of the organization* and not merely of one or a few positions within it. Organizations like co-ops need to pay attention to *how they think* about their surrounding reality, themselves, and their future.

A basic cognitive model for co-ops involves several main elements. The co-op must have a sense of what it is, where it came from, what it does, and where it is going—a sense of identity, or to put it another way, an organizational culture. It must also have a sense of what its mission is in relation to its sector and industry, and its members. To achieve this requires a mental model of who the competition is, what the issues and trends are, and what the co-op aims to do about these. It is not enough, however, that such mental images exist. For them to be useful to the co-operative, they have to be *shared* by the different groups that need to play a role in the co-operative's success, i.e., its various stakeholders. Managers who deal full time with directing the co-operative will have a more detailed understanding than members who deal occasionally with the co-op. But the co-op will be stronger and more cohesive if managers, members, elected leaders, staff, and other stakeholders buy into similar or shared visions. Finally, a cognitive model for a co-op involves the mechanisms by which the organization refines and tests its understandings of itself, its mission, and its sector—mechanisms for collecting and analysing information and ideas (research); mechanisms for maintaining a sufficient degree of consensus (broad, periodic discussion and revision); and mechanisms for trying out new ideas and new approaches on a small scale (innovation). Small-scale experiments with new ideas are important, because co-operatives can rarely risk radically new approaches without testing them first.

Cognitive Models in Co-operatives

- the co-op operates with a clear mental *model of itself* (sense of identity) and of its *role in the wider sector* or industry (mission)
- these models are *widely understood and shared* among stakeholder groups (members, elected leaders, managers, employees, others)

- the co-op undertakes *research* in an organized way to analyse changes in its membership and its environment
- organized research activity is connected to the way the co-op regularly *revisits, discusses, and revises* its identity and its mission
- the co-op encourages *innovation* and has mechanisms for innovations to be tested on a small scale

A cognitive model, as described here, is not just a planning tool (though it certainly helps with that function); it is also the glue that keeps the co-operative and its members together when both are changing.

I have regularly stressed differences among the co-op's members and stakeholders, because such differences, which may be experienced as fragmentation, are a key characteristic of modern or (if you will) postmodern society. It is important to remember that members make judgements about their co-operative not as entirely isolated individuals, but as part of a community of people who have some assumptions or knowledge about each other, who share a similar context, and who think using some common experiences and concepts. In some way, either potentially or literally, they are in communication with each other. We might call membership a community of discourse. Because the success of the co-operative depends not only on one's own choices, but also on those of other members, each member is thinking on some level about other members and how they will behave. What motivates them? Can they be relied upon? Will one's own commitment be wasted, or worse yet, taken advantage of? Members need not just a mental image of their *own* relationship to the co-op, but a mental image of *other members'* relationships to the co-op. They need to see what different services are required by different member groups, how these are accessed and paid for, and whether important cross-subsidization occurs; otherwise they may not fully trust their co-operative to be a good agent for their interests.

A co-op that caters only to the common denominator among diverse members may be missing important opportunities to develop services designed to meet particular needs. Co-ops need to resist an understandable tendency to homogenize their memberships, to ignore or downplay difference. To resist this tendency, they may need to be active in seeking out, highlighting, and understanding differences among their members. Co-operatives that need members to make strong commitments, whether of input, patronage, or investment, may have to reorganize themselves so that members can participate in the parts of the co-op that most interest them. In an extreme case, a co-operative whose members have highly divergent interests might be better off breaking up into a number of organizationally distinct (but perhaps still connected) entities. But where a co-operative aspires to remain whole, it may not be enough to offer different services for different people, to have members or stakeholders involved in different aspects of the co-op's activities. This may complicate the member relationship in the co-operative in ways that actually reduce member commitment overall. A co-operative can cater to and derive strength from the heterogeneity of its stakeholders only if these stakeholders are, in some way, connected with each other.

The concepts of *mental models* and *member identities* are one way to understand the challenge, and the solution. For co-operative renewal and adaptation, the co-op's leaders must have conceptions or mental models of their co-op and their industry that are up-to-date and based on good understanding and analysis. Second, the corresponding mental models held by members and other stakeholders, though they may not be identical, must sufficiently resemble or overlap the models held by the co-op's leaders. These mental models must connect with the members' or stakeholders' sense of their own identity in such a way that they can see themselves—as consumers, as employees, as young or old, as men or women, and so on—reflected adequately in the co-operative. This may require a great deal of nuance and sensitivity; it is unlikely to be achieved by catering only to the least common denominator among the members.

The arguments outlined in this section have demonstrated that pursuit of co-operative advantages in business leads to co-ordination, shared understandings, and trust among members as well as between members and the co-operative. With accelerated change, competition of new kinds, and fragmenting member and stakeholder identities, it is likely that co-ops will have to become more sophisticated in how they think about and pursue linkage, transparency, and cognitive processes. All of this depends on individual investments (of time, energy, and commitment) in creating social capital. Will it also make a difference to social cohesion—that is, will benefits aggregate at a higher level, and benefit not only a narrow group? There are two reasons to believe they will. First, co-operative networks generally overlap and diffuse into wider community networks. The co-operative principles of open membership and concern for community reflect the historical experience of co-operatives, that their members' interests tend to correlate with or approximate wider community interests. They do this because the co-operative is typically open to all, in which case it cannot provide an exclusive privilege; and because the type of benefit it provides is needs based, often therefore of interest to many. Naturally, deviations from these conditions will make for interesting studies. Second, co-operative social capital does demonstrably aggregate at higher levels and bridge between subgroups and communities. This is demonstrated by federated, regional, and national co-operative systems based on autonomous local organizations. Such co-operative systems are living examples of forms of local social capital that are simultaneously part of regional and national social cohesion.

VOLUNTARY ADHESION AND IDENTITIES

Co-operatives are autonomous institutions created and maintained by individual choice. They have no automatic or guaranteed existence, but rather sustain themselves in a competitive environment where they do not survive unless people support them. In other words, they are not merely about cohesion, but also adhesion, the conscious act of associating oneself with a mutual entity. This creates a situation slightly more nuanced than Dayton-Johnson's models, where social capital is created by interactions between individuals, and social cohesion aggregates over time out of these choices. In the case of an existing co-operative, the individual has a choice to join a voluntarily created institution that embodies the results of past members' decisions and behaviour. The co-operative organization, in other words, makes manifest the social investments espoused by past groups of members. It renders social cohesion visible, and not merely in an abstract aggregate, but in a concrete organizational form that individuals directly perceive and experience. To each member, the co-operative "stands for" all the other members, past and present. We may suppose that this could greatly speed up the processes of individuals thinking through decisions regarding social capital and social cohesion, and so it can; but there are also complications.

Before expanding on these points, let me say that this discussion of how co-operatives work has a number of implications for Canada's discussions about social cohesion. First, there may be a benefit in looking at the *voluntary choices* of Canadians as important creators of cohesion—not just shared values or national institutions or policy frameworks, but direct engagements by citizens in society, however simple these may at first appear. Much of the literature concerning social cohesion, so far, has taken a critical stance towards voluntarism, seeing it as a source of divisiveness and inequality, as an alternative to public social programs, and as a tool of only limited, small-scale usefulness.[25] Co-operatives generally represent a voluntary alternative to the *private,* not the public, sector. And where they are an alternative to public-sector activity, this does not necessarily mean the gutting of social principles.[26] Second, resulting as they do from the largest social movement in Canadian history (currently, something like ten to fifteen million Canadians are members), co-ops provide an example of *large-scale* voluntary activity that bridges local, provincial, and regional boundaries. Using co-operatives as an example, we can address questions about different kinds or levels of social cohesion by reconceptualizing cohesion issues as identity issues. Instead of asking, does local social cohesion strengthen or weaken national social cohesion?—a question so abstract that it is hard to know where to begin—we can ask about the multiple identities local people feel and demonstrate, and whether these conflict or reinforce one another. Intermediate-level voluntary organizations may, indeed, be excellent places to see these processes at work.

As I mentioned at the outset, I spent much of the year 2003 crisscrossing western Canada with a tape recorder, talking to people in consumer co-operatives that are members of what is called the Co-operative Retailing System (CRS), and working with the transcripts of their interviews. Only a couple of them ever mentioned the term social cohesion, and yet it was present, nevertheless, in what they described—present, but often below the surface. Co-operators are pragmatic people, by and large, who are wary of woolly generalizations. Many of today's managers, especially, see the idealistic past rhetoric of co-operative movements as something worse than mere baggage. It may, in their eyes, actually be dangerous in its potential to distract co-op leaders and members from what they need to do to be successful. Yet for all that, underneath the stress on marketing and profitability is another set of values, shaped by the relationships and ultimately by the ownership structure and community base of the co-operatives.[27]

Commercial co-operatives—as opposed to small, idealistic, "non-profit" co-operatives—do not usually look much different from competing businesses, and often their management styles, organizational structures, and labour or human-resources policies are not much different, either. As Malo, Lévesque, et al. noted in their study, mentioned earlier, the distinctive features of mature co-operatives lie, first of all, in their charitable donations, patronage refunds, and investments in communities. As those authors also demonstrated, co-operatives may preserve high-quality, front-line service to members, including small members, while centralizing backroom functions to remain competitive. This strategy differs from the behaviour of profit-maximizing competitors, and embodies the distinctive dedication of co-operatives to localities and regions. Consumer co-operatives in western Canada illustrate the same pattern; and beyond that, they vividly demonstrate that local ownership, combined with a well-functioning federated system, can be a source of good governance and effective innovation. The Co-operative Retailing System succeeds—it *thrives* in small, medium, and some very large communities—*because* of its co-operative character, local ownership, and federated structure.

The success of the CRS reflects several kinds of cohesion. There is, first of all, the cohesion within local, geographic communities, among the members of the co-op, or between the members and the co-op. This is especially evident in smaller or more isolated communities, but the same thing occurs in large cities, where the co-op may act in similar fashion as the focal point for a neighbourhood. In such cases, managers, staff, and members report that the co-op is seen as the centre of the community. It is the only full-service outlet, or it is the place people go to put up notices on the community bulletin board, or it has the cafeteria where seniors drink coffee together or local voluntary associations assemble for meetings or marches. Co-operatives can and do serve groups in the community whom social-cohesion researchers would characterize as marginalized, including new immigrant communities, Aboriginal people, and families on tight budgets. Interestingly, co-op leaders are often reluctant to talk about such groups, perhaps because the commitment to equality in co-ops is so strong that it makes people reluctant to draw attention to differences.

Cohesion in the co-op system is not only local; there is, second, the cohesion among the co-operatives—the cohesion of the whole system, across the communities, the multiple provinces and territories within which it operates. To some extent, there is a true bridging going on. Members who patronize and support co-operatives are identifying with a brand, an image, a set of values that is consistent in some ways from Lake Superior to the Beaufort Sea to the Inner Passage. However, co-operative loyalty is a highly local matter. While further study is needed, it seems probable that most members regard their co-op as an institution of their community, and are unaware of or give little thought to the equivalent co-ops elsewhere. If this supposition is true, the cohesion of the CRS is less a matter of cohesion among hundreds of thousands of co-op members than among the *leaders* who are developed and gain experience within the system. Leadership development is the co-ops' main contribution to bridging among communities. But perhaps when ordinary members travel to distant Canadian communities and see a co-op there, they do, after all, recognize some connection to their own co-op at home. Research to study such perceptions has not been done.

A lesson from the retail co-ops is that they do not simply promote cohesion because it is a good thing to do; that isn't how commercial co-operatives work. Rather, they are challenged to meet competition, to innovate, to reduce costs, and to increase quality and service. The means they can draw on to do these things often involve social cohesion and certainly contribute to it. Perhaps the best case in point is that managers at all levels in the CRS describe the ways in which they must strive to persuade members and create buy-in, rather than being able to give orders as they might do in a more hierarchical organization. The wholesale has to persuade retail managers to adopt its programs. To ensure this happens, it involves them in various ways in discussing, designing, and modifying the programs. Through this process, the wholesale also establishes its credibility: it creates trust. As a result of the trust and collaboration among levels of the organization, innovations are better designed and adopted more quickly. This is an example of the mechanisms by which social cohesion (in this case, cohesion among levels and branches of the co-op system) is theorized to contribute to productivity and growth.[28]

This brings us to a third dimension of cohesion in the co-op system: cohesion among staff and among managers. Formally, CRS co-ops are organizations of member consumers; in the organizational chart, employees appear only the way they would in any other firm. But the reality may be somewhat different. As interviews indicated, the CRS benefits from the stability and experience of employees who spend exceptionally long careers in the system, receiving training and development along the way for their changing roles. Of twenty-three retail co-op general managers whom I interviewed—the CEOs of their local firms—twenty-one started off as checkout clerks, shelf stockers, gas-pump attendants, truck drivers, or the like. This is not so much a policy or principle of the co-operatives as a necessity resulting from their distinctive structure (which makes it difficult to bring in outside managers past a certain level) and their community-based ownership (which roots them in communities of various sizes in a stable way, with few transfers, mergers, or acquisitions such as often shake up the workforces of profit-maximizing companies). The community orientation of the co-ops also creates an environment in which it is normal and expected that staff, again especially managers, will play certain kinds of roles in their communities, as leaders, as advisors, and as community figures. It is not a universal or hard-and-fast truth, but it seems that being an employee of the co-op system may mean working in a relatively stable workplace, with good opportunities for training and advancement, and within a context of both customer service and community orientation. This, too, looks like cohesion, of a type that increases efficiency for the firm, satisfaction for the employees, and benefits to the community. Again, more research is needed.

While in many senses, both economic and social, the CRS co-operatives are eminently successful, I have mentioned a certain colourlessness in how managers and leaders describe their members. Leaders in the system commonly distinguish among their members in three respects: by age, by economic size, and by location. The system's current marketing is aimed at young families, first of all—making stores child-friendly and catering to families with little time by offering ready-made meals. Beyond that, seniors are recognized as a distinct group, perhaps not as important in the volume of what they purchase individually, but historically (as co-op pioneers who built the current social cohesion of the organization) and socially as a distinct group in the community. In addition, young people (teens and early twenties) are often identified as a group in which co-operatives have a distinct interest, especially as future employees and leaders. With regard to economic size, this typically enters the discussion in connection with the agricultural and commercial arms of the consumer co-ops' business, especially in bulk sales of petroleum to, for example, farms or trucking firms. Here, co-ops feel a tension between serving the large purchasers competitively (with discounts or differential patronage refunds on the specific products they purchase, for example) and maintaining services to the smaller purchasers, both of which they would like to do. This is similar to co-ops' understanding of locational issues, in which they want to maintain prime urban locations while at the same time keeping locations in smaller, outlying communities. The tension arises because competitors would just serve the larger customers or centres; the co-ops want to serve both if they can keep doing so. Some other distinctions do enter into the mix, mostly in terms of display and merchandising. The system has paid increased attention to the specific preferences of women members in a variety of ways, ranging from better night lighting at gas bars and convenience stores to fresh-cut flowers in washrooms. Managers in the system also procure, stock, and display products for particular ethnic or immigrant communities, following demographic trends.

While these examples do show awareness of differences among members, some co-operatives do more. First, the approaches mentioned above generally involve products and marketing, not participation, involvement, empowerment, or education. But some co-ops offer classes for seniors, network with particular ethnic communities and invite representatives to join committees, or have distinct representation for different communities in their elections (such as delegates from small communities where branches are located, or special directorships set aside for youths). Such approaches help empower the members concerned. Second, while accommodation of differences seems to be understood in co-operatives mainly as a matter of personal consumer preferences, some co-operatives do market themselves more on the basis of values, inviting members to identify with these. Typically, these values involve support for the local community, but co-operative values such as mutuality, tolerance, equality, and respect could also have wider resonance. As a rule, most co-operatives seem to do little image advertising, and instead focus on the basics of products and services, giving the impression that the co-op is neutral and treats all consumers equally. Some groups may be more receptive to such a neutral, commercial approach than others. Third, and more specifically, some co-ops make organized attempts to involve themselves with Aboriginal communities. Several co-operatives deal commercially with First Nations governments—for example, selling petroleum for resale by an on-reserve Aboriginal gas station. I found at least one where board members and managers have made concerted attempts to network in First Nations communities; and I talked to a number of co-op presidents who have done their best to recruit Aboriginal candidates for the board of directors or Aboriginal youth to support for education and training. Naturally, individual First Nations or Métis customers or members are more visible in some co-ops than others, but many co-ops do look more white (if I may put it crudely) than the geographic regions they serve in western Canada.

I have argued that the underlying issue, for co-ops, is the complex relationship between the identities of an organization and the identities of different members it serves. Co-ops cannot be all things to all people—a phrase usually quoted to mean they must specialize economically, but it could equally apply to their image in the community. It is probably the case that organizations tend to have shallow or one-dimensional identities, which cannot easily stand for the actual heterogeneity of the members. Such a least-common-denominator kind of co-operative identity, however, may invoke only weak adherence from members. One of the trends in western Canadian society is certainly towards greater cultural diversity, whether through the growth of the Aboriginal population or through immigration; and many other kinds of identity are also expressed more confidently today. Apart from other considerations, there is a marketing opportunity for co-operatives in this, and despite co-operative values, it is the marketing opportunity that ensures they can respond. Co-ops cannot be all things to all people, but there may be a growing advantage to being slightly different things to different people. This would require much more careful and sophisticated marketing than in the past—just as CRS co-ops have got to where they are today by continual improvement in their marketing.

Interviews and study visits need to be complemented by wider, more systematic, and more in-depth studies of co-operative membership in order to unpack the actual connections or tensions in people's attachments to the co-operatives they have voluntarily joined. But given the special characteristics of the co-operative sector, it is inevitable that understanding these relationships will expand our understanding of social cohesion in Canada. Unlike other instances of social cohesion, co-operatives are voluntary, local, but also connected to large-scale networks. They formally articulate multiple levels of association and cross boundaries of communities. They do not function in what is commonly understood as the public sector, but instead produce public goods in the private sector—dealing head-on with the forces of competition and corporate globalization that many people perceive as threats to social cohesion. Like small business, they represent not just Canadian ownership but local ownership in a globally competitive economy. Unlike small business, they require formal commitments by ordinary Canadians to support them. If economic autonomy has a future in the globalized economy—and it is difficult to imagine how social cohesion can be maintained without a foundation of economic autonomy—then co-operatives will be part of that future.

Endnotes

1. A co-operative is defined by the International Co-operative Alliance as "an autonomous association of persons united voluntarily to meet their common economic, social, and cultural needs and aspirations through a jointly owned and democratically controlled enterprise" ("The ICA Statement on the Co-operative Identity," from Ian MacPherson, *Co-operative Principles for the 21st Century* (Geneva: International Co-operative Alliance, 1996), p. 1). This definition reflects more than a century of discussion and has several important elements, including the substantives association and enterprise, the concept of needs-based activity, as well as the qualifiers autonomous, voluntary, joint, and democratic. Importantly, it may apply to organizations incorporated as business corporations, associations, or nonprofits, or those not incorporated at all, where the specified conditions are met.
2. Jeff Dayton-Johnson, "Social Capital, Social Cohesion, Community: A Microeconomic Analysis," in *The Economic Implications of Social Cohesion*, ed. Lars Osberg (Toronto: University of Toronto Press, 2003), pp. 43–78, and the same for the following.
3. Jane Jenson, *Mapping Social Cohesion: The State of Canadian Research* (Ottawa: Canadian Policy Research Networks Inc., 1998), p. v, and the same for the following quotation. Academics routinely use the term "neoliberal" to describe policies of free trade, deregulation, and privatization (key aspects of economic globalization as practised in the late twentieth century) because of the similarity of these policies to tenets of nineteenth-century liberalism. This usage can be confusing to nonacademics, since the same policies are today often regarded as aspects of neoconservative economic policy.
4. Cited by Paul Bernard, "Social Cohesion: A Critique" (Ottawa: Canadian Policy Research Networks Inc., December 1999), Discussion Paper No. F–09, p. 5.
5. Jenson, p. 8, and ff for the following.
6. Jenson writes, "Solidarism developed as a direct response—and rejection—of 19th century liberalism" (p. 9). I have to admit to scratching my head over this comment. The Third Republic and its political elites favoured constitutionalism and the Republican tradition, economic and social modernization, anticlericalism—in short, many of the core concepts of nineteenth-century liberalism—while being opposed by clerical conservatives, monarchists, Marxists, and other traditional enemies of mainstream liberalism. In fact, solidarism looks much more like a variety of nineteenth-century liberalism than a rejection of it.
7. Jenson, pp. 15 and ff.
8. Ibid., p. 16.
9. Social economy is discussed in English by Benoît Lévesque and Bill Ninacs, "The Social Economy in Canada: The Québec Experience," in *Social Economy: International Debates and Perspectives*, eds. Eric Shragge and Jean-Marc Fontan (Montréal: Black Rose Books, 2000).
10. Jenson, p. 24.
11. Some of the key works in which Putnam developed his ideas include R.D.

Putnam, "The Prosperous Community: Social Capital and Public Life," *The American Prospect* 13 (spring 1993); Putnam, *Making Democracy Work: Civic Traditions in Modern Italy* (Princeton: Princeton University Press, 1993); G. Gamm and R.D. Putnam, "The Growth of Voluntary Associations in America, 1840–1940," *Journal of Interdisciplinary History* 29, no. 4 (1999); Putnam, *Bowling Alone: The Collapse and Revival of American Community* (New York: Simon & Schuster, 2000); and Putnam, "Social Capital: Measurement and Consequences," *ISUMA* (spring 2001). They have been extensively discussed, developed, and critiqued by others.

12. Bernard, p. 3.

13. Ibid., p. 16.

14. Sophie Bessis, "From Social Exclusion to Social Cohesion: Towards a Policy Agenda," Management of Social Transformations (MOST), UNESCO Policy Paper No. 2 (1995).

15. Posted at http://www.social.coe.int/en/cohesion/strategy/htm, accessed 24 December 2002.

16. Summary of strategy posted at http://www.social.coe.int/en/cohesion/strategy/CDCS/sumstrat/htm, accessed 24 December 2002.

17. *Social Cohesion Developments,* newsletter of the Council of Europe, posted at http://www.social.coe.int/en/cohesion.htm, accessed 24 December 2002.

18. Jenson, pp. 29–37.

19. Neil MacGregor, "The Perpetual Present," *Oxford Today* 15, no. 1 (2002): pp. 23–25.

20. Marie-Claire Malo, Benoît Lévesque, Omer Chouinard, Pierre-Marcel Desjardins, et Éric Forgues, *Coopératives financières, cohésion sociale et nouveau territoire local à l'ère de la mondialisation* (Montréal: Cahiers du CRISES, mars 2002), Collection "Working Papers," No. 0108.

21. Malo et al., pp. 54ff.

22. Brett Fairbairn, *Three Strategic Concepts for the Guidance of Co-operatives: Linkage, Transparency, and Cognition* (Saskatoon: Centre for the Study of Co-operatives, 2003). What follows includes abridged excerpts from this booklet.

23. On the importance of trust in the economic success of co-operatives, see Roger Spear, "The Co-operative Advantage," *Annals of Public and Cooperative Economics* 71, no. 4 (2000): pp. 507–23.

24. I have expanded on these ideas in Brett Fairbairn, "Communications, Culture, and Co-operatives: Liminal Organizations in a Liminal Age," paper for "Mapping Co-operative Studies in the New Millennium: A Joint Congress of the International Co-operative Alliance Research Committee and the Canadian Association for Studies in Co-operation," 27–31 May 2003, University of Victoria, Canada; Revised June 2003.

25. Valid points, of course, though the dualism (either we have a welfare state, or we have voluntary activity) sometimes seems a bit forced. Besides Jenson, another intelligent argument in this vein is Frances Wooley, "Social Cohesion and Voluntary Activity: Making Connections," in Osberg, pp. 150–82.

26. See the discussion in John Restakis and Evert Lindquist, eds., *The Co-op Alternative: Civil Society and the Future of Public Services* (Toronto: Institute of Public Administration of Canada, 2001).

27. What follows are preliminary results and reflections from in-depth interviews with eighty-one individuals, visits to more than two dozen retail co-operatives in Manitoba, Saskatchewan, Alberta, and British Columbia, as well as documentary research conducted between January and July 2003. The co-operatives are all members of the Co-operative Retailing System, that is, they are affiliated to Federated Co-operatives Limited. Generally speaking, they operate consumer stores handling food and groceries, and/or petroleum outlets; some have lumber, hardware, agricultural supplies such as feed, fertilizers, and chemicals; others have pharmacies, clothing, appliances, or particular lines of business unique to their communities. All are owned locally by consumer members. More detailed results of this research are available in Brett Fairbairn, *Living the Dream: Membership and Marketing in the Co-operative Retailing System* (Saskatoon: Centre for the Study of Co-operatives, 2004).

28. Dick Stanley and Sandra Smeltzer argue that social cohesion reduces transaction costs by reducing the need for defensive behaviour and increasing political and labour-relations stability; it reduces costs to firms by increasing worker productivity (less dysfunction, increased employee satisfaction, faster spread of ideas). See "Many Happy Returns: How Social Cohesion Attracts Investment," in Osberg, pp. 231–46.

BENOÎT LÉVESQUE, PATRICK DE BORTOLI,
AND JEAN-PIERRE GIRARD

Translated from the French by Nancy Senior

SOCIAL COHESION AND DELIBERATIVE DEMOCRACY
A CHALLENGE FOR CO-OPERATIVES IN BUILDING THE COMMON GOOD[1]

THE CONCEPT OF SOCIAL COHESION plays a central and unifying role in the research project on which this book is based—Co-operative Membership and Globalization: Creating Social Cohesion through Market Relations. It is essential to explain the relevance of this concept, since it is the structuring principle of this work on co-operative organizations. In the first part of the article, after defining its raison d'être, we will show the ties between the contributions of collective organizations such as co-operatives and social cohesion. But the contribution of co-operatives, and more generally of social economy enterprises, to the construction of the common good depends also on the exercise of democracy. We show various concepts that do not all have the same consequences. The means and the impact of the practice of democracy differ considerably between liberal representative democracy and deliberative democracy. The various ideas of democracy, and the consequences and the importance of favouring deliberative democracy, will be the subject of the second and third parts of the article.

Relevance of the Concept of Social Cohesion

The idea of social cohesion has resurfaced in recent years, largely because of awareness of its opposite—that is, a social dislocation, or fragmentation, or even exclusion of a growing part of the population.[2] The adjustments made necessary by the upheavals in the structure of global economic exchanges over the last twenty years call for a renewed questioning of the means of organizing and harmonizing the social, political, and economic spheres, including those in developing countries. The spread of the market economy as the dominant and all-powerful sphere has not been without hindrances and consequences for the social and political realms. Globalization has led to considerable structural adjustment in most countries in the name of economic growth, balanced budgets, and fighting inflation. This concern has even reached the Organization for Economic Co-operation and Development (OECD), an organization whose members have been among the principal players in this globalization: "Although these policies have been successful in supporting economic growth, combating inflation and reducing current-account imbalances, there is now pressure on many governments to take stock of the longer-term societal implications that are beginning to emerge."[3]

Among the social implications, the organization mentions polarization of income, which is itself responsible for disenchantment with politics, a large increase in unemployment, and the problem of social exclusion. In a context where growth and economic prosperity are accompanied by insecurity and social divisions, the question arises: How can we combine economic growth and social development?

The social question also raises that of the legitimacy of political powers. The choice of globalizing the economy, followed by elimination or reduction of public services, has made politicians responsible for disenchantment with politics and the rise of "pathological" forms of political power through spontaneous violence.[4] But disenchantment with *one kind* of politics—that represented by the politicians, in whom citizens are continuing to lose confidence.[5] On the other hand, there is also a desire to reinvest in the democratic process through civil society, that is, more actively and directly.[6] From this point of view, the question of social cohesion is part of the mandate of a society that is democratic, free, and egalitarian, in accordance with the three ideological pillars of the French Revolution: Liberty, Equality, and Fraternity (Solidarity).[7]

As a result of better understanding the "material" consequences of forced restructuring and structural adjustments caused by globalization, neoliberal ideology is subject to more and more questioning. "As people attempt to start such conversations, however, they discover that they also face an ideological tidal wave."[8] By proposing to give the market economy and technical systems priority over individuals and collective organizations, while leaving the market responsible for sharing resources and powers, neoliberal ideology contributes to reinforcing social disparities both within and between countries, leading inevitably to exclusion, isolation, and thus to fragmentation of the social sphere. Breton defines the limits of this ideology by showing by extension those of the self-regulating market, emphasizing that this market "may perform certain functions in allocating resources, but it is clearly incapable of performing the functions of redistribution, and thus of ensuring social protection," and even more so of ensuring social cohesion.[9] But is the dislocation of the social bond caused by neoliberalism alone?

To this (neoliberal) "market conservatism" is added another ideology, which has serious consequences for the re-establishment of the social bond: the conservatism of the welfare state. Making the welfare state the guarantor of all social rights that have been won, this ideology masks the effect of bureaucratization and government management of social actors, leading to the dislocation and dissolution of solidarity (an increasing dissociation between contributors and beneficiaries, for example). This state conservatism, costly and considered inefficient, leads to a philosophy of blame and a culture of entitlement that make the state both a scapegoat for all social problems and the only possible means of solving them: "This philosophy and this culture are being questioned today because they are seen to lead us to a scenario that does not make sense: one where the freest individual is the one most managed by the state ... a soft totalitarianism that would result directly from the logic of the welfare state."[10]

Both the critique of the self-regulating market and that of the invasive bureaucratic state lead us to consider a third sector that can generate the social bond: civil society and its organizations.[11] By their great variety of activities and their diverse forms of organization—consumer co-ops, worker co-ops, solidarity co-ops—co-operatives find themselves in various situations: some deal with the world of the market, while others are like quasi-public services. But by the nature of their organizational form, they all, to different degrees, relate to civil society and its actors.

The co-operative, like other so-called social economy organizations, combines a social dimension with an economic one, which makes these collective enterprises different from other kinds of organizations.

The social dimension is present in any economy, but it is not always easy to recognize because it is protean and never in its final form. While it is present at the level of *input* or what makes it possible for an enterprise to start up and expand (for example, collaboration by the family, by a collectivity, by institutions, and by state aid), the capitalist enterprise nevertheless does not recognize these contributions either in sharing power or in sharing profits. In the social economy enterprise, these contributions are recognized in theory, but in order for them to be fully recognized, there must be a public space that allows such a construction.[12] Similarly, any enterprise has positive or negative social effects, which economists call externalities because they do not appear on balance sheets (in capitalist enterprises, balance-sheet *output* is limited to the market area). In the case of the social economy, these externalities are not only identified, but generally planned for. As they are not necessarily visible at the beginning, and a fortiori in the long term, they cannot be taken care of without deliberation and the participation of the parties concerned. Deliberation and democratic functioning make it possible not only to identify the social in the economy, but also to set priorities among, for example, job creation, local development, respect for the environment, equity, quality of life, etc. In short, an enterprise and an association—the combination that gives the co-operative its form—cannot belong to the social economy without investing in democracy, that is, their democracy. But what do we mean by democracy?

Four Forms of Democracy

At the societal level as well as that of individual organizations, at least four forms of democracy can be identified:

1. *representative democracy*, in which representatives are elected by the citizens or parties concerned;
2. *direct democracy or participatory democracy*, where the citizens or parties concerned speak and decide without mediation;
3. *social democracy*, which is based on a common understanding or consultation by the collective actors in a society; and
4. *deliberative democracy*, which calls for deliberation to produce enlightened and socially validated choices.

These four forms are not mutually exclusive, since a representative democracy may give great importance to deliberation, while direct democracy and social democracy may be accompanied by representative democracy, as allowed by referendums initiated by elected representatives. From this comes the idea of *plural democracy*, which would allow the potential benefits of these various forms. This option is not a panacea; it presupposes *"democratic doubt,"*[13] or at least a questioning that accepts the uncertainty at the heart of any deliberation.[14]

While direct democracy and social democracy[15] have often been used to criticize representative democracy (also called liberal democracy), we must recognize that the various forms of democracy are insufficient and that it is worthwhile to call on each one, in particular deliberative democracy.[16] Representative democracy tends to be based solely on individual choices defined by individual interests and preferences that are considered fixed. A society that limits itself to representative democracy implicitly states that it is composed exclusively of individuals. This form of democracy, essential though it is, causes those represented to be excluded, or better stated, soon creates a gap between citizens and their representatives.[17] Social democracy, which is based on co-operation among large social actors (expression of collective interests), complements representative democracy (expression of individual interests). However, social democracy is itself limited in that it gives the impression that the sum of collective interests constitutes the general interest, whereas in fact, the combination of collective interests does not reflect the general interest any more than does the combination of individual interests.[18] In addition, if it is not subject to representative democracy, social democracy can turn into a narrow corporatism or even into a privatization of citizenship.[19] Finally, direct democracy and wider participation do not necessarily ensure an increase in the moral and intellectual abilities of the person making the decisions.[20] It may also serve as a way of diverting representative democracy to serve only the interests of professionals.[21] For these and other reasons, deliberative democracy is as essential as representative democracy.

Democracy consists not only of choosing but of offering the possibility of enlightened choices, or choices for the common good or the general interest. To avoid the risk of these decisions being produced by short-sighted or narrow interests, the desire to promote the common good, the public good, or the general interest must be encouraged.[22] To construct a higher good, one must also support the circulation of information and the construction of public spaces that will allow for debate. Thus "by deliberation and the clash of opinions, temporary consensuses are built, definitions of the *common good* that are not present at the start in society and which are literally the product of democratic development."[23] By this means it becomes possible to not only go beyond or even to reconcile individual interests and collective interests, but also to derive a general interest defined in terms of the common good and on the basis of citizenship, that is, from the point of view of "the person who prefers the common good to his or her personal or group interest."[24]

Unlike liberal theory, which tends to limit democracy to representative democracy, *deliberative democracy* receives legitimacy not so much from a will that is already formed, as from the process of forming this will, that is, deliberation. Consequently, "the idea that we have to say goodbye to the idea of fixed preferences implies a learning process that does not aim for a preconceived model of substantial rationality, a continuous and open learning process without a teacher and without a program."[25] The term "learning" is no doubt more appropriate than "training," in that determining what should be learned is itself one of the objects of the learning process. From this point of view, deliberative democracy aims "to organize and regulate

Table 1. Forms of Democracy[26]

Forms of Democracy	Means	Radicalization
Representative Democracy (Institution)	Representative authorities Choice of elected representatives Basis: individual interest Vote and majority	Extending categories of persons entitled to participate
Direct Democracy (Organization)	No mediation Direct participation Interest formulated directly Choice by consensus	Extending levels and sectors where people have the right to participate
Social Democracy	Co-operation among large social actors bearing collective interests Voluntary associations and groups Mobilization	Encouraging people who share common conditions to unite and express themselves
Deliberative Democracy (Process and education)	Deliberation and discursive dimension Public spaces detached from immediate interests Free expression by all Objective: to derive a higher good that can be justified	Stimulating deliberation Procedures that make it possible to formulate well-thought-out and socially validated preferences Collective learning

the various preferences of each citizen-voter so as to organize and regulate social conflict not only around the confrontation between majority and minority (or between workers and entrepreneurs in the case of economic democracy), but also as an interior conflict between what individuals themselves consider their more desirable desires and those that are less so."[27]

TOWARDS A "DEMOCRATIZATION OF DEMOCRACY"

The four forms of democracy that we have just examined make possible a strategy of *"democratization of democracy"*[28] in at least three ways. First, there is the introduction of *"democratic doubt,"* which encourages us to question all forms, and which leads us to refuse one exclusive form. Second, it becomes possible to envisage a hybridization of the different forms of democracy—what might constitute a *plural democracy* open to a plural economy. Finally, the idea of *radicalization of the principle of democratic participation* might take the following direction: for representative democracy, a "generalization of categories of persons authorized to participate"; for social democracy, policies that favour expression by collective actors and the formation of voluntary associations; for direct democracy, a "generalization of real levels and of institutional sectors that have the right to participate"; for deliberative democracy, "procedures that favour the formulation of well-thought-out, coherent, generalizable, justifiable, and socially validated preferences."[29]

These four forms of democracy are suitable not only to societies that have chosen democracy, but also, with certain adaptations, to various organizations and enterprises dealing with the social economy, including co-operatives. These organizations cannot develop and reach their full potential without democratic functioning. To this end, it is possible to put in place a strategy of "democratization of democracy," as described above. From the beginning, democratic doubt is required for examining the democratic functioning of the social economy. It must be acknowledged that the enterprises and organizations of the social economy often tend to be based on representative democracy alone, to the detriment of other forms. It is obvious that these enterprises and organizations are *institutionally* in advance of other forms of organization because of rules that give power to the people according to the principle of one person, one vote. As well, the organizational form of solidarity co-operatives[30] requires, by definition, dialogue and arbitration between the interests of users and workers, in addition to individual and collective actors from the community who are sustaining members of these co-ops.[31] On the other hand, on the level of direct democracy (the *organizational point of view*), these collective enterprises are sometimes less advanced than capitalist enterprises with regard to, for example, participation by workers (e.g., semi-autonomous teams).[32] In some worker co-operatives, we have observed forms of organization closer to Taylorism than to democratization of work.[33] Similarly, for certain enterprises and organizations of social economy centred on users, the organization of work often represents a blind spot.[34]

Finally, deliberation is often limited to a few people, so that boards of directors make the decisions and annual general meetings are an empty formality. Gradually, debates can be considered a waste of time; there is a danger of this happening if deliberative assemblies are not adequately prepared. In other words, deliberative democracy cannot be spur-of-the-moment; it requires a large investment of effort, a process of collective learning, and the formation of social capital and a climate of confidence. From the point of view of deepening democracy, Archon Fung and Erik Olin Wright[35] have examined some cases of social economy in the North and in the South to show the characteristics of an empowered deliberative democracy (EDD) as well as its limits. Deliberation as a process for democratic decisions requires that the participants learn to listen to each other's positions if they want to arrive at well-thought-out collective choices. The participants must also learn to persuade each other by supplying reasons that the others can accept, instead of asking them to accept things on trust. As deliberation often gives rise to clashes of ideas and to conflicts, there are sometimes winners and losers. According to Fung and Wright, "The important feature of genuine deliberation is that participants find reasons that they can accept in collective actions, not necessarily that they completely endorse the action or find it maximally advantageous."[36] It may happen that the various interests or collective goods are hard to reconcile with an effort to construct a *common good*, which requires effort and compromise. In such situations, there is a danger that participants may manipulate others, using their power to impose particular interests.

While the deepening of democracy must occur first in enterprises and organizations of the social economy, as well as in their sectoral or intersectoral groupings—that is, in the case of co-operatives and federations—nevertheless the *institutional context* may or may not favour this deepening towards plural democracy. In the first place, it is necessary that the state be decentralized and that it respects the relative autonomy of enterprises and organizations of the social economy, even when they take on certain functions or provide services formerly provided by the state. This requires a change in the places where decisions are made; that is, rather than at the macrodemocratic level of representative and executive institutions, they should be made at "the *molecular* level, where a collective will is formed in the various contexts of civil society, including some that are by definition out of the reach of institutions and of control and intervention by the state."[37] Second, the state must recognize the contribution of the social economy to the development not only of active citizenship but also of a *common good*. The state's recognition of the social economy is meaningful only when appropriate resources are allocated, and innovation and learning are encouraged for the benefit of all of society. In the long term, the state and its agents could be transformed, in particular by the reintroduction of deliberative democracy at these various levels.

Endnotes

1. Parts two and three of this article (the sections titled Four Forms of Democracy and Towards a "Democratization of Democracy") are based on part of the paper "Économie sociale et solidaire dans un contexte de mondialisation pour une démocratie plurielle," which was presented by Benoît Lévesque at the 2nd International Meeting on the Globalization of Solidarity, held in Québec, 9–12 October 2001.
2. Jane Jenson, *Mapping Social Cohesion: The State of Canadian Research* (Ottawa: Canadian Policy Research Networks, Study no. F–03, 1998), p. 15.
3. Organization for Economic Co-operation and Development (OECD), *Societal Cohesion and the Globalizing Economy* (Paris: OEDC, 1997), foreword.
4. Slavoj Zizek, *The Fragile Absolute: Or, Why Is the Christian Legacy Worth Fighting For?* (London: Verso, 2000).
5. Leslie Pal and F. Leslie Seidle, "Constitutional Politics 1990–92: The Paradox of Participation," in *How Ottawa Spends, 1993–94: A More Democratic Canada…?* ed. Susan D. Phillips (Ottawa: Carleton University Press, 1993).

6. Ekos Research Associates, "Rethinking Government '94: An Overview and Synthesis" (Ottawa: Ekos Research Associates, Inc., 1995), p. 20; and Suzanne Peters, *Exploring Canadian Values: A Synthesis Report* (Ottawa: Canadian Policy Research Networks, 1995), p. 12.
7. Paul Bernard, "Social Cohesion: A Critique" (Ottawa: Canadian Policy Research Networks, Discussion Paper no. F–09, 1999), p. 4.
8. Jenson, p. 7.
9. Gilles Breton, « La protection sociale sert à se protéger du marché, » dans *L'État aux orties?* sous la dir. de Sylvie Paquerot (Montréal: les Éditions Écosociété, 1996), p. 134.
10. Ibid., p. 136.
11. Joseph-Yvon Thériault, « De la critique de l'État-providence à la reviviscence de la société civile : le point de vue démocratique, » dans Paquerot, p. 145.
12. Jean-Louis Laville et Renaud Sainsaulieu, dir., *Sociologie de l'association. Des organisations à l'épreuve du changement social* (Paris: Desclée de Brouwer, 1997).
13. Thériault, p. 150.
14. Michel Callon, Pierre Lascoumes, et Yannick Barthe, *Agir dans un monde incertain: Essai sur la démocratie technique* (Paris: Seuil, 2001).
15. P.C. Schmitter, "Interest Systems and the Consolidation of Democracies," in *Reexaminimg Democracy: Essays in Honour of Seymour Martin Lipset*, eds. Gary Marks and Larry Diamond (London: Sage Publications, 1992), pp. 156–81.
16. Claus Offe and Ulrich Preuss, « Les institutions démocratiques peuvent-elles faire un usage efficace des ressources morales? » dans *Les démocraties modernes à l'épreuve,* sous la dir. de Claus Offe (Montréal et Paris: L'Harmattan, 1997), pp. 199–231; and Thériault.
17. Callon et al., p. 170.
18. Lionel Monnier et Bernard Thiry, « Architecture et dynamique de l'intérêt général, » dans *Mutations structurelles et intérêt général : Vers quels nouveaux paradigmes pour l'économie publique, sociale et coopérative?* » sous la dir. de Lionel Monnier et Bernard Thiry (Bruxelles, Belgique: De Boeck Université, 1997), pp. 11–30.
19. Jules Duchastel, « De l'universalisme au particulier. De l'individu citoyen au citoyen incorporé, » dans *Vivre la citoyenneté : Identité, appartenance et participation,* sous la dir. de Y. Boisvert, J. Hamel, et M. Molgat (Montréal: Liber, 2000), pp. 37–52.
20. Offe and Preuss, p. 226.
21. Jacques Godbout, *La participation contre la démocratie* (Montréal: Editions Saint-Martin, 1982); Paul R. Bélanger et Benoît Lévesque, « Une forme mouvementée de gestion du social, » *Revue internationale d'action communautaire* 19/59 (1988): pp. 49–64.
22. Monnier and Thiry.
23. Thériault, 147–48.
24. Ibid.

25. Offe and Preuss, p. 227.
26. B. Lévesque, « Économie sociale et solidaire dans un contexte de mondialisation, » following Offe and Preuss.
27. Ibid.
28. Callon et al.
29. Offe and Preuss, p. 227.
30. A legal form that has been possible since June 1997 in Québec.
31. Jean-Pierre Girard, « La cooperative di solidierietà : una formula nuova, » *Impressa Sociale* 59 (septembre-octobre 2001): pp. 33–42. This is also called "joint construction of supply and demand by users and professionals."
32. Michel Grant, Paul R. Bélanger, et Benoît Lévesque, *Nouvelles formes d'organisation du travail : Études de cas et analyses comparatives* (Paris et Montréal: L'Harmattan 1997).
33. Yvan Comeau and Benoît Lévesque, "Workers' Financial Participation in the Property of Enterprises in Québec," *Economic and Industrial Democracy* 14, no. 2 (1993): pp. 233–50.
34. Benoît Lévesque, Paul R. Bélanger, et Lucie Mager, « La réingénierie des services financiers: un secteur exemplaire de l'économie des services. Le cas des Caisses populaires et d'économie Desjardins, » dans *Lien social et politiques—RIAC (Revue internationale d'action communautaire)* 40 (1999): pp. 89–103.
35. Archon Fung and Erick Olin Wright, "Deepening Democracy: Innovations in Empowered Participatory Governance," *Politics and Society* 29, no. 2 (2001).
36. Ibid.
37. Offe and Preuss, p. 228.

References Not Appearing in the Endnotes

Cope, B., et al. "Immigration, Ethnic Conflicts and Social Cohesion." Sidney, Australia: NLLIA Center for Workplace Communication and Culture, 1995.

Lévesque, Benoît, and William Ninacs. "The Social Economy in Canada: The Quebec Experience." Prepared for the Conference on Local Strategies for Employment and the Social Economy, Montreal, 18–19 June 1997.

Putnam, Robert D. *Making Democracy Work: Civic Traditions in Modern Italy.* Princeton, NJ: Princeton University Press, 1993.

Part Two: Issues

New Directions in Research and Practice

Four practitioners discuss their experiences and challenge researchers on topics such as co-op membership and social cohesion, membership and public relations, co-operative social responsibility, and governance, leadership, and volunteerism.

KAREN PHILP

THE CHALLENGES OF CO-OPERATIVE MEMBERSHIP, SOCIAL COHESION, AND GLOBALIZATION

THIS PAPER will present some of the Canadian Co-operative Association's (CCA) ideas about the challenges of co-operative membership, social cohesion, and globalization. It is framed, generally, as a series of questions that members of co-operatives in Canada would like to see answered by the forthcoming research project titled Co-operative Membership and Globalization: Creating Social Cohesion through Market Relations, being undertaken by the Centre for the Study of Co-operatives in Saskatoon.

First, a few general comments about globalization. I asked a couple of CCA members for their thoughts about what I should bring to this conference.[1] While this method would not meet formal sampling selection criteria, it did help me to conclude that there are many views of globalization amongst co-operative members. Most believed it was here to stay and that the only course of action was to make the rules of globalization work more fairly for Canadians and for others around the world.

Mark Goldblatt of the Canadian Worker Co-op Federation, for example, said that while trade is beneficial on a generic basis, it takes place in a real world context, where it is never neutral. He listed a series of problems associated with globalization—from living standards, to environmental destruction, to increased child labour, and the violation of human rights. His conclusion, however, was realistic. We need to accept globalization as a fact of life, but we must try to make its effects more fair.[2]

The co-operative sector generally acknowledges that the changes affecting the operation of the global economy are irreversible, and this new reality provides both challenges and opportunities—not all of which we can presently foresee. These global forces continue to unfold, and recent actions by the United States in steel and agricultural subsidies suggest that we are still travelling along a bumpy road to a global end that remains out of sight.

There is also a sense growing among some Canadians that the path to globalization may take a brief detour as the United States responds to the aftermath of September 11th. There have been calls recently in the Canadian media and on the academic conference circuit by public policymakers—Wendy Dobson of the Conference Board of Canada, for example—for a public discussion about a new Big Idea.[3] These policy wonks generally argue that the only way we can attract US attention to our economic concerns is by proposing a major strategic bargain that offers them physical and economic security in exchange for easy access to US markets.

This new Big Idea proposes a greater economic integration between Canada and the United States, possibly leading to a single currency by building on the North American Free Trade Agreement. The proponents ultimately believe that in order to continue economic growth in Canada, a North American Community—similar to the early European Economic Community—will be required. For members of the co-operative sector, the concretization of large, regional, economic blocks in the international arena will likely be a brief detour in the globalization drive, but it may require Canada to increase exports to the US from 85 percent to almost 100 percent, and that will have a significant impact on co-operatives and their members.

In the pursuit of greater economic growth to date, for example, globalization has deeply affected the relationships between state and citizens, and while it has brought opportunities for some in terms of wealth creation and prosperity, it has also brought to others insecurity and inequality. Rapid job creation in some sectors and communities—in southern Ontario, for example—contrasts with job losses and difficult economic adjustments in communities such as Gold River or Tumbler Ridge. Reaction to these discrepancies varies, but the point for co-operators is that this is our reality, and that we need to closely examine globalization with all its accompanying threats and opportunities.

Only by thoroughly understanding what is happening can we identify opportunities to work together to advance the interests of co-op members and our communities. In small communities, co-operatives may be able to offer support by building on existing industrial activity. The Malcolm Island Shellfish Co-op, the Harrop-Proctor Community Co-operative, or the Cowichan Lake Community Forest Co-op, for example, are locally owned and managed businesses creating and maintaining jobs in resource-based communities.

This leads to the first set of questions members of the co-operative sector would like to see answered by the research currently underway. Are co-operatives effective in supporting communities facing change as a result of globalization? Can they respond effectively to globalization without losing their co-operative identity? How can communities appropriately respond to global economic changes? How do co-operatives grow to compete in a market-place of increasing size and diversity, and yet make membership meaningful at the same time?

On the surface, co-operatives appear to have a great opportunity in the global future precisely because they have a special identity, because they have both economic and social objectives, because they are values and community based, because they are people-oriented, and because they have a network of linkages not only across Canada but around the world. The co-operative model offers people the opportunity to take control over some of the economic decisions directly affecting them.

Co-operatives should, by being true to their seven principles,[4] provide locally based solutions to globalization. But do they?

How strong is the co-operative identity? During Co-op Week in October 2002, the Canadian Co-operative Association and its French counterpart, le Conseil Canadien de la Coopération (CCC), along with the federal Co-operatives Secretariat, released the first survey of Canada's nonfinancial co-operatives.[5] More than seven thousand co-ops received the survey, which was designed to better understand the types and extent of their community contributions, and to ascertain whether they are different from those made by other organizations.

More than eight hundred co-ops in ten provinces and one territory responded to the survey; 7.4 percent of the respondents saw no unique contribution from their co-operative to their community, and 31.5 percent of them did not answer the question. More importantly, 60 percent said their co-op and their members did contribute to their communities in ways that are very different from other businesses.

The sector's conclusion is that many co-operatives are perhaps challenged when it comes to articulating their uniqueness in their community. This may relate to the fact that co-operatives see themselves as an integrated part of their community and therefore do not identify their community activities as unique in that context.

The strength of the co-operative identity is also challenged by demutualization amongst the larger agricultural co-operatives and remains a real threat.[6] Why?

Co-operators are driven by vision and values, yet are fundamentally pragmatic; they've been described as having their heads in the clouds but their feet on the ground.

With this in mind, the co-operative sector appreciates that the research for this project over the next few years will examine what has happened in the past and what is happening today. We also hope, however, that researchers will be able to provide suggestions as to what steps will be required to help co-operatives survive in the increasingly competitive market-place.

One of the greatest assets of the co-operative movement, for example, is its networks of vertical and horizontal links within communities, across the country, and internationally. Should co-operatives be seeking out strategic alliances with other partners in their various spheres? Should co-operatives be looking at cross-border alliances? Is GROWMARK[7] an example to follow in the future? In Sweden, Norway, and Denmark, consumer co-ops are merging operations in an attempt to maintain their share of a highly competitive consumer market. Dairy co-ops in the Netherlands and Germany are working more closely than ever before in order to maintain market share. Will strategic or even cross-border alliances be necessary for Canadian consumer co-operatives to have a long-term future under the North American Free Trade Agreement and the new Big Idea?

If the answer is yes, how do co-ops maintain local control and make membership meaningful while business is growing economically and expanding geographically? The co-operative sector is seeking answers as to how it can compete with multinational enterprises yet still serve local needs and interests. The experience of Canada's wheat pools would suggest that the co-operative model cannot compete against multinationals, but the sector wonders whether that experience is due to the limitations of the co-op model or whether it is related to the nature of the agricultural economy itself. Would Mountain Equipment Co-op, for example, be more successful than the pools if it entered international markets?

The co-operative sector's second area of interest concerns social alliances. The co-op movement is one of the longest surviving social movements in the world today. Yet without partners, can we survive in the new global reality? Should co-operatives be establishing and building links with other players in civil society in order to promote the co-op model as a viable alternative?

The research underway may show that co-operators are already doing this, and if it finds that this is the case, is the sector recognizing its full value? The 2002 survey of co-operatives revealed that more than 90 percent of Canadian co-ops provided in-kind contributions or donations to community and civil society groups in the form of meeting rooms, office space, and equipment, as well as providing direct advice and management support for the organizations and specific projects. The survey did not ask about or identify individual co-op member involvement in community or civil society organizations. It would be extremely useful if the research on co-op membership and globalization was able to identify how many co-op members volunteer or contribute to their community, to charitable activities, or to civil society organizations. This information would allow us to identify the importance of social alliances for co-operatives that are already in place, albeit informally, and identify the value of these alliances to the growth of new co-operatives in Canada. If there is value in social alliances, the question would then be, how does the co-operative sector support and encourage the formation of these relationships?

I would like to turn briefly to the issue of the Internet, where more and more business is being conducted. E-commerce offers a supplemental marketing opportunity to traditional co-operative marketing strategies. Dot co-op was, and continues to be seen by some, a way for co-operatives in Canada to differentiate in the market-place. It was also seen as a means to link members, to provide information, and in essence to add to the democratic nature of co-operative membership. But it does not appear—at least on the surface—to be taking off either as a tool to help co-operatives engage their members or to contribute to building member identity or loyalty to their co-op. Why not?

Is member identity weakening among co-operatives in Canada? This is certainly the intuitive perception of some co-operators, and this research project may provide evidence to support or contradict the observation. If the research reveals a weakening of identity, why is it happening? Are there causal issues at play, or is it simply a correlation? Is co-operative membership negatively impacted by the fragmentation of social cohesion in society as a whole?

Perhaps the issue is the divorce between ownership or membership of the co-operative and the real control or management of the organization. Is there sufficient space for member participation in the direction of the co-operative, or has the adoption of the Carver Model of governance[8] by for-profit co-operatives colluded with the lack of co-op education in Canada's business schools effectively to shut out members from the discussion of priorities and choices in order to get on with *doing business.*

This is an important issue from both the membership and the business perspective. The participation of members is a critical co-operative value as well as an important means to an end—a dynamic co-operative business. Members provide resources, get involved in decisions, and the result is a business that is more responsive to consumer/member needs. As a result, member benefits improve—both in terms of dividends and quality of goods and services provided—thereby demonstrating to the member the co-operative advantage of values, trust, and community. This in turn generates loyalty and attracts new members, resulting in a stronger co-operative in the long term.

It would be useful for the co-operative sector if the proposed research were to consider whether there is any value in examining the different levels of participation by members in each co-operative. We in the co-operative sector think—but do not know—that there are a minority of members who participate fully; a greater number who are involved in some small way; and a majority who are loyal and committed to the values or economic benefits of membership. Is this really the case today in Canada? If the current research suggests that this is true, should the co-operative sector be thinking about formally acknowledging these different types of membership in some way? Should we be looking at different levels of benefits depending on the level of involvement and commitment to the co-operative, or would this negatively affect the principles of the co-operative movement?

Finally, how does all this relate to social cohesion? The analysis and research about social cohesion in Canada is confusing. Robert Putnam's thesis[9] about the subject does not appear to be supported by the evidence provided in the National Survey of Giving, Volunteering and Participating published by Statistics Canada in 1997,[10] which indicated that 78 percent of Canadians donate, 31 percent volunteer time, and 51 percent participate in civic organizations. The rate of volunteering by Canadians rose from 1987 to 1997, although the evidence also suggests that the number of hours donated dropped. One can conclude from this that growing numbers of Canadians continue to contribute to their communities, but that the time crunch affecting the work-life imbalance as described by Linda Duxbury[11] is also impacting the number of hours they can donate. This same time crunch arising from the work-life imbalance may mean that individual co-operative members have less time to volunteer for board or committee activities, unless the co-operative is pro-active in addressing the issue.

The Canadian Co-operative Association eagerly awaits the findings of the current research and analysis, and believes that the recommendations will not only enable the co-operative sector to identify its existing contributions to social cohesion, but will also suggest positive steps for consolidating and expanding its role in Canadian society.

ENDNOTES

1. Co-operative Membership and Globalization: New Directions in Research and Business Strategies. A Dialogue for Researchers, Practitioners, and Policy Makers, held 24–25 October 2002 in Saskatoon.
2. Mark Goldblatt, "Globalization: Some General Comments," 21 October 2002.
3. See Wendy Dobson, "The Border Papers: Shaping the Future of the North American Economic Space: A Framework for Action," C.D. Howe Institute Commentary, April 2002; David Zussman, "The Challenges of North American Integration," *Ottawa Citizen,* 8 April 2002; Thomas J. Courchene, "A Common Currency for North America," at the 2002 Policy Forum: A Border Too Far? How Much Continental Integration? School of Policy Studies, Queen's University, 26–27 April 2002, and the Borderlines Conference: Canada's Options in North America, sponsored by the Institute for Research on Public Policy, Montreal, 1–2 November 2002; Hugh Segal, "New North American Institutions: The Need for Creative Statecraft," at The Ties That Bind: Closer Economic Relations between Canada and the USA, Fifth Annual JLT/CTPL Trade Law Conference, 18 April 2002; and Strengthening the North American Partnership: Scenarios for the Future, conference sponsored by the Policy Research Initiative of the Government of Canada and held at Carleton University Centre for the Study of North American Politics and Society, 12–13 May 2002.
4. The seven principles are: voluntary and open membership, democratic member control; member economic participation; autonomy and independence; education, training, and information; co-operation among co-operatives; and concern for community.
5. Available at www.coopscanada.coop.
6. *Canadian Agricultural Co-ops Capitalization Issues and Challenges: Strategies for the Future,* final report by Ernst and Young (November 2002) prepared for le Conseil Canadien de la Coopération and the Canadian Co-operative Association.
7. GROWMARK is a federated, regional agricultural co-operative that provides products and services to member co-ops in the Midwest US and Ontario. Local member co-operatives, in turn, provide farmers and others with goods and services such as crop inputs, energy products, feed and animal health products, grain handling systems, lawn care products, and grain marketing services.
8. John Carver's Policy Governance® is a specific set of concepts and principles and their application to the servant-leadership of boards and the board-management partnership.
9. Robert D. Putnam, *Bowling Alone: The Collapse and Revival of American Community* (New York: Simon and Schuster, 2000). See also review by Alison Van Rooy in *ISUMA* 2, no. 1 (Spring 2001).
10. See Caroline Beauvais and Jane Jenson, *Social Cohesion: Updating the State of the Research* (Ottawa: Canadian Policy Research Networks, discussion paper, July 2002), and Jane Jenson, *Mapping Social Cohesion: The State of Canadian Research* (Ottawa: Canadian Policy Research Networks, discussion paper, November 1998). See also Statistics Canada, *Survey of Volunteer Activity* (1987), *National*

Survey of Giving, Volunteering and Participating (1997), and the *World Values Survey* (1991); Kathleen M. Day and Rose Anne Devlin, "Volunteerism and Crowding Out: Canadian Econometric Evidence," *Canadian Journal of Economics* 29, no. 1 (1996): pp. 37–53; François Vaillancourt, "To Volunteer or Not: Canada, 1987," *Canadian Journal of Economics* 27, no. 4 (1994): pp. 813–26; and Jack Quarter, *Canada's Social Economy: Co-operatives, Nonprofits and other Community Enterprises* (Toronto: J. Lorimer, 1992).

11. Linda Duxbury and Chris Higgins, *Work-Life Balance in the New Millennium: Where Are We? Where Do We Need to Go?* (Ottawa: Canadian Policy Research Networks, October 2001).

CHRIS MCCARVILLE

MEMBERSHIP AND PUBLIC RELATIONS
AN EXAMINATION OF ARCTIC CO-OPERATIVES LIMITED

ARCTIC CO-OPERATIVES LIMITED is particularly interested in member loyalty and how co-op membership fosters social cohesion. Member loyalty is what has helped our co-ops thrive, and we need to work hard to understand how co-op loyalty will transfer down to the next generation. Those who helped get the co-ops started are now Elders in their communities, and the next generation is one that grew up with a co-op in their community. What is their understanding of the movement, and where does their loyalty lie? How do co-ops foster social cohesion in the communities they serve? This study—Co-operative Membership and Globalization—offers our co-ops the opportunity to examine the root structure of co-operative membership.

OVERVIEW

How did Arctic Co-ops begin? The first co-operatives in Canada's North were legally incorporated in 1960. During the 1960s and early 1970s, many communities formed co-operatives as community-based, member-owned businesses to provide their residents with services and employment opportunities.

Today, there are thirty-four community co-operatives in the Northwest Territories, Nunavut, and Manitoba, representing the interests of more than eighteen thousand member/owners. Co-ops provide an important source of income for hundreds of northern families through wage employment and the sale of arts and crafts, furs, and country foods. The co-operatives in the North are involved in general merchandise retailing, hotels and tourism, fuel distribution, contracting, art and craft marketing, taxi and cartage services, and cable television services.

- Across the North, co-operatives have invested more than $98 million in the infrastructure of their communities by developing assets such as retail stores, hotels, fuel distribution systems, cable television networks, residential and commercial buildings.
- Ordinary people in the North have built up equity of $28 million in the assets of their co-ops.
- In their 2002 business year, the co-ops had combined revenues of more than $118 million, and paid $17 million in wages to northern residents.
- Our community-owned co-ops employ more than eight hundred people, and in 2002, co-op business activities recorded a consolidated profit of $5.3 million. All of this profit belongs to northern people and stayed in the North.

The co-ops in the North are small businesses that provide a wide range of services to their members and their communities. Early in our history, the leaders of the northern co-op movement realized that there were many obstacles to overcome, including the small size of our communities; a lack of capital; our remote location; limited trained staff; limited communication facilities; and limited transportation infrastructure.

Working Together

Thirty years ago, the community-based co-ops in the North decided to work together to achieve their goals and formed two co-operatively owned service organizations—Arctic Co-operatives Limited (ACL), and the Arctic Co-operative Development Fund (ACDF).

The services provided by Arctic Co-ops include:
- accounting and audit;
- computer support services;
- marketing of art and crafts;
- purchase and transportation of merchandise for sale in co-op retail stores;
- construction and project management services;
- management advisory services;
- member and public relations;
- operational, marketing, and technical support in fuel distribution, hotel operation, and cable TV operations;
- recruitment and human resource services; and
- training and education of elected officials and staff.

Services provided by the Co-operative Development Fund are financial in nature, and include providing affordable self-financing to member co-operatives through pooling the financial resources of the individual co-operatives. To encourage local community development, all investments made are in the co-operative movement. Since 1986, the fund has loaned $247 million and returned 60 percent of the interest on those loans to those who paid it. It is the largest Aboriginal-owned capital fund in Canada and has the most successful repayment rate.

The decision to work together was a good one. Thirty years later, 80 percent of those co-ops are still in business—an amazing success rate anywhere in Canada. Add to that the obstacles that co-ops in the Arctic face every day and this achievement is even more impressive. Statistics suggest that small businesses in Canada have a survival rate of less than 20 percent.

What is special or unique about the co-ops in the North? Why do they have a much better rate of survival than other small business in Canada? Co-operatives have one critical ingredient that other small businesses do not—each other. The co-ops in the North, like those in other parts of Canada and around the world, have each other to lean on in good times and in bad. Co-operatives in the Arctic live the sixth co-op principle, co-operation among co-operatives.

The Challenges

Our co-op system today is the result of the dedication and commitment of many leaders. One of our challenges is to help source out and develop the skills of people—those who will lead the movement for the next forty years and beyond. There are a number of other significant challenges as well.

Travel

Travel costs between communities are very high. A short-notice airline ticket from Winnipeg to Iqaluit is $3,900. The physical distance between our co-ops also makes the delivery of training more difficult, although managers and two directors from each community are brought together annually to participate in workshops.

Lack of Financial Services

There are no financial services available to our members—no credit unions, and just a few bank branches in Yellowknife and Iqaluit. In Nunavut, the government was decentralized, and now complete departments administer large annual budgets in communities without financial services. In Arviat, for example, the entire student-aid program grants funds without a bank or credit union branch in the community. Cash must be flown in, and access to cash planned well in advance. Many Elders still travel without money, and if a group is planning a community event that includes Elders, cash allowances must be made available in advance. Our co-ops provide charge accounts to members, but many people in southern Canada learned how to manage their first chequing account by joining a credit union or opening a bank account. That education process has yet to take place in the North, and government leaders often cite the lack of financial services as one of the reasons people do not get ahead financially.

Promoting the Co-op Model to the Next Generation

There is a lack of awareness of the co-op model in many of our audiences, and the development of a youth movement and succession planning are two major concerns in our system.

Access to Training Funds

There is no central fund we can use to access training dollars and help develop local staff and management. The process of incorporating cultural values and business practices in a sustainable way could be significantly accelerated with a program of training and education for boards and Aboriginal management.

For the last few years, our members have been working to develop and deliver training programs to ensure that people are involved in every aspect of the operation and direction of their co-operatives. Similar efforts were made twenty years ago, but government programs changed and we do not have the resources to finance them on our own. What the government offers today is not sufficiently flexible to meet our needs. The time is right for the original training program to be redesigned and delivered to a new generation of people. The co-op system can bring a developed program, job-site training facilities, and specific placement of trained people to this project.

Our difficulty today lies in the way many government programs are delivered. There has been a great deal of emphasis on the community-based approach. Our co-operative system has members in two territories and one province. Funds for capacity development in both the Department of Indian Affairs and Northern Development and the Aboriginal Human Resource Development Strategy have been devolved to local, regional, and territorial organizations. In order to access the latter, for example, we would need to negotiate twelve separate agreements with twelve different organizations to get the funds to deliver the program to our members.

As a co-operative, we fully support community-based initiatives, but economies of scale must be considered when programs are planned. It is not feasible to design and deliver thirty-four different training programs. The philosophy for the human resource development programs must recognize the specific training requirements of the various groups. Programs cannot offer a canned solution with a one-size-fits-all approach.

Arctic Co-ops will continue to work with those people in the federal government who have supported us over the life of our movement. The goal will be to find a co-operative solution to the need for developing management and technical skills in our communities, creating job opportunities for local Inuit, Dene, and Métis residents, and continuing down the path towards sustainable co-operative community development.

In conclusion, co-operatives offer a model of development in Aboriginal communities that provides transparency and accountability, democratic participation by the broad community, a means for developing capacity in both infrastructure and administrative skills, and a way for individual and isolated Aboriginal communities to come together through a federation, which allows them to pool limited resources and provide an increased level of support for economic development.

Meet Annie Goose

Our co-op system would not have grown without the strength and determination of hundreds of leaders throughout northern Canada. One of these leaders is Annie Goose, the president of Holman Co-op, which is located on the western shore of Victoria Island, north of the seventieth parallel and more than two thousand kilometres north of Edmonton. In this community of fewer than five hundred people, Holman Co-op operates a variety of businesses, including a printmaking shop and a gift store, where members sell arts and crafts. Lithography is the main type of art in production and includes stone lithos and woodcut stencils. Other operations cover the essential community services of a hotel, retail store, cable TV, fuel delivery service, post office, and video rentals.

At the 2002 annual meeting in Yellowknife, Annie brought the crowd to tears as she picked up a guitar after fourteen years of musical silence. She explained to the delegates how she had stopped playing when her husband had died, but the warmth and community she felt as the other delegates played led her to come forward and "take her music back."

To celebrate the federation's thirtieth anniversary, some co-op leaders provided personal accounts of their involvement in the co-op movement. Here is Annie's story.

I thought about this for sometime now regarding the story about my co-op involvement in my community of Holman. I thought it might be appropriate to begin from where I began as a child and end with where I am in my personal healing. So here goes.

I was born in the nearby outpost camp of Minto Inlet, where my biological parents were living most of their younger days. In this family, I have ten sisters and four brothers. Then I was adopted to my parents Jacob and Agnes Nipalayok Aleekuk, and in this family I have two sisters and one brother, all whom I am very close to. I especially have great respect for all of my brothers- and sisters-in-law. I have great respect and honour for the Elders. My dad owned a schooner and they came to pick me up right after I was born. My grandfather wanted his sister to adopt me because she was able to have only one child. As I grew a little older, I used to go out on the trapline with my father, till I left on a single-engine Otter airplane with a lot of my fellow students for the residential school to Kugluktuk tent-frame experimental school, and then on to Inuvik Stringer Hall Residence.

I did not go home for two years at that time. Anyway, I never used to like harnessing up sled dogs because I did not like the smell of dogs, but I loved helping my dad make igloos, setting up camp, and he used to encourage me to run alongside the sled every so often when I started getting cold. Although I was dressed in caribou-skin clothing from head to toe, I still would get cold every so often. In the evenings we camped in the igloos, making dog pot, and while we waited for the dogfood to cool, we would make fishing holes with an ice chisel at the lakes and catch our supper of lake trout.

There were a few young mothers back then who started with a little material to begin what was to be the early stage of the co-op movement, with the help of a priest by the name of Father Henri Tardy. These ladies sewed home-tanned sealskin tapestry and then went on to bigger and larger items. Later in the years there was even a tannery here in our community, but it is no longer here. I was about eleven years old at that time. I started out by helping my mother, who now is deceased. She would have scraps of sealskin pieces left over from sewing and I would ask her if I could sew little things, and when she said I could use the scraps, I would sew little hand purses with little straps and a little design on them, even little mittens. I would get tiny little colourful mints for payment because at that time they did not have any money to pay anybody who sewed these products. I would be so grateful for being given some candy and I always appreciated having some sweets. I also used to share with my little brother.

Later on in life I started sewing bigger items and helped to provide for my family because my husband didn't have a job back then. You know, in those days we didn't have very much in store-bought foods other than tea, coffee, flour, sugar, baking powder, lard, and klim—the very basic necessities.

Later in the years, the men who started the prints made stonecuts that were black and white models. Also, burlap material was used for silk-screen products such as tablecloths, napkins, curtains, tea cozies, aprons, sealskin fur garments, duffle parkas, and mukluks. Later on into the years, very artistic and colourful prints started to come out with very talented printmakers coming on stream, and then they moved into large productions as exhibitions created more demand for Inuit art. A lot of these people who helped start the co-op are not around any more, but the work that they have done is still around in buildings and galleries. Even though they are not here, we can remember them still and appreciate them for all their hard work.

I did not really have a fatherly figure to look up to because my father died in Charles Camsell Hospital while I was away at residential school. But my mother was my mentor; she taught me a lot how to be thankful for everything we receive and to respect people no matter what happens. She did everything to provide for me and my little brother as a widow, from cleaning and cooking at Hudson's Bay Company to washing sealskins and sewing. Oh, she can sew beautiful parkas and sunbursts and she was very involved in politics and an outspoken speaker in the Cope land-claims meetings in communities. I may have picked up that from her; today I can be very vocal when it comes to ensuring our Aboriginal peoples' rights are met and that they are validated and acknowledged for all they have gone through.

It wasn't until later on in life that I started getting involved in the politics of the co-op movement as a member and director, and in the last few years, as president for Holman Co-op. I really enjoy being on the co-op board; it gives me a sense of belonging to be of service to my community members who make up the majority of the co-op. And also to appreciate staff we have in our operations in our community, and we need to work real close with our managers. I feel honoured to have that working relationship with our co-op manager and hotel manager to this date in my community. Today, we have the grocery and hardware store, postal services, the Arctic Char Inn, a craft shop, a print shop, cable services, and fuel and gasoline contracts. We are steadily climbing uphill and hope to move even further ahead.

To this day I have been involved in my land-claim committees past and present, such as on the board of directors for land use planning for the community of Holman; Settlement Council vice-chair; hamlet councillor; Beaufort Sea advisory director; chairperson of Holman Community Corporation; Inuvialuit Regional Corporation director; Inuvialuit Enrolment Committee member; vice-chair of the Hunters and Trappers Committee; vice-chair of the District Education Committee; community social services worker; chairperson of the Kingalik Jamboree Committee; Anglican Church vestry member; and field service clerk. One of the jobs I've really enjoyed having was the announcer-operator position for CBC Inuvik Inuvialuktun Programming. I am also the secretary-treasurer of the Native Women's Association of the NWT, involved with the Western Arctic Interagency Committee with the Grollier Hall Healing Circle, and working with the Native Communication Society for Story Board on the residential school four-part video project. Presently, I am an addictions and drug worker for the Hamlet of Holman, also working with the residential schools issue by going out to conferences.

I hope to be around the co-op movement for awhile if my higher guide permits me to be around for awhile yet. In the last fourteen years I have been alone as a widow bringing up my family and my grandchildren whom I adore. Some days they are my inspiration; I love them dearly, but most of all I love my dear family without whom I would not have come this far. The greatest one I appreciate every day is my higher power, who permits me to be who I am today and what I can be. I have been on my healing journey for the last seven years, and today I can honestly live with who I am, and I love every moment of it. Some days it can be rough, and at times it is so peaceful. Some days I feel the Creator telling me it is okay.

Today being able to live in the present is so comforting. My hobbies are going out on the land, reading, and yes— dancing, especially old-time fiddle dances and gospel music. I love country music; I also love to speak my languages— Inuvialuktun, Inuinaktun, and some Inuktitun. When I feel I need to rejuvenate, I go to my respected Elders, visit and share with them, and regain my focus. When you work in the help-care giving field, sometimes you need to get a new sense of direction through whatever message the Creator gives you —through meditation, through reading the Bible, through people, through musical songs, gatherings, when people speak at large gatherings. Mine comes in especially when I'm out in the countryside or just walking about outdoors. I also respect everyone's beliefs no matter what faith they have, because in the end I can only be responsible for myself, my attitude, and actions.

ANDREA HARRIS

CO-OPERATIVE SOCIAL RESPONSIBILITY
A NATURAL ADVANTAGE?

CO-OPERATIVES offer a compelling alternative for conducting business in a more socially just way than other forms of enterprise, particularly publicly traded companies. This is the belief that first drew me, and doubtless others, to study and be a part of the co-operative movement. Indeed, the "co-operative difference" has been a cornerstone of co-operative marketing efforts to engage existing members and attract new members based on an appeal to social and community values. However, with more companies engaged in serious efforts to integrate corporate social responsibility (CSR) into all aspects of their business, and after working on CSR initiatives within two leading co-operatives, I worry about the ability of co-ops to effectively engage members by claiming a unique appeal to social values. For this reason, I would like to suggest that researchers take a closer look at the interplay of co-operative principles and practice with those that define CSR, examining questions such as:

- Do co-operative businesses, by virtue of their unique structure and adherence to the co-op principles, have a CSR advantage over other forms of business? If so, what aspects of a co-operative business structure make it uniquely "more" responsible?
- With the rapid adoption of CSR in the corporate[1] world,

how do co-operative businesses stack up against their investor- or privately-owned counterparts on social and environmental performance?
- Are co-operatives well positioned to play a leadership role in advancing corporate social responsibility?

As a starting point to exploring some of these questions (and quickly raising others), I would like to offer a rough comparison of the co-operative principles and the various standards and ethical codes that have been developed to define socially responsible business. This comparison suggests that while co-ops have some distinct advantages over investor- and privately-owned firms, adherence to the co-op principles is not in itself a sufficient condition for leadership in corporate social responsibility. I propose that emerging CSR practices, such as those intended to foster broader stakeholder engagement and improve board accountability, and their application in the co-operative context, warrant further investigation by co-op researchers. This research should aim to offer ideas, practical solutions, and best practice examples that will inspire more co-op managers and directors to play a leadership role in advancing values-based business, and ultimately, to distinguish their co-ops among existing and potential members.

A Comparison of Co-operative and CSR Principles

Co-operatives worldwide generally define themselves according to a set of co-operative values and principles,* developed and adopted by the International Co-operative Alliance. Socially responsible businesses, on the other hand, have not universally adopted one standard or set of principles, but rely instead on a bewildering array of ethical codes to guide them towards social responsibility. To add to the complexity, these codes employ a variety of terms—sometimes interchangeably—to talk about corporate social responsibility, including business ethics, corporate citizenship, corporate accountability, and sustainability.[2] While numerous studies have compared the various sets of CSR standards and principles, I know of none that has included the co-operative principles as part of their comparison.

---

* See Appendix A at the end of this chapter.

The SIGMA (Sustainability—Integrated Guidelines for Management) Project[3] represents an intensive effort to develop an integrated management system to guide businesses through the complex array of standards, guidelines, and principles relating to corporate social responsibility and sustainable business. The first phase of this research, conducted in 2000, compared a multitude of these ethical codes,* using a framework based on the triple-bottom-line approach.

The triple-bottom-line approach centres on the idea that companies "derive their license to operate not just by satisfying shareholders through improved profits and dividends (the economic bottom line), but by simultaneously satisfying other stakeholders in society (employees, communities, customers, etc.) through improved performance against the social and environmental bottom lines."[4] Despite some limitations,[5] the triple-bottom-line approach has gained broad support in the business community, with many leaders being familiar with the term and concept.

What follows is a synopsis of the SIGMA research results overlaid with some observations of how the co-operative principles may have factored in had they been included in the comparison of CSR standards and principles.

Environmental Bottom Line

Comparing the various CSR and sustainability standards, the SIGMA project concluded, in general, that the environmental bottom line is well covered by existing approaches, but that each approach has specific strengths and weaknesses. Some set out aspirational principles, others are sector specific, while yet others focus narrowly on only one or two elements of a management system. ISO (International Organization for Standardization) and EMAS (Eco-Management and Audit Scheme),[6] for example, are tightly focussed on resource and operational control, the idea of "doing what you do right" rather than "doing the right thing." The Natural Step,† on the other hand, focusses on sustainability parameters but does not set out a detailed management system for implementation.[7]

---

* See Appendix B at the end of this chapter.
† See Appendix B, at the end of this chapter, for details about ISO and The Natural Step.

In contrast, the environment is not specifically mentioned anywhere within co-op values or principles—although some may suggest that the seventh principle touches on environmental responsibility by stating that "co-operatives work for the sustainable development of their communities through policies approved by their members." Regardless, in comparison to CSR principles and standards, it is fair to note that the environment is conspicuously absent from the co-op principles, suggesting that co-operatives do not have a clear advantage for managing or enhancing their environmental bottom line.

It follows, then, that if a co-operative has aspirations towards leadership in social responsibility, it must pay particular attention to environmental performance and pro-actively adopt some of the practices being developed in the corporate world. Examples might include:

- adopting policies centred on the "precautionary principle"—referring to the notion that the burden of proof for determining the environmental consequences of an action lies with the company; it must definitively prove environmental safety rather than environmental harm;
- engaging stakeholders on environmental issues;
- appointing a designated person or people with responsibility for the co-op's environmental performance;
- providing employee training on environmental issues;
- establishing an environmental management system or environmental code of conduct for all operations; and
- advocating for public policy changes on environmental issues.

Economic Sustainability

The SIGMA project concludes that relatively few standards encompass the economic aspects of sustainability to any depth. The authors note that although financial and accounting standards are well established and detailed, they deal with only one part of the economic equation. "The wider economic impact of organizations and the measurement and management of intangible assets is still embryonic."[8]

An examination of the co-operative principles offers a somewhat opposite result. While the co-op principles have little to say about financial performance, they go some way in addressing the wider economic impact of the organization. The silence of the co-op principles around the need for financial sustainability may be a shortcoming. In a comprehensive report from the UK's Co-operative Commission, this issue is identified as a critical deficiency in the management of co-operative enterprise. The report urges co-operatives to pay closer attention to managing their financial performance, and to investing in infrastructure in order to remain viable.[9]

Despite the lack of reference to financial performance, the co-op principles do have a number of things to say about the economic conduct and impact of co-operative businesses. Specifically, the co-op principles:

- promote co-operation among co-operatives as a means to increase the well being of their members;
- broaden the definition of responsibility beyond paying taxes by stating a concern for the sustainable development of their communities;
- address how the financial capital generated by the enterprise is to be allocated; and
- limit the amount of capital subscribed as a condition of membership.

It is these last two features that are clearly unique when compared to CSR principles and standards developed for the corporate world. The co-op principles hinder the accumulation of wealth by a few at the expense of the many. They also prevent people who do not have a direct interest (beyond the amount of capital invested) in the enterprise from controlling the business. Although the most recent version of the co-op principles does allow external capital, previous versions also took the added step of preventing anyone without a vested interest in the enterprise from sharing in the financial wealth generated through its operations.

With the exception of The Natural Step, none of the CSR standards and principles prevalent in the corporate community go anywhere near addressing the thorny issues of wealth accumulation and distribution. The Natural Step makes indirect reference to the notion of distribution by stating that "in the sustainable society, people can not be subject to conditions that systematically undermine their capacity to meet their needs." By including this as a necessary condition for sustainability, The Natural Step framework recognizes that we need an improved means of dealing with issues such as equity and fairness in order to achieve positive social change. The framework does not, however, offer suggestions for the implementation of such notions in the context of business and economy. Perhaps the three co-operative principles of democratic member control, member economic participation, and autonomy and independence offer the beginnings of a prescription.

Social Bottom Line

In their examination of the social bottom line, the SIGMA researchers conclude that there is no currently accepted definition for social sustainability, although it is agreed that at a high level it concerns the attainment of sustainability with respect to social impacts.[10] It is also agreed that social performance is not simply about philanthropy, nor is it enhancing reputation with a view to increasing profits. There is an ethical core to social sustainability that goes deeper than the business benefits.[11]

Much of the dialogue around social responsibility centres on two approaches:

a) a prescriptive approach measured through the achievement of certain standards regarding the ethical behaviour of business in the market-place and treatment of employees and suppliers; and

b) a process approach, which concerns the way in which organizations relate to and are accountable to their stakeholders.

Social Principles—The Prescriptive Approach

The notions of individual human rights, employee rights, and supply-chain management are key tenets of the majority of the CSR standards that take a prescriptive approach to social responsibility. Most standards in this category include statements on:[12]

- working conditions;
- freedom of association and the right to collective bargaining;
- the unacceptability of child labour;
- the right to freely choose employment;
- the right to a living wage;
- the prohibition of abuse or inhumane treatment;
- limits on working hours;
- responsibility for supplier actions and impacts;
- deduction of wages as punishment;
- compliance with tax laws and regulations; and
- the respect of intellectual and other property rights.

A cursory look at the co-op principles suggests that co-operatives share an aspiration towards meeting some similar and/or complementary goals around:

- anti-discrimination—the first co-op principle addresses discrimination against membership;
- employee development—co-ops hold as a principle the education and training of their employees so they can contribute effectively to the development of their co-op; and
- community development—the seventh principle, concern for community, encourages co-ops to work for the sustainable development of their communities.

The notions of individual human rights, employee rights, and supply chain management, however, are not specifically touched on within the co-op principles. This suggests that co-ops aiming to strengthen their social bottom line will face many of the same challenges as their corporate counterparts when they attempt to ensure the maintenance of basic human rights. The co-operative that aspires towards social responsibility will need to align itself with the standards being developed by the broader corporate community.

STAKEHOLDER ENGAGEMENT—THE PROCESS APPROACH

The process approach to improving a company's social bottom line focusses on the notions of stakeholder accountability and engagement.

This approach views social sustainability as the "totality of the relationships that an organization has with all its stakeholders."[13] Key stakeholders for businesses include employees, customers, suppliers, community, shareholders, government, and civil society. Accountability is a property of these relationships, and being accountable means explaining or justifying to people with a legitimate interest the actions, omissions, risks, and dependencies for which you are responsible. Accountability, therefore, is a process of actively engaging and involving stakeholders in organizational affairs.[14]

The SIGMA research points out that the development of the AccountAbility 1000 (AA1000, see Appendix B) standard has helped to highlight the importance of an inclusive and responsive dialogue with stakeholders around triple-bottom-line issues. Engagement with stakeholders is a central element of the AA1000 framework, which identifies principles of accountability and an inclusive process of social and ethical accounting, auditing, and reporting. The first step in implementing the framework is a comprehensive mapping of stakeholder groups affected by a company's operations. The second step is the development of systems (such as surveys, focus groups, town-hall meetings, and expert panels) to consult with key stakeholder groups with a view to having their feedback inform organizational decisions and policies that they deem important. These same processes are also used to generate indicators, targets, and reporting systems to measure organizational performance in critical social and environmental areas. Together these elements are intended to help hold a company accountable to its stakeholders and systemize continual improvement.

Both with and without the AA1000 standard, a number of companies have taken a leading role in engaging various groups of stakeholders to help focus their approach to social responsibility. Despite these recent developments, however, doubts as to the meaningfulness of this engagement continue. In their study comparing social sustainability standards, Henriques and Raynard raise a concern regarding the lack of standards around the quality of stakeholder dialogue.[15] They note the challenges associated with determining what good-quality stakeholder dialogue actually involves and how it differs from traditional market research techniques. The SIGMA team notes that "it is arguable whether this has led to a significant change in organizational decision making and whether, indeed, a stakeholder model for organizations within a shareholder-driven economic system is feasible."[16]

Viewing notions of stakeholder engagement and accountability through a co-operative lens reveals a unique opportunity for co-operative organizations. By definition, co-ops exist to meet the common needs of their members, who are both the primary beneficiaries and the owners of the organization. The principle of democratic member control offers all members the opportunity to participate in setting policies and decision making. This participation is primarily conducted through the election of a member-directed board, a process in which voting rights are equal for all members, regardless of their level of investment in the co-op or the degree to which they use the services provided. These distinguishing features of co-operative enterprises can be viewed as built-in mechanisms that promote meaningful stakeholder engagement. In other words, two key stakeholder groups are always able to have a significant impact on organizational decision making—the member-customers (or, in case of worker co-ops, the member-employees) and the member-shareholders.

In *Co-operatives and Community Development,* Fairbairn et al. describe the opportunities for co-ops to demonstrate leadership in social sustainability through engagement and accountability as follows:

> Indeed, a co-operative can be viewed as a kind of crude social auditing process in itself: through the democratic side of the organization, the members of the co-operative—the people affected by its business—provide feedback on its impact on the community.... Co-operative democracy gives members the power to change the behaviour of the co-operative to meet the community's standards.... This is far in advance of the control that affected people have over almost any private business or corporation. Co-operatives have a head start in social auditing, and a unique advantage—provided their democratic structures are working and they are willing to formalize and improve their procedures.[17]

Enhancing the Co-operative Advantage

The above analysis is by no means intended as a rigorous comparison or understanding of the co-operative principles vis à vis other corporate social responsibility standards and principles. I do hope, however, that it offers a slightly different perspective on the notion of the co-operative as a socially responsible business model. As noted above, even close observance of the co-op principles is not enough to secure a leadership position in corporate social responsibility. From a CSR practitioner's perspective, co-operatives that aspire to CSR leadership will need to pay particular attention to managing (a) their environmental bottom line; (b) the social aspects of individual human rights, employee rights, and supply chain management; and (c) their financial performance, as none of these aspects is addressed within the co-operative principles. Since co-op principles go further than most of their corporate CSR counterparts in addressing basic sustainability issues of fairness and the equitable distribution of wealth, unique CSR leadership opportunities exist for co-operatives in the area of economic sustainability. Another opportunity lies within the notion of stakeholder engagement as a process to enhance a company's social bottom line; the principle of democratic ownership and control ensures member engagement in co-operative organizations.

For a co-op manager or director the question then becomes, what are some of the ways in which co-operatives can build on their unique advantages to enhance their social bottom line and ultimately distinguish themselves as values-based, socially responsible enterprises? Again, we can look to some of the emerging CSR practices in the corporate realm for potential ideas. Two areas of particular interest to me are broader stakeholder involvement in setting policy and program direction, and board accountability and representation.

Stakeholder Involvement in Setting Policy and Program Direction

As mentioned earlier, social auditing and reporting is one way in which co-operatives can formalize and enhance their ability to involve stakeholders in a meaningful way. In her study of social auditing in Canadian credit unions, Leslie Brown gently poses a challenge to co-operatives to take a leadership role in advancing social auditing:

> Social auditing has a particular relevance for businesses such as co-ops which have at their core a range of social commitments including that of accountability.... Further, changes are occur-. ring in the business environment and it behooves co-ops and credit unions to lead rather than lag in responding to them.... To lead in social auditing means that co-operative claims to espouse co-operative principles are likely to be taken more seriously, while to lag may mean that these claims are viewed as mere market positioning.[18]

The AA1000 framework could offer co-operatives some guidelines to enhance the principle of democratic member control and possibly extend the benefits of stakeholder engagement to other groups such as employees, suppliers, local communities, and those with environmental interests. Examples of co-operatives that have taken the lead in successfully adopting the AA1000 framework to guide their sustainability efforts include the Co-operative Bank in the UK, Co-operative Insurance Services (UK), and VanCity Savings Credit Union.

On a practical level, engaging stakeholders in policy and program development needn't involve the adoption of a comprehensive sustainability framework or a commitment to social accounting and reporting. Regularly adopting simple processes to engage members on issues of importance to them, such as posting questionnaires on a co-operative's web site or holding periodic town-hall meetings, can go a long way towards making democratic ownership more meaningful.

As part of the process to rewrite their Sourcing Policy, for example, Mountain Equipment Co-op recently engaged a broad range of stakeholders in a number of different ways—it consulted members through an on-line survey; it held focus groups to collect staff input; and representatives from nongovernmental organizations provided input as part of an external panel of experts.[19] The benefits of this relatively inexpensive process were multiple:

- It proactively identified and addressed potentially contentious topics before they became public issues requiring reactive management.
- It created a policy statement that the board could confidently endorse as representative of their constituents.

- It developed an external network of supporters who were willing to advocate for the policy and the process by which it was crafted.

The end result was a highly successful process, both from a risk-management perspective and as an example of engaging stakeholders in a meaningful way.

As an example of involving stakeholders in decision making on a more operational level, VanCity Savings Credit Union and its subsidiary, Citizens Bank, both regularly involve their employees and members in determining the direction of their community involvement and granting programs. Both companies, for example, ask their members to vote annually on the distribution of certain granting dollars, such as the VanCity million-dollar award and Citizens Bank's shared interest program. With the VanCity EnviroFund VISA card, members are polled to determine the programmatic themes of interest to them and funding streams are set accordingly.

Board Accountability, Development, and Composition

In the corporate world, few areas have received as much attention in recent years as that of board accountability. A closer look at the evolution of corporate practices related to board accountability, development, and composition could enhance the principle of democratic ownership within co-operatives. Specific examples of emerging best practice in this area include:

- performance evaluations of individual directors and the board as a whole;
- the adoption of a directors' code of conduct to help ensure that the interest of the company is always placed before that of individual directors;
- the development of job descriptions for directors and their roles;
- a published list of attributes, including desired skills and demographic representation, required by a particular board to function effectively and reflect its constituents; and
- the subsequent screening and identification of candidates who possess the attributes identified as important.

While some co-operators may argue that such practices go against the co-operative feature of democratic member control, I would like to suggest otherwise, particularly for large co-operatives. It is true that many small co-operatives are challenged in finding enough people willing to run for the board. In these cases, it seems reasonable to leave the call for nominations to anyone who expresses even the mildest interest. But how valid is this strategy (or lack of strategy) for a large, complex business operation that often has more than a dozen candidates vying for three positions? If we agree that a potential strength for co-operatives is their connection with community through ownership, then leaving the element of effective, good governance to chance would seem like a missed opportunity.

In fact, one could argue that the board of a large co-operative has a responsibility to make the election of candidates a worthwhile and fulfilling task for its members. In many ways, this responsibility could be thought of as an extension of a commitment to member service. How good a service is a co-operative providing its members when the task of electing its representatives becomes cumbersome and meaningless to the broad majority of the membership? Using the analogy of a retail business, it would be similar to a general store offering every brand available within a product category versus internalizing some of the tough buying decisions and limiting the offering to those few brands most likely to meet the needs of the member.

Taking a proactive approach and offering a representative array of qualified candidates would allow members to understand more clearly the candidates' positions on key issues facing the co-operative. To continue the retail analogy, by offering a range of products that all meet a minimum quality standard, consumers are freed from having to assess product quality (of which they are often ill-informed) and are able to focus more clearly on the features that appeal to their needs and aspirations.

Beyond election practices, broader representation of different stakeholder groups could be addressed through their direct involvement in governance. Indeed, the findings of the Co-operative Commission in the UK call for employee involvement in governance as a way of achieving a revitalized membership, informed and fully involved in democracy. To quote the authors:

Employee members—as stakeholders within the (co-op) movement—should be encouraged to become members of the Society and have a reserved employee member constituency from which they should be able to elect employee Directors. This change will be a positive means of reinforcing the key role of employees in achieving the improved commercial performance of Societies. But it will also mean becoming fully involved in developing the overall commercial strategy of the Co-operative businesses for which they are working and in the drive to achieve the social goals of co-operation."[20]

Employee involvement in the governance of consumer- or producer-owned co-operatives or credit unions in North America is relatively rare. A common argument against it is the difficulty employees would face in having to wear "the different hats" of director and employee at the same time. Concerns focus on the ability of employees to make decisions for the benefit of the organization versus those that serve their own personal interests as employees. And yet, successful worker co-operatives, notably in Europe, do not appear to share these concerns.

As part of an annual study tour of co-operatives operating in the Bologna region of Italy organized by the BC Co-operative Association, I had the pleasure of speaking with the managers of several large, highly successful co-operatives owned and governed by employees. When asked about the benefits of having employees govern, many of the managers responded by praising factors such as greater employee loyalty and engagement as well as improved operational efficiency and productivity. These same managers were also quick to talk about the need for ongoing training, clear governance policies and procedures, and a commitment to internal communications in order for the model to be successful, which can also be said for any governance model. Suffice it to say that co-op researchers could tap into both co-operative and corporate governance examples to find effective and creative ways to engage stakeholders, particularly employees, on their boards of directors.

In conclusion, although it seems clear that co-operatives can no longer claim a unique appeal as organizations based on social and community values, they still have some distinct advantages over investor- or privately-owned firms. With a measure of creative thinking, co-ops have the potential to act within the framework of their values and principles to address their shortcomings and play a leadership role in advancing corporate social responsibility.

APPENDIX A: STATEMENT ON THE CO-OPERATIVE IDENTITY[21]

Definition
A co-operative is an autonomous association of persons united voluntarily to meet their common economic, social, and cultural needs and aspirations through a jointly-owned and democratically-controlled enterprise.

Values
Co-operatives are based on the values of self-help, self-responsibility, democracy, equality, equity and solidarity. In the tradition of their founders, co-operative members believe in the ethical values of honesty, openness, social responsibility and caring for others.

Principles
The co-operative principles are guidelines by which co-operatives put their values into practice.

1st Principle: Voluntary and Open Membership
Co-operatives are voluntary organizations, open to all persons able to use their services and willing to accept the responsibilities of membership, without gender, social, racial, political or religious discrimination.

2nd Principle: Democratic Member Control
Co-operatives are democratic organizations controlled by their members, who actively participate in setting their policies and making decisions. Men and women serving as elected representatives are accountable to the membership. In primary co-operatives members have equal voting rights (one member, one vote) and co-operatives at other levels are also organized in a democratic manner.

3rd Principle: Member Economic Participation
Members contribute equitably to, and democratically control, the capital of their co-operative. At least part of that capital is usually the common property of the co-operative. Members usually receive limited compensation, if any, on capital subscribed as a condition of membership. Members allocate surpluses for any or all of the following purposes: developing their co-operative, possibly by setting up reserves, part of which at least would be indivisible; benefiting members in propor-

tion to their transactions with the co-operative; and supporting other activities approved by the membership.

4th Principle: Autonomy and Independence
Co-operatives are autonomous, self-help organizations controlled by their members. If they enter to agreements with other organizations, including governments, or raise capital from external sources, they do so on terms that ensure democratic control by their members and maintain their co-operative autonomy.

5th Principle: Education, Training and Information
Co-operatives provide education and training for their members, elected representatives, managers, and employees so they can contribute effectively to the development of their co-operatives. They inform the general public—particularly young people and opinion leaders—about the nature and benefits of co-operation.

6th Principle: Co-operation among Co-operatives
Co-operatives serve their members most effectively and strengthen the co-operative movement by working together through local, national, regional and international structures.

7th Principle: Concern for Community
Co-operatives work for the sustainable development of their communities through policies approved by their members.

APPENDIX B: KEY CSR STANDARDS AND PRINCIPLES COMPARED AS PART OF THE SIGMA PROJECT

AccountAbility 1000 (AA1000) is a management framework to improve the accountability and overall performance of organizations. AA1000 identifies principles of accountability and a quality (inclusive) process of social and ethical accounting, auditing, and reporting. Engagement with stakeholders is a central element of the framework.

The Global Reporting Initiative (GRI) was established in 1997 with the mission of designing globally applicable guidelines for preparing enterprise-level sustainability reports. The GRI focusses on establishing common indicators for reporting but does not include guidelines on benchmarking or on the quality of systems management.

The Global Sullivan Principles are voluntary guidelines launched at the United Nations in 1999 that include eight directives on labour, ethics, and environmental practices targeted at all private-sector organizations.

Investors in People is a UK quality standard developed in 1990 that sets a level of good practice for improving an organization's performance through the training and development of its people to achieve business goals.

ISO 14001 is a system that provides a standard for quality management within an organization. The International Standards Organization is a nongovernmental organization comprised of a network of national standards institutes from 148 countries working in partnership with international organizations, governments, industry, business, and consumer representatives.

The Natural Step Framework provides a simple framework to enable businesses to integrate environmental issues into the structure of business reality. It aims to move a company towards sustainable development and has a strategy for action that consists of four core processes and four system conditions. The framework provides a common language with which to talk about sustainability and facilitates the creation of shared goals around the issue. As an organization, The Natural Step engages in training and consulting, research and development, and community outreach.

Social Accountability 8000 (SA8000) represents an attempt to create an auditable standard for global manufacturing operations. SA8000 builds on the quality and environmental auditing process developed by the International Standards Organization in its ISO9000 and ISO14000 principles. SA8000 relies on certified monitors to verify factory compliance with the standard and, addresses issues including prison labour, wages, child labour, and health and safety.

The UN Global Compact, endorsed by Secretary-General Kofi Annan, consists of a set of nine principles, including specific practices, which Anan encouraged world business leaders to voluntarily embrace and enact.

Endnotes

1. Throughout this paper I will use the term "corporate" to refer to investor- or privately-owned companies as distinct from member-owned co-operatives.
2. See Business for Social Responsibility, posted at http://www.bsr.org.
3. The SIGMA Project—Sustainability: Integrated Guidelines for Management—was launched in 1999 with the support of the UK Department of Trade and Industry. It is a partnership among the British Standards Institution (the leading standards organization), Forum for the Future (a leading sustainability charity and think-tank), and AccountAbility (the international professional body for accountability). See website at http://www.projectsigma.com.
4. The SIGMA Project, page 4.3.1. "Building SIGMA—Where We Are" (9 April 2001, Draft 9, pg. 3). This draft document is no longer available on the website.
5. A key limitation of the triple-bottom-line approach, for example, includes the implied equal weighting among the three respective bottom lines when, in fact, long-term ecological sustainability is a precondition to sustainability.
6. EMAS is a voluntary initiative designed to improve companies' environmental performance. Its aim is to recognize and reward those organizations that go beyond minimum legal compliance and continuously improve their environmental performance.

7. The SIGMA Project, Phase 1 Report, May 2000. The SIGMA Project, p. 10.
8. Ibid., p. 11.
9. The Co-operative Commission, "The Co-operative Advantage—Creating a Successful Family of Co-operative Businesses" (London: The Co-operative Commission, January 2001), pp. 26–27. Posted at www.co-opcommission.org.uk.
10. A. Henrique and P. Raynard, "Social Sustainability—Research from the SIGMA Project," *Journal of Corporate Citizenship* (autumn 2002): p. 34.
11. James Wilsdon, "The Capitals Model: A Framework for Sustainability," written at Forum for the Future for the SIGMA Project Gap Analysis, September 1999.
12. Business for Social Responsibility, "Comparison of Selected Corporate Social Responsibility-Related Standards," November 2000. Posted at www.bsr.org.
13. Henriques and Raynard, p. 34.
14. Ibid.
15. Ibid., p. 38.
16. SIGMA Project Guidelines, "Appendix A," Pilot Draft, May 2001.
17. Fairbairn et al., "Accounting for Change: Co-operatives and the Social Audit," in *Co-operatives and Community Development: Economics in Social Perspective* (Saskatoon: Centre for the Study of Co-operatives, 1991), p. 101.
18. Leslie Brown, "The Co-operative Difference? Social Auditing in Canadian Credit Unions," *Journal of Rural Cooperation* 28, no. 2 (2000): pp. 98–99.
19. A recent similar example in the co-operative world is Starbucks, which in April 2004 invited more than twenty organizations to Seattle in an attempt to solicit constructive stakeholder feedback on its revised Coffee Sourcing Guidelines and Preferred Supplier Programme. Representatives of Rainforest Alliance, Fairtrade Labelling Organizations International, TechnoServe, Oxfam America, TransFair USA, US AID, Conservation International, and others provided comment. Participants discussed social standards, verification methods, and environmental considerations.
20. The Co-operative Commission, ch. 3.6.3.
21. In Ian MacPherson, *Co-operative Principles for the 21st Century* (Geneva: International Co-operative Alliance, 1995).

BILL TURNER

CO-OPERATIVE MEMBERSHIP
ISSUES AND CHALLENGES

IN CANADA, people have enjoyed the freedom to choose to work together for their own mutual benefit. Over the years they have formed many different kinds of co-operatives in response to many different needs. In many cases, co-operatives have been extremely successful and have attained prominent positions among the myriad organizations and enterprises that comprise Canadian society and the economy. As the contemporary world order changes, however, established co-operatives and their members face new realities, and opportunities emerge for fresh approaches and for the formation of new co-operatives.

Co-operatives are formed to provide benefits to their members, and the measurement of their success can consequently be multidimensional. Unlike an investor-owned business, where the motive is to satisfy shareholders—the providers of capital—by maximizing returns to capital, a co-operative is challenged to satisfy its owners—the members—by providing tangible benefits to members in an economically sustainable manner that will maintain their loyalty to the co-operative. Those member benefits may take several forms and could include things such as patronage refunds, the provision of services otherwise not available to the membership or the community, the creation of employment opportunities, an investment in community infrastructure, or the improvement of members' incomes by moving up the market supply chain. The bottom line for the co-operative is that it must contribute to the enhancement of its members' social and/or economic welfare, and it must do so in competition with other providers of goods and services.

Co-ops tend to form in times of change or adversity. They form when people see the need to challenge the status quo by developing innovative approaches that will enhance their welfare or fill a void in the market. Credit unions, for example, developed among farmers on the Prairies when the established banks and trust companies withdrew from the farm-credit market in response to the ravages of the Great Depression. In response to this reality and in desperate need of credit, a few brave souls dared to think that there was another way to do things and formed the first credit unions. Similar stories can be told about the formation of the wheat pools, the consumer co-operatives, and the dairy co-ops. Advancing technologies, changing rules in the market-place, new competitors, and evolving consumer preferences all cause change and create difficulties for people as they struggle to adapt to new realities. It is in these circumstances that people invent new approaches and where the opportunities for co-operation arise.

Adapting to Change

Adaptation to change, however, can be a difficult task for co-operatives. It can be especially complicated for established co-operatives that have spent many years building an effective organization and infrastructure, and that have enjoyed operating in a stable environment for some time. When co-ops become comfortable with a set of market rules or regulations that define their scope of operations, it will be a challenge to adapt to rapid change that totally redefines the conditions under which they function. On the other hand, newly emerging organizations do not have the restrictions of a culture or infrastructure that was designed to operate under a set of conditions that are no longer applicable. They are free to design strategies and systems unencumbered by vestiges of the past.

Consider the example of the western Canadian grains industry. With declining margins for traditional cereal crops throughout the 1980s, farmers began to focus on producing more specialized, nontraditional crops that were marketed in a different manner from bulk cereal commodities. Even for traditional crops, demand emerged for specific product characteristics or qualities; wheat was no longer wheat, canola no longer canola. The global market-place was changing. Farmers were also seeking ways to alter the enterprise mix on their farms in order to diversify their revenue sources and reduce their dependence on grain production.

At the same time, advancing technologies strongly influenced farming methods on the Prairies, and the capital structure of farms changed dramatically. The requirement for operating capital and liquidity meant that farmers needed to turn over their crop production quickly to meet cash-flow requirements. They also had to expand their revenue base to justify the higher capital investment that now characterized the farm. The results were an increase in farm size, diversification of farm enterprises, and a lack of new entrants into the farming business.

With their operations changing in such fundamental ways, farm members of co-operatives required different services from their co-ops. If the co-op could not supply the growing need for operating credit, specialized farm inputs, customized services, marketing for specialized crops, and services for livestock enterprises, farmers would seek them elsewhere or form new organizations to meet their needs. Members were drifting away from their established grain-marketing co-operatives and were ahead of their organizations in adapting to changing conditions.

New co-operatives and other farmer-owned enterprises began to spring up across the Prairies. In Leroy, Saskatchewan, for example, farmers, the retail consumer co-operative, and the credit union worked together with a local hog farmer to form a New Generation Co-operative. Owned by the farmers, it was an innovative partnership approach to expanding the revenue base for the farmers and to offering the hog farmer a means to scale up his production. In the neighbouring town of Naicam, the local retail co-operative expanded its business to provide farmers with customized services. In other communities across the Prairies, farmers banded together to build new grain-handling facilities in direct competition with the established grain-marketing co-ops.

Like their farmer members, the Prairie grain co-operatives were also facing changing times. Officials engaged in multilateral trade talks were negotiating the rules of the world and domestic grain market, eroding the ability of the large Prairie wheat pools to lobby for their own interests. New trade rules emerged from the final GATT (General Agreement on Tariffs and Trade) negotiations in the early 1990s, and the removal of the long-standing grain transportation subsidy (The Crow Rate) in 1995 occasioned the need for substantial investment to upgrade the outmoded grain-handling system. The competitive environment had changed dramatically. To compound things, the demographics of the farming community and thus the co-op membership were shifting noticeably as the average age of farmers continued to increase. The margins in the traditional grain-handling business could not produce net revenues that would finance reinvestment and equity payouts to retiring members.

What happened to the Prairie grain co-ops in these circumstances is well known and it raises some fundamental issues for co-operatives. One of the first that comes to mind is how can both members and their co-operative adapt to change without sacrificing the sustainability of one or the other? Should the member adapt to the institution or vice versa? What processes would engage the membership in a meaningful way that would harmonize the business strategies of the co-op in a timely manner with the needs of members? Are the forces of globalization so strong and pervasive that some co-operative structures cannot adapt? There are no easy answers here, and leaders attempting to lead change are often confronted with a dilemma. This is surely a fruitful area for investigation that could contribute greatly to the sustainability of co-operative organizations over the long run.

A look at the agenda of any board meeting of a larger, established co-op might be revealing. How much effort is put into understanding the events that are going to fundamentally influence the operations of the co-op? In response to such events, is the strategy one of adapting to the new situation or of attempting to lobby for maintenance of the status quo? How much time is spent analysing or thinking about how decisions or events will impact the members? Particular attention needs to be paid to understanding how globalization and advancing technologies are affecting the co-op's membership as well as how they are changing the nature of the competitive market-place and everyday business operations. To understand how members are being affected is to understand how the co-op's primary market-place is changing, and this will help the co-operative to develop a strategy that maintains its identity and its linkage to the members.

IDENTITY

Co-operatives are often thought of as a collection of physical assets or as a building. If you ask people, "What is the co-op or credit union?" the response will usually indicate the service station or the grocery store or the grain elevator. People interact with the organization through its physical assets, which have given the co-op its identity in peoples' minds. You are less likely to get a response that describes the co-op or credit union as a group of people working together to provide themselves and their community with a bundle of services, or to intervene in the market-place with the objective of enhancing the welfare of the members.

Identity is often defined in terms of a local presence, but a co-op also takes on a broader community identity, and over time it becomes an integral part of the community to which its members are linked. When a co-op consolidates its services into larger units or withdraws services from communities, it faces the prospect of losing its community identity and the support of its members. This raises the question of where peoples' loyalty really lies. Is it with their community or with their co-op? In the case of co-operatives, can the two identities be separated?

Some people suggest that a decentralized service-delivery structure makes it easier to develop and maintain a local identity. Where there is a local identity, the co-op's services are delivered in close physical proximity to its members. While a local presence may contribute to a strong identity, it is not the only factor in moulding it. Mountain Equipment Co-op (MEC) has been successful in developing an identity even in communities where its physical facilities are absent. MEC commits to providing "ethically sourced" products at reasonable prices and "experience-based" advice that will maximize a person's outdoor experience. In addition, an integral part of MEC's strategy is "to protect and preserve the natural environment." This suggests that providing convenient access to the co-op's services and implying that supporting the co-op contributes to some "greater good" can be just as important to the organization's identity as the presence of physical facilities. Being environmentally responsible, supporting local ownership, buying Canadian, and sourcing goods from suppliers who adhere to ethical standards are all examples of contributing to the "greater good" that links to member values. And ATMs, tele-service operations, online services, and convenience stores can provide services in an accessible and timely manner that connect with member lifestyles.

GOVERNANCE, LEADERSHIP, AND VOLUNTEERISM

Membership renewal is another issue that co-ops cannot ignore. The members who become involved in the active governance of their co-operative are relatively few in number. Many will be content to utilize the services of the co-op for their own benefit and will never consider assuming a leadership role in the organization. And due to the largely voluntary nature of co-operative governance, two situations tend to develop. In the first, a small group of committed members take on leadership positions and serve for long periods of time. While the dedication of such individuals is admirable, the co-operative risks losing the advantage of having new ideas and perspectives brought forward from the broader membership. The second situation arises when no one person or group can undertake a leadership position for any length of time. As a result, there is a constant turnover in the leadership group and a lack of continuity in directing the co-operative.

Neither of the aforementioned situations is desirable, and the co-operative needs to devise strategies that will provide continuity and allow for the orderly succession of the leadership group. In addition, it must devote resources to developing and supporting individuals while they assume their co-operative responsibilities. Many co-ops have rules regarding the number of terms that an individual can serve on a board of directors and have well-developed approaches to recruiting new people to run for elected office.

This raises a fundamental issue: How do you maintain the co-op governance model and attract competent leaders from amongst the membership, while at the same time achieving the scale of operations necessary to sustain the business? This may mean rethinking the traditional centralized structure to which most enterprises migrate as they grow, and exploring innovative ways to link to or network with smaller, autonomous or semi-autonomous units to achieve scale and create efficiencies. This also implies a more decentralized management and governance structure, in which the major challenge becomes one of maintaining cohesion, sharing information, and gaining knowledge among the smaller units. It also requires a mindset that views the co-operative in a "bottom up" paradigm.

To compound the challenge, considerable responsibility is thrust upon the volunteer leadership as co-operatives become larger and more complex. Many of the recent difficulties in the corporate world have been attributed to inadequate oversight or governance. As a result, directors in general are being held to a higher standard of accountability and are expected to possess or acquire specific skills that will enhance their effectiveness. Exercising the responsibilities of leadership involves a significant time commitment, and it will become more difficult to recruit people who can take time away from their careers to assume leadership positions in co-operatives. This is not such an issue in smaller, less complex co-ops, where the demands are not so great.

In the future, co-operatives will need to discover new and innovative ways of allowing their volunteer members to take on the challenges of leadership. New approaches to governance processes that utilize modern technology hold some promise but cannot be relied upon completely. The Internet, video-conferencing, and tele-conferencing all offer methods of involving members without taking them away from their home base for extended periods. The governance structure also needs to be examined to determine if there are ways to provide effective governance in smaller "chunks," which would allow more members to participate and require fewer part-time or full-time leaders.

MEMBER EDUCATION AND TRAINING

In a more complex, interdependent, and competitive world, the key to co-operative success will rest with a well-educated and -trained membership. No longer can co-ops assume that they function in a small, insulated market, and it will be important for members—particularly those in leadership positions—to understand the complexities of the world around them. Co-operative education and research can contribute to this understanding in the following ways:

- An examination of innovative and successful approaches to organizing co-operative business and governance activities would greatly assist all co-operatives to develop new approaches. Useful models to consider include practical examples of functional networked or federative structures that link smaller units to gain efficiencies, as well as the policies or strategies that bring them together.
- A review of existing co-op education programs with a view to expanding the generic approach to member and director training—incorporating new material that challenges traditional thinking around business and governance models—would encourage people to consider new approaches.
- An examination of the social nature of co-operatives would provide an understanding of the complex human relationships that exist within them and the linkages to a broader community.
- Experimentation with new distance-education techniques would reveal different methods of reaching members in their own communities and homes.
- A better understanding of how globalization is affecting people in different sectors and locations would be beneficial to co-operative members and leaders as they grapple with strategies to adapt to this phenomenon.

Concluding Remarks

When things are changing so rapidly in Canada's social and economic environment, it would be easy to view co-operatives as something "old," as an organizational form that does not have much relevance to the future. Considering the struggles of the Prairie grain co-operatives or the western dairy co-ops, one could be forgiven for making this assumption. In fact, there may be some validity to the observation that the co-operative model is slow to change and does not adapt easily to large, centralized business operations.

In direct contradiction to this, however, is the continued success of the co-operative retailing system and the credit union system. In both cases, the co-op model is thriving in markets that are dominated by some of the largest corporate entities in the country, or indeed the world. The reasons for this are many and varied, but in simplest terms, these co-operatives have remained connected to their members' needs and their communities. They have developed and maintained a strong identity and have used it to their commercial advantage.

There is every reason to be optimistic about the future for co-operatives. The changing world order creates an opportunity for organizations responsive at the local level to be part of a much larger and broader network. The greatest challenge is for co-operative leaders to seize this opportunity, recognizing that they operate in a globally interdependent system that requires co-operation within and between different sectors.

Part Two: Theory

New Directions in Research and Practice

Nine scholars explore theoretical concepts such as co-op membership as a dynamic social process, the role of values and principles, leadership and representational diversity, cognitive processes and business strategy, and respectful research in Aboriginal communities.

MICHAEL GERTLER

CO-OPERATIVE MEMBERSHIP AS A COMPLEX AND DYNAMIC SOCIAL PROCESS

MEMBERSHIP AS A HUMAN EXPERIENCE

MEMBERSHIP is a hallmark of humanity. We humans are gregarious and well equipped for an intense and complex social life. We are unparalleled in the range of associations that we maintain, and in the degree to which we modify our group memberships over a lifetime. While the capacities to form lasting relationships and to co-operate are important for individual and group survival, membership is its own reward. We derive satisfaction from belonging and mutual recognition. Though membership, at times, may be costly, it provides us with resources, with social supports, and with opportunities for personal development. As individuals we gain our singularity by virtue of the memberships that we seek out or that are imposed upon us. Our individual identities are constructed out of past and present memberships in different groups. We define ourselves, and are defined by others, based on inclusions or exclusions that we have experienced with respect to groups.

"Member" can denote a person belonging to a group, or each of the individuals belonging to or forming a society or assembly. "Membership" may denote the fact or status of being a member of a society, assembly, or other organized entity; the body of members collectively; or the number of members in a particular organization.[1] While some of these meanings focus on the existence of, and the size of, a group of members, others focus attention on the status of being a member, and on the content or nature of the relationships involved. The membership of a particular person, and the membership in terms of the group collectively, can have particular qualities and characteristics.

We can explore the potential and complexity of membership by considering the diverse meanings of the suffix "–ship." It is used variously to denote an office, position, or occupation, as in *authorship* or *kingship;* a quality, state, or condition of being, as in *kinship, partnership;* acts, power, or skill, as in *leadership, workmanship;* relationships between persons, as in *comradeship;* someone with a certain rank or status, as in *your ladyship;* and also the members, collectively, of a class of persons, as in *readership*.[2]

While not all of these aspects of *membership* surface regularly in relation to co-operatives, such meanings highlight multiple latent interpretations of co-op membership. These meanings draw attention to the skills and powers involved in membership, and to the complex relationships that exist between each member and the organization, as well as among the persons who are members. These meanings also link back to, and highlight, the dual character of a co-operative as an association and an enterprise: members associate in order to carry out various collective goals.[3]

Membership is a widely used—though less frequently analysed—social arrangement that encompasses an array of rights, privileges, responsibilities, and obligations. It can be viewed as a set of structured relations and practices within which an individual takes on various roles and levels of activity within a formally or informally constituted group. As a social institution, membership can also be viewed as a set of norms and rules for association which themselves may be expanded or renegotiated.

The modifiers that can be attached to the word "member" remind us that it is a status that is often qualified or amplified in some manner. One can be an active, associate, charter, clandestine, continuing, ex officio, founding, honorary, life, long-time, loyal, minority, new, past, potential, or sponsoring member. The conditions attached to membership as a category are likewise varied: open or closed, voluntary or compulsory, hereditary or by invitation. One's membership may be conditional, permanent, probationary, renewable, temporary, or trial.

When we think about what it may mean to be a co-operative member, we can start by identifying and considering a number of overlapping concepts: activist, adherent, advocate, associate, client, customer, elector, investor, leader, office holder, owner, partner, patron, practitioner, promoter, proponent, shareholder, stakeholder, user, or volunteer. Co-operative members draw on membership experiences as band members, church members, clan members, club members, faculty members, family members, gang members, library members, party members, professional association members, service club members, team members, and union members. These kinds of membership may inform expectations, attitudes, and behaviours when it comes to co-operative membership.

The approach of individual co-op members with respect to membership, and likewise the collective membership culture of a co-operative, can vary and also change over time. Membership may be formal and legal, but passive and lacking in substance or solidity. On the other hand, it may be substantive, and associated with multiple forms of attachment, commitment, and activity. Such differences have significant repercussions for a co-operative organization.

Characteristics of Co-operative Members and Memberships

In commerce it is common practice to analyse the customer base and to target specific subgroups with particular kinds of communications and incentives. Politicians gather intelligence through polls and target specific audiences with particular messages. Co-operatives also face a membership and a broader public that is increasing in its diversity and particularistic interests. It thus becomes important to identify relevant subgroups within the membership and to address their concerns, preferences, and needs. Members and memberships have temporal, spatial, and socio-demographic characteristics. Members also vary in terms of the scope and intensity of their involvement and commitment(s). These dimensions interact and overlap so that the relevant characteristics of members and membership rarely belong to only one domain. Our conceptualization of membership must perforce be multidimensional and dynamic, accommodating many possible locations and mutually conditioning connections.

Each co-op member has, and the members collectively have, a unique socio-demographic profile. Although this profile reflects the structure of the communities from which the membership is drawn, it can vary significantly from the general makeup of the population when subgroups are over- or underrepresented. A co-op's membership can be characterized in terms of gender ratios, age distribution, ethnic origins, occupations, family or household characteristics, income, or other socio-economic indicators. Averages do not tell the whole story. There may be subpopulations with characteristics that mark them as significant subgroups or subcultures. Furthermore, the members collectively can be characterized in terms of their diversity or homogeneity.

Temporal dimensions of membership include variables such as length of membership, the mix in terms of new or long-term members, time of joining relative to key events in the history of the enterprise, and trends in terms of growth or shrinkage in membership. The time of joining in relation to the individual's own age, and the extent to which membership is passed on intergenerationally, are also significant. Each member will have their own activity-level trajectory with respect to involvement in the co-operative over time. Members may be active or inactive for a range of personal, life-cycle, or issue-based reasons. A co-operative member might be active in one organization and quite inactive in another, including another co-operative. Given the time required, it may not be possible to be active in multiple organizations. Variability in terms of individual patterns of activity over seasons or lifetimes is not necessarily a bad thing from the perspective of organizational sustainability, but it is important to know something about these patterns and to identify any emerging trends.

Activity level is itself a multidimensional construct. There can be many measures of the intensity and scope of member involvement in a co-operative. Examples include volume of business, the relative share of business done with the co-op, and the degree to which a member participates in co-operative governance. The character of member affiliation and identification with the co-operative can also be conceptualized in terms of indicators such as satisfaction with services and governance processes. Members can be characterized in terms of their commitment to co-operative philosophies and in relation to their commitment to a particular co-operative.

As a process, globalization involves a wholesale reorganization of spatial as well as temporal relationships. Individual members face important changes in the spatial economies of the regions in which they live and work. Co-operatives likewise confront new spatial relations with suppliers, customers, competitors, and their own membership. Relevant socio-spatial characteristics of the membership include the location of residences and places of work, mobility patterns related to commuting and shopping, longer-range travel in terms of places of origin and geographic dispersal of family members, and travel related to recreation or retirement. Under globalization, goods, people, and information tend to travel greater distances. This has significant implications for the "local" quality of co-operative membership.

Membership from a Member's Perspective

Membership as a social fact, as an identity, or as a structural relation can be approached and examined from the perspective of the individual, the organization, or the community. Membership issues from the standpoints of communities and co-operative organizations are explored further below. From the individual's perspective, membership in a particular co-op is one among many formal and informal memberships. In the mix of other activities and associations, the co-operative may be a minor or major involvement. Membership in the co-op may be tightly coupled with other memberships, or it may be an isolated and somewhat disconnected part of the person's life. The experience and practice of co-operative membership have a range of obvious and less obvious characteristics, with dimensions that are at once social, economic, political, and cultural.

Co-op membership may be viewed as personally advantageous or as an act of generosity and faith. The membership may be seen as conferring a higher social status, as neutral in this regard, or as an instance where the individual contributes her/his reputation and resources to help a community organization. It may be a minor involvement or a central aspect of personhood and livelihood. It may involve strong or weak commitment, and the presence or absence of co-operative consciousness. Membership may be maintained only passively, through inertia, or because there is no viable exit strategy. On the other hand, it may be a status that is valued intensely, that is taken up with high hopes and strong resolve to invest in the organization. Like more widely recognized kinds of identities, membership can be contingent—sensitive and responsive to particular circumstances and conditions. As for other aspects of identity, co-op membership may be claimed and defended in some situations, and scarcely acknowledged or admitted in others.

Co-op membership may involve consciously *doing* business differently. Transactions are carried out in contexts and ways that deliberately realign interests and relationships. Patronage of a co-operative may be viewed as a contribution to building a different type of economy, one that pays closer attention to the full range of interests one has as a resident, citizen, and user of services. Patronizing a co-op can be a social and political act, even as it is an economic act. Membership may reflect confidence and optimism given a high level of social capital circulating in the community, or it may be an effort to build something solidary in a community that has often failed to act collectively.

Membership from an Organizational Perspective

Organizations have their own interests with respect to membership: Leaders and managers may experience member adherence as a source of legitimacy and strength, but also as an encumbrance. The importance of membership and positive member relations from an organizational perspective can be explored by asking two questions. What are the advantages (to a co-operative) of a positively engaged and satisfied membership? What are the risks and costs of a disengaged and alienated membership? A membership that is positively engaged may be more likely to view the co-operative as a source of useful and trustworthy information; may be more willing to try new products or services offered by the co-operative; may be more loyal to the co-operative in the face of competitive marketing and various kinds of inducements from other enterprises; and may be more likely to provide helpful and constructive feedback to staff and managers, who will consequently experience a more positive work environment. A positively engaged membership, moreover, will be more likely to think like owners, helping the co-operative to control costs, improve services, and upgrade products; may be more willing to invest in upgrading facilities and enhancing the skills of co-op staff; may be more likely to support management in new undertakings; may be more likely to see the co-operative as a partner in economic, social, cultural, and political projects; and will be more likely to promote the benefits of the co-op and co-operative membership to others.

On the other hand, there are predictable risks and costs associated with an alienated or disinterested membership. It is more likely that such members may treat the co-operative as a service provider or market outlet of last resort; more likely that they will patronize the co-operative opportunistically, only when there is a distinct advantage in terms of price, terms, or conditions; and more likely that they will terminate their relationship with the co-operative in response to any minor problem or difference in terms of price or conditions. Such members may also be less likely to support innovations that involve any new costs or risks. Alienated members may fail to pass on co-operative philosophies or commitments to family members; may ignore co-operative communications; may not provide any constructive feedback to staff or managers; may be unwilling to participate in co-op governance; and may bad-mouth the co-operative to community members.

While positive member relations may be viewed as a desirable objective in the abstract, co-op managers may have practical reasons for reducing investment in member relations and for relegating membership issues to the back burner. Depending on the organization and the situation, these reasons might include the cost of building and maintaining strong communications and member relations programs; the cumbersome character of democratic procedures, which require consultation and negotiation before an organization can respond to a challenge or an opportunity; and the contradictory expectations that are raised through participatory exercises. Assertion of general membership prerogatives may conflict with the need to take steps to secure the patronage of members who do more business with the co-op. This issue is part of a general set of unresolved pressures with respect to equal versus asymmetrical treatment of members who belong to different categories in terms of types or volume of business. Managers who emphasize membership also risk alienating customers who, for any reason, may not want to become members. Managers may also find themselves excluded from business networks if too much emphasis is placed on the co-operative difference.

Large, well-established co-operatives enjoy many advantages. Larger size and maturity, however, bring new challenges in terms of member involvement. There may be fewer opportunities for the exciting kinds of pioneering activity that the founding members experienced. Moreover, in large organizations there may be opportunities for only a small percentage of the members to assume direct roles in co-operative governance. Activist members may then seek other ways to be heard. Large co-operatives, therefore, face particular challenges in fostering, accommodating, and managing member participation. Managers may react by reducing commitment to substantive member participation, resorting instead to a kind of perfunctory staging of meetings and elections, and to collecting feedback mainly as a form of defensive intelligence gathering. The result may be a further diminution in member participation, which will be read as confirmation that people are too disinterested or too busy to take part in co-operative governance.

MEMBERSHIP AND COMMUNITIES

Communities can experience organizational memberships as sources of social cohesion or as sources of division. Both tendencies may be active. Where belonging to a particular co-op or credit union reflects divisions along political, religious, or ethnic lines, membership may strengthen ties within a particular group, but reinforce separation between social groups and networks. In contemporary communities, co-operative memberships commonly span pre-existing social divides and link together some of the diverse strands that are present. Co-operative memberships thus reinforce and stabilize certain aspects of "community of place." Membership connects people in a common project and shared interest. In this sense, co-operative membership may serve as "bridging social capital" in that it links people who would otherwise have little occasion to associate or to develop joint projects.[4] Co-operatives and co-operative membership can also contribute to a broader social climate that propitiates joining, volunteering, and collaborating.[5]

Co-operatives may compete with other organizations for what are, at least in the short term, scarce community resources—volunteers, time, energy, and capital. In the long term, however, co-operatives can help to increase the supply of such resources by building human capacity, creating new links, and expanding the pool of leaders and community activists. Positive experiences developing alternative economic institutions, or innovating with respect to service provision, can also lead to a change in outlook and mentality that comes with successful collective action. This transformative kind of *cognitive praxis*[6] leads to an expanded concept of what is possible or achievable.

Membership as a Complex Dynamic

Like the co-operative itself, membership is a hybrid entity. It is, at the same time, an economic, social, cultural, and political phenomenon. It carries formal rights and obligations, and informal but nevertheless tangible expectations and benefits. Membership is an ideal and an aspiration, as well as an emergent reality. Membership is interpreted in the sense that individuals have to make sense of its meanings and implications. Membership is also interpreted in the sense that it is acted out, revealed, and deployed as a form of social action and discourse.

Membership is not separate from members, and members are not separate from all the social relations of the community and surrounding society. Race, ethnic, and gender relations, relations between old and young, between those more or less able, between recent and less recent immigrants, and between wealthy and poor, will all enter the dynamic. Membership includes experiences of recognition and acceptance, and opportunities to interact positively with fellow citizens. There are, to be sure, instrumental concerns such as exchanging information and building relationships. There are also aesthetic, visceral, or experiential aspects to membership that have to do with owning a piece of, and belonging to, something that has permanence, solidity, potential, and a complex social purpose. A co-operative organization also has a physical presence in terms of space for meetings, services, or administrative activities. Ideally, co-operative spaces become significant places, invested with positive meanings and associations.

It is important to understand the latent as well as the more obvious aspects of affiliation, adherence, and identification. It is most common to note and address the economic and social-psychological dimensions of membership. These are attributes that get identified early when people talk about motivations and processes that underlie joining, patronizing, or supporting a co-operative. These dimensions are also, not coincidentally, the qualities that receive most attention in mainstream managerial and marketing literature. While significant, these properties do not exhaust the list that is relevant to co-operative entrepreneurs. Left aside are key dimensions of co-operative membership that may distinguish the co-op organization and furnish important elements of co-operative competitive advantage.

The reasons for joining and supporting a co-operative are typically complex. In addition to economic objectives, there may be political objectives, social goals, cultural sensibilities, and ethical concerns. Given the relative neglect of such matters in the media and education, and even in co-op communications, individuals may not be equipped to fully explain these issues. They may nevertheless harbour strong feelings about sharing, neighbouring, democracy, and community, sentiments that seek expression in co-operative forms of enterprise. Whether or not they are regularly acknowledged and articulated, these preoccupations may be operative and relevant. Those who are interested in building co-operative membership, and in developing co-operatives via member-oriented strategies, must cultivate the capacity to engage with these concerns. They are important not only as significant bases for increasing member interest and loyalty, but also because ignoring them may eventually lead to alienation and dissension among members who are expecting more from their co-operative.

Because joining and supporting a co-operative has social and collective aspects as well as an individual and personal dynamic, it is useful to recognize the relevance of social and collective processes that motivate and facilitate association and adherence. Membership is something experienced most fully as a group process. One needs to study and support membership as a collective dynamic, and as something that is regenerated through association. Methodological individualism may not serve us well, either as researchers or as personnel charged with member relations development responsibilities.

Membership in a co-operative reflects the reciprocal character of joining and belonging. One belongs to the co-operative, and the co-op comes to belong to you. Members belong to the co-op, but they also own and direct the enterprise. In the case of founding members, or of member-leaders who help to develop and renew the organization, membership also includes a vigorous strain of social and economic entrepreneurship. The term member here labours to convey a multifaceted relationship that involves organizational innovation as well as ownership, association, participation, and patronage.

Achieving membership is a process that does not begin or end with the signing of a membership form. It is also important to understand the social and cognitive processes that underlie the successful development of a strong member and a strong member-based organization. Membership is a conscious process that involves frequent intelligence gathering, assessment, and re-evaluation. One invests more in memberships that yield social or financial dividends. Moreover, one is more likely to identify strongly with an organization that contributes to a positive, and less contradictory, identity. Thus co-operative membership has a reflexive and dynamic character.

Co-operative membership, like other forms of social relationship and association, is a socially embedded and embodied experience. We are co-op members as whole people, with histories, biographies, and bodies that signal to others that we are old, young, male, female, or likely to be categorized as belonging to some racial or ethnic minority. We also experience membership from our own situated perspectives, and interpret the possibilities and meanings based on our own needs, constraints, or opportunities. When studying membership issues, it is necessary to go beyond the idea of the "average member" and to analyse the membership as a set of overlapping subgroups and subcultures.

Membership is something we accomplish, and the groups and organizations to which we belong are, in some measure, the product of vision and imagination—by ourselves and by others. Like communities of all kinds,[7] groups and organizations have an imagined quality in that we perceive their characteristics and boundaries by combining knowledge and experience with desires and ideals. Joining and building a co-operative organization are, in part, acts of imagination, vision, and faith.[8] These may be principled decisions undertaken out of solidarity with future generations unknown to ourselves. Our understanding of co-operative action must therefore go beyond narrow concepts of present-oriented utility and rationality.

Membership Challenges for Co-ops

Co-operatives face short- and long-term investment decisions with respect to developing relationships with (and among) members. How should co-operatives view the investments necessary to develop positive member relationships? For co-ops, the calculus and the practices involved go well beyond the rationales and modalities of customer relations and goodwill promotion that are deployed by conventional firms. While co-operatives might well emulate some corporate communications strategies and attempts to promote a service culture, they need to develop their own distinct logic and approach to building strong relations with (and among) members. For co-ops, membership in its more substantive forms is both a fundamental distinguishing feature and a key to economic viability in a transformed market-place. Given the strong links between robust member relations and the development of both the co-operative and its host community, an amply ramified approach to membership is both a means and an end. Membership that is tangible, authentic, and beneficial in multiple ways will be a key feature that distinguishes a co-operative from other enterprises.

Co-operatives face diverse challenges with respect to member recruitment and member relations. This diversity increases when one considers different kinds or classes of co-operative. The membership issues confronting a large retail co-op bear only partial semblance to member relations concerns in a small production co-operative. While it is important to acknowledge the diversity of these challenges, it may also be useful to entertain the proposition that co-operatives collectively constitute a distinct and significant class of membership-based organizations, with an overlapping array of membership challenges and opportunities that arise due to the particular principles by which they are governed. These include orientations towards voluntary participation, equality, serving member interests, democratic control, and community.

Co-operative organizations eager for member engagement and participation can be both welcoming and off-putting. Different people (and the same people at different times) may be attracted to or repelled by organizations that reach out to them and encourage integration and identification. While those in search of community may find this kind of organizational advance appealing, it may not be seen as desirable by someone who is already overloaded with organizational obligations. Individuals who feel that their identity is somewhat marginal to the enterprise, or that their interests are minority interests within the organization, likewise may be disinterested in strong engagement. Such a person may be willing to affiliate, but unwilling to identify with, or to be identified with, the organization. This may be non-negotiable and beyond the capacity of the organization to address in any substantive manner.

The Rights Revolution[9] and some strands of consumerism have predisposed many individuals to emphasize freedom, choice, and flexibility. Moreover, the dominant culture puts a certain premium on disengagement, on being cool, detached, or uncommitted.[10] There are people who, at a given time in their lives, do not wish for heavy engagement with an organization, who prefer an arrangement that appears to give them greater autonomy and even anonymity. This might be true of certain subgroups such as single, mobile, young people. These are potentially important members, but they may not be willing to engage fully with the organization at this particular time. Nor are they likely to be susceptible to the same kinds of recruitment messages as those who are eager for a stronger form of association and involvement.

A co-operative that seeks to connect with a large group of members representing diverse backgrounds, circumstances, and interests, must be open to a diversity of membership styles and forms. This does not imply institutionalization of more than one class of membership, but rather recognition of diverse ways of connecting with the co-op, and a healthy variation in modes of belonging and contributing. A co-operative needs many types of members. A co-op with a strong membership profile and program will find ways to deepen its relations with many kinds of members (and potential members).

In addition to positive relations between the organization and individual members (or subgroups of members), co-operatives might benefit from consciously promoting durable forms of networking among members. This will strengthen the membership base and reflects a commitment to intra- as well as inter-co-operative co-operation. The co-operative has multiple reasons to be interested in the well being and success of its own membership as members of families, communities, organizations, and enterprises.

Many people need to be asked or invited personally in order to become active as leaders, volunteers, or participants. This may be particularly true and important in a co-operative. People perceive co-ops to be social as well as economic organizations and may be waiting for social contact and social dividends. If these kinds of connections or benefits are not forthcoming, the co-op may be judged more harshly than another kind of organization. Moreover, co-operatives present a context in which personal approaches may be more readily accepted. Many other kinds of enterprise now find it useful to mimic and to implement certain dimensions of membership as they attempt to influence their customers or clients to form more lasting and loyal relationships. Though presented in language that invokes membership, most such initiatives offer only a hollowed-out version. Corporations may use different levels or classes of membership to provide perquisites to preferred customers. Co-operatives generally do not, and cannot use different classes of membership to bestow differential privileges. On the other hand, corporations typically find it untenable to instigate the more developed forms of membership that imply commitment to shared ownership and control, and to the social development of members and their communities. This is where co-ops can easily outdistance and outshine the competition.

The commercial appropriation of the language of membership may lead to a debasement and corruption of the idea. The widespread implementation of such customer relations strategies presents a strong challenge to the co-operative sector, which has held out membership and its attendant benefits as a distinguishing feature. In this context, it is important to analyse the various *dimensions, qualities,* and *gradations* of membership, and to explore their implications for individuals and communities. For co-operatives, it is important to distinguish between weaker and stronger forms of membership, and to find new ways to further develop the latter.

With increasing size and associated member heterogeneity, co-ops will often find it easier to opt for "cooler" versions of co-op membership that put less emphasis on membership as an identity or as a significant focus for activities. Membership issues and co-operative identity may fall below the consciousness threshold for many patrons and other stakeholders. This may be temporarily expedient for managers and may also reduce some of the potential points of conflict among diverse members. It will not, however, appeal to everybody, especially those more philosophically committed to co-operation. Moreover, it may rob the co-operative of identity and dynamism. The cooling of membership as a pivot and focus will also rob the enterprise of a key tool for approaching, integrating, and connecting with a diverse population of members and potential members. What starts as an easy method to facilitate growth and minimize friction can end up as an impediment to the development of the member-based enterprise and to the reproduction of co-op leadership.

MEMBERSHIP-BASED DEVELOPMENT

The membership challenge for co-operatives is to expand opportunities for constructive member engagement, and to develop substantive, authentic, and beneficial forms of membership. This must be accomplished while accommodating multiple styles of membership. *Membership development* here denotes policies and programs designed to promote member recruitment, retention, loyalty, and participation. *Member development* refers to activities or initiatives to further the growth of individual members as fully competent participants in the organization and in the broader community. Member development is important for democratic organizations that rely on the quality of their elected leaders and on the wisdom of the voting members. Members are also likely to look on their co-op more favourably when they see it as a place to access new experiences and acquire new competencies. Moreover, the co-op also gains when its members are successful as community members, family members, and economic actors.

Membership-based or *member-based development* signals a stronger alignment towards building the co-operative through close working ties with members and by fostering a strong member-oriented culture. This strategy recognizes and embraces the particular character and challenges of a co-operative organization: It can generate strong allegiances and commitments, but it is also vulnerable to the disengagement or disaffection of members.

The rise of fundamentalist movements reminds us that membership can lead to behaviours that are heedless and exaggerated.[11] Membership in organizations tinged with fundamentalist characteristics (e.g., extremist political movements, politicized military units, chauvinistic national formations, or charismatic religious sects) may lead to the sacrifice of rights and freedoms—one's own, and particularly those of other people who are not seen as eligible for membership.[12] Co-operatives rarely inspire blind faith or unquestioning adherence, and this is a good thing. The loyalty they seek from members is an engaged and thoughtful loyalty, based on transparency and substantive understandings with respect to overlapping interests and projects.[13]

Membership relations represent the best opportunity for distinguishing a co-operative among the proliferating choices available to potential patrons. The 1990s should be remembered not only as the dot-com decade but as the dot-org decade, in which millions of new organizations were founded. In Canada, the number of registered citizen groups increased by more than 50 percent between 1987 and 2003, reaching about two hundred thousand (or about one group for every hundred adults).[14] Despite the widespread experience of time pressure, there is a growing interest in meaningful participation and democratization. This is an important phenomenon of our era and a historic opening for the co-operative sector.

How can co-operatives capitalize on this will for engagement in an era that has been characterized as a time of disengagement?[15] One option would be to reconfirm their social movement character by more explicitly differentiating themselves from other forms of organization, and by adopting a discourse that more adequately communicates this realignment. While there are risks arising from re-engagement, closer collaboration with movements for democracy and social justice would allow co-operatives to confirm their role and identity as socially responsive and progressive enterprises.[16] This would also be an opportunity to connect with individuals and groups that could be strong supporters of the co-op were they to perceive it as an ally and as a socially relevant organization.

Many co-operatives have been successful in renewing their membership base. This is self-evident when one contemplates the number, size, and range of co-operative organizations that exist. Given rapid changes in the characteristics of the communities in which members and potential members live and work, however, and given equally rapid changes in the expectations, preferences, identities, and personal situations of the individuals involved, co-operatives will have to explore new ways to connect with existing or would-be members.

Some co-operatives are reticent about marketing the benefits and virtues of membership. Aggressively marketing memberships may be seen as impolitic in certain contexts. Some co-ops may be wary about recruiting new members for fear of adding unworkable diversity. Still others may have doubts about the capacity of the organization to mount an effective recruitment campaign. Whatever the cause, failure to more actively market membership may lead to slow erosion of the membership base. In the absence of messages reinforcing adherence to the co-op, this may also include problems retaining existing members. Integrating new members involves cost and effort, and there are risks involved. Greater risks, however, await a co-operative that fails to renew its membership and to reach out to people who represent new kinds of diversity in the community.

Decisions with respect to joining a co-op are influenced by peers and family members who provide models and precedents, and by other influentials who help to reduce anxieties or questions around the decision.[17] It would be useful for co-operatives to learn more about the process of joining—or not joining. This would equip them to intervene more strategically and increase the possibility that new members will be enlisted under conditions that promote a strong, positive relationship.

We need to think systematically about membership as a dynamic social process. It is a mistake to treat it as a black box yielding only two possible outcomes. Members don't only join; they investigate, affiliate, confirm, and reactivate. Along the way, it may matter how they experience recruitment, installation, recognition, consultation, and accession to leadership positions. Moreover, a co-operative may have different meanings, and yield different experiences, depending upon who we are. Members and their co-ops can use such insights to improve member relations and to promote more positive and beneficial dynamics around all membership processes. An orientation towards membership-based development offers the best prospect for fulfilling the unique promise of the co-operative as a durable organization broadly responsive to member needs and hopes.

Endnotes

1. Adapted from *The New Shorter Oxford English Dictionary* (Oxford: Clarendon Press, 1993).
2. Adapted from *Gage Canadian Dictionary,* rev. ed. (Toronto: Gage Educational Publishing Company, 1997).
3. International Joint Project on Co-operative Democracy, *Making Membership Meaningful: Participatory Democracy in Co-operatives* (Saskatoon: Centre for the Study of Co-operatives, University of Saskatchewan, 1995).
4. Robert D. Putnam, *Bowling Alone: The Collapse and Revival of American Community* (New York: Simon and Schuster, 2000).
5. Lou Hammond Ketilson, Michael Gertler, Murray Fulton, Roy Dobson, and Leslie Polsom, *The Social and Economic Importance of the Co-operative Sector in Saskatchewan* (Saskatoon: Centre for the Study of Co-operatives, University of Saskatchewan, 1998).
6. Ron Eyerman and Andrew Jamison, *Social Movements: A Cognitive Approach* (University Park: Pennsylvania State University Press, 1991). See also Neva Hassanein, *Changing the Way America Farms: Knowledge and Community in the Sustainable Agriculture Movement* (Lincoln: University of Nebraska Press, 1999).
7. Benedict Anderson, *Imagined Communities: Reflections on the Origin and Spread of Nationalism,* rev. ed. (London and New York: Verso, 1991).
8. See William Coleman, "Globalization and Co-operatives," chapter one in this volume.

9. Michael Ignatieff, *The Rights Revolution* (Toronto: Anansi, 2000).
10. Zygmunt Bauman, *Community: Seeking Safety in an Insecure World* (Oxford: Polity Press, 2001).
11. Carol Schick, JoAnn Jaffe, and Ailsa Watkinson, eds., *Contesting Fundamentalisms* (Halifax: Fernwood, 2004).
12. See Bauman.
13. Brett Fairbairn, *Three Strategic Concepts for the Guidance of Co-operatives: Linkage, Transparency, and Cognition* (Saskatoon: Centre for the Study of Co-operatives, University of Saskatchewan, 2003).
14. Harvey Schacter, "Social Entrepreneurs Devoted to Change," review of *How to Change the World* by David Bornstein, *Globe and Mail,* 10 March 2004, C3.
15. See Bauman.
16. Michael Gertler, *Rural Co-operatives and Sustainable Development* (Saskatoon: Centre for the Study of Co-operatives, 2001).
17. Roger Herman, "Choice of Organizational Form in Farmer-Owned Enterprises" (master's thesis, University of Saskatchewan, 2003).

LOU HAMMOND KETILSON

REVISITING THE ROLE OF VALUES AND PRINCIPLES
DO THEY ACT TO INCLUDE OR EXCLUDE?

The future role of co-operatives in the economy will be determined largely by their ability to distinguish their form of economic enterprise from those of other economic players, and to achieve wide public acceptance of that role.
—The Bundon Group, 1991[1]

THE ATTEMPT TO IDENTIFY DISTINCTIVENESS has become a bit like the search for the Co-operative Holy Grail, and many writers have offered opinions regarding what might be considered distinctive.

Most academics and practitioners cite co-operative values and principles as the primary source of distinguishing features. The co-operative principles have been revisited three times after having evolved from the original statutes and practices of the Rochdale Society of Equitable Pioneers in England in 1844.[2] The latest and perhaps most exhaustive review, conducted in order to arrive at a common Statement on the Co-operative Identity, was finalized at the International Co-operative Alliance Centennial Congress in Manchester in 1995.[3]

The importance of reaching such an agreement is clearly identified in the following quote:

A soundly founded movement will grow marvelously if the members act up to their principles. Of course the difficulty is there. A principle is a troublesome thing, and no wonder that so many persons have distaste for it. A principle ... is a profession of conduct: it implies a method of procedure: it is a rule of action—a pledge of policy to be pursued.[4]

And therein lies the difficulty and the essential issue I wish to address in this chapter. Co-operative practitioners and academics recognize that the movement and the institution will endure in an increasingly competitive and individualistic world only if we are able to identify and sustain elements central to their distinctiveness. Advocates of co-operatives in their "purist"[5] form point to the principles as the mechanism to ensure that co-operatives will continue to exist in a form and with functions distinctive from privately-owned or investor-owned firms.

This is an important objective. The downside, however, is that the rigidity that must accompany this goal may prevent many who are interested in the co-operative model of organization from pursuing it further when they run up against those in positions of authority who refuse to consider modifications to the model. And the movement therefore risks losing an important source of new supporters.

As co-operative practitioners and researchers, should we insist upon imposing on others the Eurocentric model that currently exists in Canada, derived as it is out of the specific needs and aspirations of the Rochdale Pioneers of the 1840s? Perhaps there are other aspects contributing to the distinctiveness of co-operatives that might draw new members and developers who possess a different cultural viewpoint, which would ultimately serve to sustain or expand the movement.

Continuing the Search

Beyond identifying co-operative principles as a source of distinctiveness, many researchers emphasize elements related to the structures and processes found within co-operatives.

In their extensive review of the literature on the management of co-operatives and other organizations, for example, Brown, Craig, and Hammond Ketilson[6] suggested that co-ops must not forget that they are, first and foremost, self-help organizations.[7] They also noted Furstenberg's argument that since democratic processes are the basis for the legitimization of authority in a co-op, legitimacy can easily be lost if democracy is forfeited.[8] Côté recognized that co-operatives generally differ from conventional businesses in their operating principles, the legislative framework within which they function, and their acquisition and use of capital.[9]

Others identify the importance of the relationship between co-operatives and their members as what sets them apart.

> Even though co-operatives perform functions similar to those of traditional business firms, they have unique differences in their relationship to the owners. The co-operative organization does not buy, process and sell to make a profit as a separate entity; instead, it procures services for the benefit of its members—who hope to increase their savings if it is a consumer co-operative, or to increase their profits of their own separate business if it is a farmer or business co-operative.[10]

Indeed, closeness to the members and responsiveness to their needs was the competitive advantage of co-operatives during the first half of the twentieth century. Initially, co-ops successfully addressed the issues of the day, but the established structures and processes became outmoded as the co-ops grew, and decision makers began to borrow methodologies from conventional business in response to changes in the co-ops, the environment, and technology. While these actions helped the enterprise side to some extent, they unfortunately neglected responsiveness to members. Ultimately, the culture of co-operatives stagnated as the co-ops paid too little attention to education and efforts to attract young people and immigrants.[11]

Beginning in the 1970s, concerned officials and researchers began to critique the malaise developing within co-operative management. They urged leaders to develop uniquely co-operative management styles and techniques in order to invigorate interest in their organizations and to encourage greater pro-activity among co-operative decision makers.

Since then, theorists have made efforts to identify management philosophies and styles most congruent with co-operative values and principles. Early writers have concluded that direct participation and the structures and facilitation of participatory democracy in various aspects of organizational life increase knowledge and commitment through experiential learning. Direct participation also provides co-operative leaders and managers with the information they need to respond to their members and their markets.[12] It has been observed that co-op management styles should be democratic in nature[13] and must go beyond representative democracy to meet not only the requirement of representativeness but also that of responsiveness.

Drawing upon contemporary management literature and linking it to the values underlying the co-op principles, as well as the structures and processes inherent in co-operatives, Brown, Craig, and Hammond Ketilson proposed that a co-operative management style should be more informal, friendly, supportive, and participative.[14] Co-op managers should be expected to stress direct democracy (participating and learning through doing) and member involvement, with an emphasis on teaching people and facilitating learning and a de-emphasis on positional authority. Further, Hammond Ketilson et al. concluded that co-operatives need to utilize effectively all human resources—women, youth, Aboriginals, and minorities—and are uniquely positioned to do this if they would just rise to the challenge.[15]

In his writings about co-operative management, Côté speaks to a distinctively co-operative dilemma: if a co-op neglects its associational needs, the consuming public can no longer distinguish it from any other business.[16] The problem becomes cyclical. In order to differentiate the co-operative, pressures mount to conform with conventional business models and strategies, moving the organization away from its co-operative roots. As it continues to neglect member needs, and perhaps fails to perform at a higher level using traditional business methods, the membership may move away from the co-op entirely, not only because it no longer acts like a co-operative but also because it fails to out-perform conventional business.

Ultimately, co-operative leaders must find answers to two basic questions: What draws members to a co-operative, and what holds their loyalty? The ongoing quest for these answers constitutes part of the research project on which this book is based and includes an exploration of what sets co-operatives apart and why people might choose to join or start one. My primary focus will be the co-operative principles and the accompanying rigidity noted earlier in the quotation from Holyoake.

As researchers interested in understanding co-operatives, we must ask ourselves, "Are the co-op principles useful in this search for uniqueness? Or do they only appeal to those with a lengthy involvement in co-ops—like a secret handshake or whispered password into the halls of co-op history? What do those principles mean? Is there some way to make them more accessible? How do co-operatives appear to newcomers—do they seem to be intriguing, dynamic organizations or curious dinosaurs of the past?"

OBSERVATIONS BASED ON EXPERIENCE

My observations regarding issues of concern to future research on co-op membership flow from a number of experiences. The first arises directly from an occurrence in the classroom with business students. I had invited a speaker who was a member of a worker co-operative to share with my students his experiences as a worker and member. He explained at length how his co-op worked, and why, from his point of view, it was such a valuable institution and so preferred in its organizational form to others. The following class I asked my students to comment on what they had learned. You can only imagine my surprise when one individual remarked with great enthusiasm that a worker co-op functioned in exactly the same way as an Amway distributor!

I wondered for many days how what he and I had heard at the same time could have been understood in such different ways. I finally concluded that it had a lot to do with where the listener starts from; in order to understand, the listener looks for familiar elements in what is being described. My students had little or no direct experience with co-operatives. And from their point of view, aspects of what I considered to be the most interesting or most significant, indeed the strengths of co-operative organizations, they considered to be, at best, curiosities, and at worst, alarming weaknesses.

Conclusion #1: My understanding of co-operatives, and that of established co-ops or the larger co-op system, is not universal. We have to constantly keep that thought in mind: How does a co-op appear to someone to whom it is unknown?

Would newcomers to a co-op annual meeting feel that a lengthy and animated discussion of policies related to purchasing was an exercise of democratic rights, or would they feel that the members were interfering in the job of the purchasing manager? Would consulting with members regarding significant changes in business strategy be considered a wise investment of the manager's time to ensure that the membership supported the new ideas, or simply an unnecessary delay in the business decision-making process?

co-op advocates have to be able to explain how participating in the democratic process strengthens rather than weakens the organization, since the positive outcome may not be immediately obvious to those unfamiliar with the dynamics of co-op–member interaction.

My second observation derives from experiences and intellectual struggles encountered as a colleague and I conducted our initial research into the state of Aboriginal co-operatives in Canada.[17] I began my investigation with the viewpoint of a researcher who has been looking at issues related to co-operative membership for a long time—perhaps too long to be able to see with fresh eyes. I knew in detail the benefits of co-operation and of participating in co-operative organizations personally; I also had many years of experience studying other people's understanding of what a co-op is and why they might choose to be involved as a member.

I went into the research with a number of assumptions fixed firmly in mind, in particular regarding what makes co-operatives an attractive organizational form for people and communities. I believed that democratic structures would have great appeal and that the concept of membership would resonate with First Nations peoples, who have been marginalized from so many aspects of Canadian life.

In the process of gathering our information, we discovered many examples, particularly in northern Canada, where Inuit and Dene communities had embraced the co-operative model and built a movement across the country. Co-operatives had been used as a foundation to provide a wide variety of services in remote regions previously unserviced or underserviced. In the south of Canada, however, we did not find so many examples. And we wondered why.

I discovered that the notion of membership with which I was most familiar—my experience of co-operatives in Canada and Europe—may be perceived, in the on-reserve, southern Aboriginal experience, as being in competition with membership in the First Nations cultural and ethnic context. The latter is a type of membership that comes intact with its own structures, processes, and traditions, which may or may not complement or support the structures and processes in place within co-operative organizations as they have developed across Canada historically.

> *Conclusion #2:* Had First Nations' understandings of membership and identity been integrated into the co-operative models developed at the turn of the century, we might have had a very different model in place today. Since this is not the case, are we able, first of all, to understand what those variations might have been and why, and secondly, can we identify unique modifications within existing Aboriginal co-operatives and the reasons for the change? Finally, can we make room to embrace rather than exclude them as appropriate cases for study?

Since my own research is in its early stages, it is premature to have answers to the first two questions. I have recognized, however, that the extreme importance of kinship and family must be reconciled within the current model of membership and governance. Furthermore, the governance model must accommodate the central role of the band within the community, while maintaining an arm's length relationship. And I feel strongly that co-op–like initiatives must be studied to expand our understanding.

Applying the Co-operative Principles

My final observations are linked to my own efforts to identify the ways in which co-operative organizations can integrate co-op values and principles into their strategic behaviour in the marketplace, successfully transforming this behaviour into increased member participation and greater member loyalty. My approach to this challenge emerges from the early work by Robert Briscoe regarding consumer co-operatives on the east coast of the United States.[18]

Briscoe concluded that "the conservativism which characterizes the behaviour of so many co-ops stems, in part, from the active participant's ways of perceiving the world of business, and from the disabling dilemmas he experiences when trying to reconcile his social ideals with the day-to-day running of a supermarket."[19] He classified as "frozen" the group of co-operatives that were either stable or in decline. He suggested that their managers in particular, but decision makers in general, were unable to say what a co-op could do to distinguish itself in the competitive market-place; the leaders could not articulate and pursue a co-operative vision. Finally, they were unable to adjust their thinking in order to meet new challenges as opportunities rather than threats.

Co-operatives suffering from the *frozen co-op syndrome* experience a situation in which:

> most of the traditional dreams, goals and functions of co-operatives have been overtaken by events and ... virtually all that is left to the co-operator is an attachment to the institutional value of democracy. This value is seen as impairing the efficient operation of co-ops and, as a consequence, co-op values are seen as incompatible with efficiency in business. Hence, co-operators believe that their Store is superior, from a moral point of view, but inferior as a business.... This dichotomized view of the world ... also appears to lead to a split in the leadership of the co-op (a split which is often formalized). As a result, business activities tend to be characterized by opportunistic adaptation, uniformed by co-operative principles, and the idealism of active members is frequently channeled into relatively harmless, expressive activities.[20]

The two world views are present in two types of leaders/managers: The *trader* believes that economic criteria alone should drive decision making and considers adherence to co-operative principles a burden and barrier to business success. The *idealist* is prepared to compromise economic criteria in order to adhere strictly to co-operative principles. Neither approach results in rapid improvements in sales or profitability.

Briscoe observed that successful co-operatives were able to devise business strategies focussed on translating social values into business operations, which resulted in improved business performance and increased member benefit by providing distinctive services to the member/customer. He concluded that it was more profitable to approach the problem by devising strategies that were viable from an economic point of view as well as being desirable from a values point of view—in other words, values formulated in instrumental as well as institutional terms.

I began my research using this conclusion as a point of departure to determine if applying co-operative values[21] rather than co-operative principles might be a more productive means of identifying how co-op distinctiveness could form the basis for competitive advantage.

Reviewing the actions of a number of Canadian co-operatives that I felt had been successful in formulating their values in instrumental terms, I identified strategies that ranged from modest proposals for meeting more adequately the needs of a small community to ambitious schemes to remake the world.[22] I concluded that these activities implied a rethinking of how to work with the co-operative principles. The actions of the co-operatives in my study[23] demonstrated that it is not enough to value co-ops because they are member owned and democratic—a structure and set of processes derived from co-operative principles. If member ownership is to mean anything, a co-operative or credit union must be more responsive than other organizations to the needs of members and consumers in general, and more sensitive to the inadequacies, from a consumer point of view, of the business activities of itself and its competitors. In other words, a successful co-op must move beyond the paralysis that Briscoe identified, a paralysis that prevents decision makers from linking co-operative principles in a practical, proactive way to the reality of everyday decision making.

As I reviewed first the co-op management literature, then actual examples of best practice in co-operative organizations, I looked for cases where co-operative principles had been integrated in operational terms. And as I examined the principles more closely in the context of co-operative organizations across a number of sectors, I found myself struggling to identify the principles in the behaviour of managers. It was easier to do with some principles than with others.

I concluded that if I had this much difficulty, then one could see why managers, whose daily lives consist of solving one problem or another, moving from one crisis to another, were unlikely to devote a great deal of time to sorting out where the co-operative principles might fit with a decision that had to be made quickly. There had to be a different way to focus behaviour.

In the examples of best practice, I observed the ability of the successful co-operatives to identify *a value or set of values* that resonated with the members. By starting with the values, then devising ways to operationalize them, decision makers could more easily recognize when a behaviour was consistent or not, thus making their lives more manageable.

As I reflected on the values identifiable in the actions of the co-ops, I realized that some could be categorized as unique to co-operatives, while others were not. The focus on eco-friendly and sustainable enterprise advocated by Mountain Equipment Co-op, for example, is shared by other organizations; the emphasis on responsible corporate citizenship is not exclusive to VanCity Credit Union; and Desjardins is not the only organization to subscribe to the values of solidarity and mutual aid. The value of democratic participation and control, however, is distinctive to a co-operative. And the way in which these values are operationalized is singularly co-operative. Participation in decision making creates a unique relationship between member/owners and their co-op, along with a corresponding set of responsibilities that both must uphold to sustain the connection.

This conclusion may be considered heretical to those who have a specific, perhaps more narrow, understanding of what co-operative values and therefore actions should be. According to my observations, the co-operatives that have successfully wed values to actions are those that have responded uniquely to the strongly held standards of the *community of members*. This finding implies that these values are, to some extent, situational rather than universal. Further, this means that it is more difficult to claim a set of values as being fundamental to co-operatives, and therefore essential to identifying one organization as being a "true" co-op, while another might be but a poor second cousin.

Which leads me to my final conclusion.

Conclusion #3: As researchers, we need to acknowledge the importance of being open to broader and/or new understandings of co-operative values and to fresh interpretations of co-op principles. We must be open to considering greater flexibility—new applications of the values and different interpretations of the model and perhaps the principles. These applications should not stray from the essential core of what a co-op is, of course, but should allow individuals who come from different contexts and cultures the ability to define the co-op model in their own way.

Indeed, in *The Meaning of Rochdale,* Brett Fairbairn reminds us that "the important thing to remember is that the meaning of Rochdale is constructed by each generation to meet its own needs." Further, he says, "there have been many approaches to co-operation; and … the widespread acceptance of Rochdale principles in today's co-operative movement is the result of battles, defeats, and compromises."[24]

As researchers, we must look at co-operatives with fresh, unclouded eyes if we are to effectively identify what it is about them that draws and will continue to draw members in the future. This does not mean that we need to abandon all that we have come to define as beneficial regarding co-operatives—all that makes them attractive as organizations. Nor does it mean that we must forsake our current definitions, the structures and processes that set them apart. It does mean, however, that we must open ourselves to diverse viewpoints and understandings of what the organizational model could be or should be. And in our quest to find what motivates membership, we must include in our research samples organizations that may not technically be considered to fall within the population. Finally, we must conceptualize and measure in ways that are respectful of these diverse understandings.

Endnotes

1. The Bundon Group, "A Framework for Analysis," presented to the Canadian Co-operative Association First Triennial Congress, Calgary 1991, p. 8.
2. Brett Fairbairn, *The Meaning of Rochdale* (Saskatoon: Centre for the Study of Co-operatives, 1994).
3. Ian MacPherson, "Background Paper on the ICA Statement on the Co-operative Identity," *Review of International Co-operation* 88, no. 3 (1995): pp. 5–68.
4. George Jacob Holyoake, *The History of Co-operation in England: Its Literature and Its Advocates*, 2 vols. (1879; reprint, New York: AMS Press, 1971), pp. 79–81.
5. In 1966 the co-op principles were presented to the Congress of the International Co-operative Alliance as universal and "inseparable" principles that "all possess equal authority" and "should be observed in their entirety by all co-operatives." Any organization that failed even one of the six tests would not, according to the 1963–66 commission, be a co-operative. Fairbairn, p. 32.
6. L. Brown, J. Craig, and L. Hammond Ketilson, "Theory," in *Making Membership Meaningful: Participatory Democracy in Co-operatives,* by The International Joint Project on Co-operative Democracy (Saskatoon: Centre for the Study of Co-operatives, 1995), p. 290.
7. H. Hanusch, "Market and Bureaucratic Failure as a Problem of Self-Help Development," in *Co-operatives: In a Clash between Members,* eds. E. Dulfer and W. Hamm (London: Quiller Press, 1985), pp. 57–75.
8. F. Furstenberg, "Problems of Member Participation at Different Stages of Co-operative Development," in Dulfer and Hamm, pp.103–17.
9. Daniel Côté, «La gestion stratégique de l'organisation coopérative,» dans *La gestion stratégique d'entreprise,* ed. M. Côté (Boucherville, PQ: Gaëtan Morin, 1995), pp. 197–217 (texte repris de la revue *Coopératives et Développement* 24, no 1 (1992 –93), pp. 17–40).
10. J.C. Thompson and H.B. Jones, Jr., "Economic Appraisal of Co-operative Enterprise in the United States: Principles and Issues," *Agricultural Administration* 8 (1980): pp. 385–400.
11. Brown, Craig, and Hammond Ketilson.
12. L. Brown, "Organizational Ideology, Structure, Process, and Participation: Twin City Food Co-operatives" (Ph.D. diss., University of Minnesota, 1983).
13. See R. Briscoe, "Traders and Idealists: A Study of the Dilemmas of Consumers' Co-operatives" (Ph.D. diss., Harvard University, 1971). See also J. Quarter and G. Melnyk, *Partners in Enterprise: The Worker Ownership Phenomenon* (Montreal: Black Rose Books, 1989).
14. See note 6.
15. L. Hammond Ketilson, M. Gertler, M. Fulton, L. Polsom, and R. Dobson, *The Social and Economic Importance of the Co-operative Sector in Saskatchewan* (Saskatoon: Centre for the Study of Co-operatives, 1998).
16. See Daniel Côté, "Strengthening Co–op Identity and Loyalty: A Management Approach," presentation to the conference Co–operative Membership and

Globalization: New Directions in Research and Business Strategies, Saskatoon 2002.

17. Lou Hammond Ketilson and Ian MacPherson, *A Report on Aboriginal Co-operatives in Canada: Current Situation and Potential for Growth* (Saskatoon: Centre for the Study of Co-operatives, 2001).

18. See Briscoe.

19. Ibid., p. 1.

20. Ibid., p. 92.

21. The Statement on the Co-operative Identity indicates that co-operatives are based on the values of self-help, self-responsibility, democracy, equality, equity, and solidarity. Co-operative members believe in the ethical values of honesty, openness, social responsibility, and caring for others. See I. MacPherson, *Co-operative Principles for the 21st Century* (Geneva: International Co-operative Alliance, 1995), p. 1.

22. These comments are based on a presentation titled "Integrating Co-operative Principles into Strategic Decision Making in Credit Unions," made to the Fall Delegates' Meeting of Credit Union Central of Saskatchewan, Regina, November 2002.

23. The sample included co-operatives and credit unions from across Canada examined in various studies, including my thesis "Strategy Formulation in Consumer Co-operatives: An Integrative Model of Organizational Ideology and Context (Ph.D. diss., University of Saskatchewan, 1988); *The Social and Economic Importance of the Co-operative Sector in Saskatchewan;* and "Calgary Co-operative Association" and "Saskatchewan Wheat Pool," in *Making Membership Meaningful.*

24. Fairbairn, pp. 1–2.

ISOBEL M. FINDLAY

Remapping Co-operative Studies
Re-Imagining Postcolonial Co-operative Futures

I'll not listen to reason.... Reason always means what someone else has got to say.
—Elizabeth Gaskell, *Cranford*, 1853

The pathway to a new relationship is paved with the long-term commitment to share the definitional power that creates the legitimacy whereby words and phrases gain their accepted meaning.... The re-examination of the way language sanctions particular worldviews and understandings is central to this process of change.
—Patricia Monture-Angus,
Journeying Forward: Dreaming First Nations' Independence, 1999

Introduction

THIS ESSAY is an exploratory and provisional engagement with some key issues facing co-operatives at this historical juncture, including the opportunities and challenges of equitable participation of and meaningful choices for a diverse membership in a global market. Building on a commitment shared with colleagues at the Centre for the Study of Co-operatives (CSC) to rethink co-operative histories, styles, and structures for new times, peoples, and visions, I want here to reflect on the power of naming—of ways of mapping and remapping the world—so as to redress co-operatives' absence from or disfigurements within mainstream academic and business discourse.[1] In particular, drawing on the boundary-crossing capacities of cultural, postmodern, and postcolonial studies, I address two forms of co-operative deficit that impact significantly on co-operative fortunes. The one is connected to the so-called "hidden curriculum" in education,[2] which "hides," or renders invisible, the unquestioned privileges of mainstream (classical economic) versions of economy and society, one whereby students can leave high school and even university without awareness of co-operatives and their places in economies and communities. The other results in student experience that often remains narrowly disciplinary without the enrichment of interdisciplinary co-operation in probing the possibilities to imagine new versions of value. Investing in theory and history, the essay aims to negotiate controversy and challenge by changing the terms of engagement and taking back and sharing "the definitional power" of which Mohawk professor Patricia Monture-Angus writes. The essay aims thereby to resist, like dissenting writer Elizabeth Gaskell (and the Rochdale Pioneers) in industrializing England, forms of dominant reasoning that serve mainstream interests. My epigraphs mark sources of intellectual, social, and cultural indebtedness incurred in rethinking what "we" take for granted in order to re-imagine things otherwise. Yet others will emerge in my account of how some of us have put theory into practice in collaborative work enabling co-operative futures.

Like Brett Fairbairn,[3] I believe that co-operatives have nothing to fear and everything to gain from engaging with rather than eschewing dominant discourses. Today that means the challenges not only of the modern but also of the postmodern and postcolonial. Instead of being fearful of new terms and trends, we can derive strength and creativity in new opportunities to work with a diverse membership if we do not reduce people to consumer needs and the management and exploitation of economic value, as all kinds of corporations, including universities, are discovering. Their marketing and communications strategies increasingly encounter the irreducible complexity of human values and behaviour, and the need to address a broad range of ethical, environmental, and social values around, for instance, concerns for food security, fair trade, balancing work and family, community investment, and environmental sustainability. If corporations used to think in terms of ethics *or* profits, recent institutional disasters (associated most conspicuously but by no means exclusively with Enron, Andersen, and WorldCom) have added to the corporate and community lexicon and shifted the emphasis to ethics *as* or *and* profits in value-driven understandings of corporate social responsibility. Trust, confidence, credibility—and hence loyalty—are critical business values reshaping governance and stakeholder relations, especially in a context of heightened public scrutiny, and especially in Canada, which has the second highest expectations for corporate behaviour among twenty-three polled countries in a 1999 Environics International "Millennium Poll."[4]

In a postmodern, globalized information age, co-operatives have opportunities to press the co-operative advantage in resisting bureaucratic rationality, respecting diverse interests, re-imagining co-operative culture, and rebuilding interrelationships. And cultural politics can be a site and source of significant change. If Alexis de Tocqueville looked to America and saw a stable and shared moral world that made the American political system exceptional in its capacity to unite within conditions of political turmoil,[5] Barbara Cruickshank has argued that today

> the relationship of American culture and politics is reversed. Government seems fixed, particularly elections, yet in culture anything is possible.... In the political world, obedience is passive, yet voluntary.... In the cultural/moral world, however, everything is contested. From language to religion, education, to American history and identity, in each there is independence, contempt of experience, and jealousy of all authority.[6]

Where rigidity informs the domain of the socio-political, change has to find new avenues and registers and shift to the cultural as a locus of contestation and transformation, as a place for difference to have a voice and imagine things otherwise within an unforgiving set of actualities—something W.E.B. Du Bois recognized in 1930s United States. Calling for "intelligent cooperation" as African Americans' new gift to the world (adding to the gifts of "song and laughter ... work, hard, backbreaking labor"), Du Bois galvanized group identity to challenge dominant discourses and domineering industrial and economic practices:

> It is now our business to give the world an example of intelligent cooperation so that when the new industrial commonwealth comes we can go into it as an experienced people and not again be left on the outside as mere beggars.... If leading the way as intelligent cooperating consumers, we rid ourselves of the ideas of a price system and become pioneer servants of the common good, we can enter the new city as men [sic] and not mules.[7]

To be sure, I deal in broad strokes in this essay. In conscious alignment with the macro politics of the postcolonial, I favour enabling universals that connect peoples in transformative possibilities over what Pierre Bourdieu calls "the imperialism of the universal," or other cults of inevitability, impotence, or efficiency.[8] After all, broad strokes can be very useful, as apologists for dominant views or for the next big thing have always known. And changing the terms of engagement is always more than a rhetorical act, limiting or liberating as it does our capacities to think, act, and interact. Symbols and stories remain critical to imagining things other than they are—or appear to be. Retelling the history and theory of co-operatives shows that the co-operative movement is not simply a footnote to modernity. The movement remains moreover both necessary and productive in so-called postmodernity, where crises of cohesion and community cannot simply be trumped by further privatization of the means of production or modes of consolation for the dispersal of commonality.

Postmodernity

If accounts by history's victors have tended to stereotype co-operatives as a minor presence in the march of progress, then we might expect that paradigm shifts, such as that from modernity to postmodernity—

hailed by theoreticians and exploited by vanguard practice—might offer hope that those written off by dominant versions of modernity might become full and fully recognized participants in the fashioning of a postmodern present and future. Postmodernity is associated with new ways of mapping and thinking (involving skepticism about Enlightenment norms of rationality, objectivity, truth, and about the naturalness, stability, and unity of identity). It is associated too with a new way of doing capitalist relations in the so-called new economy, a knowledge economy, consumer culture, and world of technological communications displacing traditional industrial manufacturing processes and products. Given these emphases, postmodernity could conceivably be expected to bring new forms of freedom, diversity, and legitimacy that could benefit co-operatives, but such hopes have been largely dashed in practice by the ultra-individualistic emphases of post-modernity, its weak choreography of atoms and fragments in accidental and/or ephemeral identities. Consistent with such fragmentation and eclectic laxity, the local has been valued not as communitarian continuity or critical praxis, but as a function of the ephemeral and the multiple, the nonhierarchical or posthierarchical. Indeed, in its more extreme versions, as in the work of Jean Baudrillard, postmodernity leaves us with no more than a simulation of reality, a mapping that precedes and preconstructs territory: "the generation by models of a real without origin or a reality: a hyperreal. The territory no longer precedes the map, nor survives it. Henceforth, it is the map that precedes the territory—*precession of simulacra*—it is the map that engenders the territory."[9]

Paradigm shifts—such as the structure of scientific revolutions[10]—have a habit of leaving elite interpretation in control, shifting from one orthodoxy to another, leaving the "lowly" lost in complacency and confusion with little share of "the definitional power." In the recurrent shifts to an allegedly new world order, traditional medicine or Indigenous knowledge, women's, working-class, or other alternative—and feminized—ways of knowing somehow always remain beyond the pale or get lost in the shuffle. So, too, co-operatives are nowhere to be seen in postmodernity, although their liminal status should fit well with the border crossing of a liminal age, as Brett Fairbairn argues.[11] Despite postmodern claims about the end of history, the nation state, and the liberal subject, big stories persist in favouring the mainstream or central interests and reproducing inequalities of gender, class, nation, and ethnicity, while mediating and restructuring our understanding of natural and inevitable "realities" and our (in)capacities to act and intervene in changes (deregulation, monetarism, contingent labour, patterns of development and underdevelopment) construed as beyond individual or even collective control. And despite claims about the "free play" of the postmodern imagination daring to envisage things otherwise, even our imaginings do not entirely escape such dominant frames of reference. There is no place of pure, unfettered contemplation outside dominant views, but that does not mean we have to forego the real for the hyperreal. So I want here to explore the productivity of major interdisciplinary initiatives—cultural studies and postcolonial studies—for re-imagining co-operative research and business futures, for making membership meaningful and offering real choice, and for restating the co-operative advantage in ways that might reverberate more thoroughly and for more of the co-operative community now. If the master's tools, in Audre Lorde's terms, have put co-operatives in their marginal places, those tools should not be relinquished to dominant interests. Those tools can and should be reshaped and redeployed to promote co-operatives for transformative ends and collective benefit.[12]

POSTCOLONIAL STUDIES

If co-operation is another name for marginality under modernism, a blip on the path of progress, co-operators can learn from the fate of those (and especially Aboriginal peoples in Canada and Indigenous peoples elsewhere) who inhabit the margins broadly understood. While postmodernity denies centrality to *any* activity or movement, and therefore denies its capacity to contest power deriving from centrality, the postcolonial refuses to give up the centre, historicizes its privileges, and in the interests of redistributive justice, renegotiates centre-periphery relations that modernity has defined to the benefit of First World capital and economic individualism. The postcolonial is associated with multiple processes and products, diverse aspirations and applications, and a distinctive double gesture that marks a shift from the binary thinking of modernity (either/or) to the productive and processive logic of both/and—and with such related outcomes as political emancipation, cultural renewal, and justice for all. What postmodernity does is mistake detecting for dislodging, the exposure of pretensions to centrality for the achievement of democratic change and expanded access to economic levers. Creating demand or controlling choice can be exposed by consumer watchdogs, for example, yet patterns of consumption remain relatively unchanged because of who owns the means of production and where the definitional and decision-making power is centred. Where the postmodern dissolves pretension and promotes a permissive cultural carnival, the postcolonial, an agent of new solidarities, is principled and persistent in its commitment to agency, change, and enabling collective capacities, to re-inflected and re-imagined versions of the real rather than an unstoppable epidemic of the hyperreal.

The postcolonial, like the postmodern, has proven an important tool for challenging the stability and self-evidence of boundaries and definitions, the naturalness and neutrality of modernity's all-embracing yet exclusionary story of *universal* reason, progress, and civilization. The two exclusions essential to industrial expansion—domestic and colonial-Indigenous—persist nevertheless across shifts from modernity to postmodernity. These excluded internal and external communities were fodder for a colonial system, including the institutions of education, religion, and the law. These institutions—the "laboratory and production line of the colonial system," in George Manuel's terms[13]—ministered to the project of nation building by feeding industrial society's appetite for a steady supply of labour, orderly conduct, hierarchy, and respect for private property regimes. The postcolonial can expose and alter that situation by accessing the historical and contemporary capacities of co-operatives. These two exclusions are neither absolute nor immutable, and resistance to them occurs individually but also through combination and co-operation, sharing concerns, and developing commercial and collective capacities to buck dominant trends and bring together other versions of reason in the name of market rationality. The postcolonial can help by unpacking modernity as a literal, discursive, and cognitive mapping of the so-called Old and New World. That mapping—a way of representing and thus conceptualizing and imagining the way things are—supported the "civilizing mission" and allowed settler nations to imagine and legitimate their claims to the New World—and much of the rest of the planet too.

The Work of Culture

The colonial project depended massively on cultural capital at home and abroad, on the penetration of English as world language, and the diffusion of Western binary thinking as the natural and neutral way of conceiving of, categorizing, mapping, and thus managing the world. And attending to such cultural mediation has, in recent decades, proven a powerful means of rethinking discursive, conceptual, and other categories, intervening so as to open up new imaginary, institutional, social, political, and economic spaces. Cultural studies, refusing traditional distinctions between high and low culture, the centre and periphery, investigates social, economic, and political power structures that shape phenomena and endow them with meanings, value, and status. Cultural studies—antidisciplinary and antihierarchical rather than presumptuously posthierarchical—explores such determinants of high and low culture as race, class, gender, sexuality, and nation, and the defining tensions between the historical and the contemporary.

It is colonial presumption that these interdisciplinary initiatives probe, exposing what we have taken for granted, showing that the language we use, the stories we hear and retell, and the institutions (including educational ones) we inhabit are never neutral, but materially shape how we experience and understand our identities and realities. They have shown, too, how expert and increasingly professional disciplinary and other knowledge has legitimated structures of authority by undermining the legitimacy of local, experiential knowledge or the cultural knowledge represented by storytellers such as Elizabeth Gaskell. In particular, privileging Western rationality has exacerbated threats to Indigenous ways of knowing, while consolidating "New Right economic thinking that puts emphasis on competition rather than on cooperation, on the individual rather than on the collective, on regulations rather than on responsibility," as Maori scholar

Graham Hingangaroa Smith has argued.[14] Such dominating structures of authority support and supplement military, economic, political, and legal means of persuading us that the way things are is natural and inevitable and could not—even should not—be otherwise. In resisting this logic, cultural and postcolonial studies have unpacked how the project of modernity depended on a negative strategy of difference ("lower" at home; "other" abroad), whereby the dominant explained the difference of various "others" (women, the working classes, and Aboriginal peoples, for instance) in terms of their own superiority and others' inherent inferiority or lack of civilization.[15] And how the discourse of race has naturalized and legitimated inequalities, exclusions, and exploitation—and continues to do so in backlash against so-called race-based determinations of access, employment, reward, and justice. Those who demand equality before the law when faced with constitutionally affirmed Aboriginal treaty rights or other legal entitlements remain blinded by the "hidden curriculum." They remain blind to the histories of inequities (in the racialized spaces of inner-city distress, for instance) and their own everyday privileges—their own "studied ignorance" and "privileged innocence" that help reproduce the massive inequalities of the market economy they live with daily.[16]

SPEAKING, WRITING, AND RESEARCHING BACK

Postcolonial writers revalue differences in positive terms to reconstruct meanings and identities and demystify power structures in order to remythologize who we are and would like to be. If postmodern thinkers have often focussed on European intellectual history and practice and been content to do no more than expose connections between language and power, knowledge and legitimacy, postcolonial theory has been a productive tool for the global redistribution of expertise, for liberating thinking and the voices and stories of those so long silenced within Western structures and canons of value.[17] Postcolonial writers have been concerned with the culture, history, and politics of Europe's former colonies that won their freedom after World War II, and with Indigenous peoples in settler colonies such as Canada. Postcolonial writers have been concerned to "speak back," "write back," or "research back" as subjects and not objects, as Maori scholar Linda Smith recommends, in order to effect real change.[18] If identities can be constructed, they can be reconstructed. And if the way things are is not natural, they can be changed. If the first phase of the postcolonial focussed on territoriality and political independence of new or reconfigured nation states after World War II, the current phase is preoccupied with the intersecting domains of the social, cultural, and economic, as well as with globalization and cyber-community and the dangers of these latter repeating the claims of discovery and empty territory (or *terra nullius*) to justify neocolonial infractions. The postcolonial is an open forum that builds on connections as more than accident or entrenched illusion; it rehabilitates tradition and history while recognizing the temptations and dangers they represent, as well as the stories vital to a sense of belonging and the kinds of formal and informal membership that attend it. Alienation can seem glamorous, heroic even, to people who enjoy the levels and kinds of privilege that lead them to believe they don't need or can never get to know other people. But of course colonization, in the form of alienated labour, is precisely what elite self-absorption and First World angst depend upon.

Putting Theory into Practice

Indigenous Humanities

At a time when Canada is failing to close the gap in life opportunities between Aboriginal and non-Aboriginal peoples, and when the Aboriginal population would rank forty-eighth in the world behind Panama in the United Nations Human Development Index,[19] we face both an opportunity and an obligation. At this historical juncture, we have the opportunity and obligation to enrich current debate and open up possibilities by revaluing Aboriginal knowledge and heritage; decolonizing theory and practice; resisting conflict, competition, and control as natural and inevitable; and recognizing the benefits of co-operative, crossdisciplinary, and crosscultural practice. If the Indigenous cultural renaissance has been a critical turn in postcolonial studies, then the Indigenous humanities can help and be helped by the co-operative community in undoing colonial cultural legacies that (mis)shape us all. Under the aegis of the Indigenous humanities, co-operatives and Aboriginal communities can rewrite a shared history of being overlooked or regarded as curiously unmodern when they are not elided almost entirely in education. They can do so by making inquiry more relational, sociable, modest, more critical and committed.

The Indigenous humanities as term and practice is designed to unsettle taken-for-granted mainstream thinking, routines, and presumptions about what counts for knowledge, expertise, and evidence. It does so by bringing together familiar terms in unfamiliar relationship, in a catechresis, or misnaming, such as Gayatri Spivak welcomes as the place of progressive change.[20] In the name of the Indigenous humanities, new coalitions and capacity-building within and beyond the CSC, the Native Law Centre of Canada, the colleges of Law, Commerce, Arts and Science, and Education at the University of Saskatchewan take decolonizing as their objective and Indigenous issues as a major focus.[21] These initiatives were themselves born out of the frustration of a disciplinary diaspora that has found welcoming interdisciplinary spaces within a persistently colonial university mainstream that continues to know what is best for Aboriginal peoples. While favouring "native-newcomer" relations as the focus of research, the administrative mainstream worries about making education accessible to Aboriginal peoples without considering how access can be made meaningful, how the institution might change, or how transformative Indigenous knowledge or capacity might be. Hence, the university is content, as it puts it, to respond to "the Needs of Aboriginal Peoples"[22] with a reactive and reductive add-on model that leaves power and privilege unchanged, preserving insider expertise, while deferring indefinitely opportunities for real change.[23]

The Indigenous humanities represent both theory and practice, a way of putting theory to work in the world, and of transforming our intellectual and imaginative ecologies. The Indigenous humanities represent a creative way of communicating and locating ourselves thoughtfully and spiritually in relation to each other, to the ecology we share, and to forces beyond our control. While laying claim to the rigour and authority of the traditional humanities, the collaborative, crosscultural, and crossdisciplinary practices of the Indigenous humanities resist persistent paternalism and resurgent neocolonialism.

Using the master's tools to dismantle the master's house, we reread and reinterpret literary, legal, historical, and other canons to expose the complicity of the traditional humanities in acts of colonization and co-optation, and to revalue Aboriginal knowledge and heritage as well as local, experiential, and cultural knowledge. We attend to multiple and conflicted histories and critical geographies, respecting the authority of the Elders and educators, court workers as well as cultural workers, co-operative members as well as managers, while withholding *undue* deference to male authorities of any culture.

In working together in the Indigenous humanities, we acknowledge that we all have a stake in dismantling colonial structures that have taught us habits of hierarchy and deference, and patterns of commodifying and compartmentalizing that rationalize the most irrational of practices. The Indigenous humanities are committed to "sharing the definitional power" and recirculating critical histories the mainstream prefers to discount as political advocacy or special pleading, while continuing to define and hence defend the status quo.

Council for the Advancement of Native Development Officers (CANDO)

CANDO has been another fruitful site for remapping Aboriginal identities and aspirations, economic development and co-operative studies, and redefining postcolonial co-operative futures. CANDO, in its annual conferences, educational programming, and publications, including the *Journal of Aboriginal Economic Development,* the first journal devoted to economic development sustaining Aboriginal communities, represents a powerful version of speaking back. The council and its journal break new ground while also reclaiming and remapping cognitive, cultural, economic, and ecological territory forfeited to European colonial encroachments. We can learn much from the journal and its sponsoring council about the multiple strategies driving Aboriginal business ventures and connecting them to their multiple and ever-increasing constituencies. They attest compellingly to the gifts Aboriginal peoples (like Du Bois's African Americans) have offered and continue to offer. If Aboriginal peoples have traditionally understood dependency—as in "all my relations"—to be mutual rather than unidirectional, colonizers have simultaneously asserted their own independence of and superiority over Indigenous populations while *depending on* and exploiting Aboriginal knowledge, resources, and skills. Now CANDO and its journal are rendering visible that cruel contradiction of colonialism, which is giving way to the overwhelming evidence of Aboriginal independence, creativity, and capacity for collaboration.

Aboriginal difference and distinctiveness are being recoded and applied positively. Traditional and new knowledge is giving rise to new practices that are both confirming and redirecting basic and often oppressive notions such as economic development itself. Development achieved how, and in whose interests? The double gesture of recognizing and also critiquing mainstream economics and development theory means that an exciting intellectual, social, and economic agenda is emerging from a margin where its proponents are no longer content to reside, and in terms and in ways that those who are marginalized are no longer content to have defined for them or imposed upon them by others—whether by *Indian Act,* White Paper, *First Nations Governance Act,* or other means.

Offering leadership in new forms of communication, commerce, and community, the *Journal of Aboriginal Economic Development* is a model for that institution traditionally identified with leading—namely the university—which continues to assimilate the "anomalous" to dominant views and ways without acknowledging, far less exploring, its own complicity in systems of domination. Despite explicit commitments to interdisciplinary work and critical thinking, the university remains structurally tied to disciplinary and departmental interests and investments in microdistinctions and exclusionary practices—and with profound consequences for what we know, how we communicate, and who we understand to constitute that "we." As the *Report of the Royal Commission on Aboriginal Peoples* argues, we need to understand economic development in less reductive ways than those typically employed by economists and sociologists:

> [Economic] development is much more than individuals striving to maximize incomes and prestige, as many economists and sociologists are inclined to describe it. It is about maintaining and developing culture and identity; supporting self-

governing institutions; and sustaining traditional ways of making a living. It is about giving people choice in their lives and maintaining appropriate forms of relationship with their own and with other societies.[24]

If, as the Maori saying goes, our future is behind us, the *Journal of Aboriginal Economic Development* effectively recapitulates the colonial past to help us understand where and why we are—and where we might be in the future as well as how we might get there. The journal organizes its contents around four sections paralleling the multiple ways that economic development is pursued in Aboriginal settings: Best Practice: Learning from Experience; Lessons from Research; Reviews of Current Books and Literature; and the Royal Commission on Aboriginal Peoples. Like Aboriginal business, the journal blends insights of contemporary thinking with traditional knowledge symbolized in the Tree of Life emblem that graces the cover (of its first issue) and represents wisdom unleashed by the Sky Woman of Iroquois culture, and further, connecting spirit and world and underlining the equality of peoples and parts of creation. Similarly, the journal represents the active and the reflective, partnerships and collaborations, as well as the connections between economic and political self-determination. As CANDO and its journal show us, we are not helpless in the face of mysterious natural forces, but can creatively reshape what cultures shaped in the first place. If ignorance continues to mean denial, resistance, and backlash in the mainstream countering efforts to unpack and displace prevailing myths about Aboriginal realities and rights, the tax situation, and land tenure issues, we need to redouble efforts to get alternative stories out—and to use every site and occasion to do so.

Value(s) Added: Sharing Voices on Aboriginal Community Economic Development

That is what a group associated with the CSC set out to do in a conference titled Value(s) Added, sponsored by the College of Commerce at the University of Saskatchewan. Angela Bellegarde, Louise Clarke, Isobel Findlay, and Warren Weir determined to put theory into practice, testing what they'd been learning from postmodern, postcolonial, and other theory in their WOTsUp (Weird Organizational Theory!)

discussion group. Brett Fairbairn, Michael Gertler, and Lou Hammond Ketilson joined us in presenting and participating in ongoing discussion. An important first for the university, the conference aimed to encourage mutual education and public understanding of Aboriginal community economic development (CED) by promoting dialogue across cultures, communities, and disciplines. It marked the beginning of a process of sharing voices and visions, drawing on practitioners from across Canada and academics from a range of disciplines, to add values to current debate. It featured keynote speakers—David Newhouse, James (Sakej) Youngblood Henderson, Marie Battiste, and Wanda Wuttunee—and panel presenters whose work animated talking circles, and a final agenda-building session that aimed to break down some of the unproductive barriers that impede innovation and effective building on tradition.

In addressing CED in the context of globalization and resource depletion, the program promoted possibilities rather than problems, nourishing alternative models of development and communities dependent on reciprocity rather than inequality. Conference participants also rethought key terms—community, economic, development—recentring Aboriginal world views, spirituality, land, and languages, and forging new networks to re-imagine CED for the twenty-first century. What struck a number of us (though we cannot claim a scientific study) was how alienating it seemed to be for some academics to use new terms of engagement with old questions, while Aboriginal economic developers eagerly grasped new tools whose value they could recognize and connect to their own knowledge and experience. Keeping the agenda alive and enhancing a new Aboriginal CED culture, we agreed, means multiple strategies in multiple sites; interdisciplinary and crosscultural co-operation; rediscovering traditional economies while developing treaty, knowledge, and other economies. It means restructuring and rethinking Canada and Aboriginal/non-Aboriginal relations, rewriting discourses and curricula to remake meanings and relationships, and re-imagining big stories that nourish local realities. And so the conference concluded with a postcolonial hope and determination to dream, create, and celebrate together again (this time around Aboriginal women's CED).

Conclusion:
Re-Imagining Postcolonial Co-operative Futures

To build on these initiatives in remapping and rethinking co-operative futures, we need all sorts of co-operative intellectuals promoting co-operation as agent and object of decolonizing. By the co-operative intellectual, I mean a version of Antonio Gramsci's "organic intellectual," whose "general practical activity" is "perpetually innovating the physical and social world, [and becoming] a new and integral conception of the world."[25] By naming the co-operative intellectual, I mean to recognize and respect, to render visible and valuable, that which modernity aimed to hide: the knowledge and capacity-building rooted in communities and their ecologies. I mean to galvanize the far-reaching consequences of such knowledge for community education and action, and for interrelationships that sustain enterprise. As key change agents, co-operative intellectuals, like those in the context of nineteenth-century industrialization, are born in resistance to dominating forces to produce new or renewed models of intellectual, social, political, and economic association and action. Unlike Gramsci's "traditional intellectual" invested in distance, disinterest, and detachment, the co-operative intellectual—connected, committed, collaborative—brings to bear situated knowledge of multiple realities. If co-operative sharing of "the definitional power" can be a critical strategy, we need also to confront co-operative roles in a colonial past and ongoing present. For that decolonizing work, we need a critical mass of faculty and a mass of critical students committed to changing the way we do business inside and outside the academy. And that means attending to co-op members and managers, to the Elders, storytellers, and professional, practising, and academic teachers (Aboriginal and non-Aboriginal).

In asserting the role of the co-operative intellectual and a place for co-operative curriculum and research within schools and universities,[26] we aim to expand what counts for academic and other value, and make cognitive space to re-imagine postcolonial co-operative futures. A postcolonial co-operative map can be produced only co-operatively, building on local knowledge and practice as the next stage of the open forum that contests economic, social, cultural, and other forms of what Marie Battiste calls "cognitive imperialism." Think global/act local has two forms of co-operation that need to be asserted: the co-operation of global and local in the understanding *and* achievement of desirable change. The map does not start with *tabula rasa* or *terra nullius*. The map is already densely and widely populated by co-operative entities and activities still undervalued or disregarded by cartographers royal. The work of Arctic Co-operatives Ltd. and La Fédération des coopératives du Nouveau Québec, poptel.coop, the Canadian Co-operative Association, the International Co-operative Alliance, Mondragon in Spain, or centres in Saskatchewan, British Columbia, and Wisconsin is not an abandonment of mapping, but a commitment to remapping. It is a remapping as remedy for the cognitive mapping that presses some co-operatives desperately to keep up with "progress" and act like corporations, or otherwise fail to react to an appropriate sense of the co-operative advantage and co-operative commitment to economic activity with values added. It is a remapping not of a homogenized world but of one constituted by difference and deeply in need of co-operative intellectuals and Du Bois's "intelligent co-operation" as the most fully shared definition of the knowledge economy.

Endnotes

1. Earlier versions of the arguments in this essay were presented as papers at the Centre for the Study of Co-operatives Seminar Series, 4 April 2002, and at the conference Co-operative Membership and Globalization: New Directions in Research and Business Strategies, 2 October 2002. Among related work produced at the centre, see, for example, Brett Fairbairn, *Three Strategic Concepts for the Guidance of Co-operatives: Linkage, Transparency, and Cognition* (Saskatoon: Centre for the Study of Co-operatives, University of Saskatchewan, 2003); Fairbairn, "Social Movements and Co-operatives: Implications for History and Development," *Review of International Co-operation* 94, no. 1 (2001): pp. 24–34.
2. See Eric Margolis, ed., *The Hidden Curriculum in Higher Education* (New York: Routledge, 2001).
3. See Brett Fairbairn, "Cohesion, Adhesion, and Identities in Co-operatives," chapter two in this book.
4. See, too, a poll conducted by Market Explorers, Canadian Centre for Business in the Community, January-February 2000, where Canadians were 72 percent more likely to buy from responsible companies and 68 percent more likely to invest in them, for example.
5. *Democracy in America,* ed. and trans. Harvey C. Mansfield and Delba Winthrop (Chicago: University of Chicago Press c. 2000).
6. "Cultural Politics: Political Theory and the Foundations of Democratic Order,"

in *Cultural Studies and Political Theory*, ed. Jodi Dean (Ithaca and London: Cornell University Press, 2000), pp. 63–64.

7. Quoted in Jessica Gordon Nembhard, "Entering the New City as Men and Women, Not Mules," forthcoming in *The Urban Black Community*, eds. Lewis Randolph and Gayle Tate.

8. See Pierre Bourdieu, *Acts of Resistance: Against the Tyranny of the Market*, trans. Richard Nice (New York: New Press, 1998), p. 19. On current ideological habits of turning "injustice into an inevitability," see John Ralston Saul, *The Doubter's Companion: A Dictionary of Aggressive Common Sense* (Toronto: Penguin, 1995). See also Linda McQuaig, *The Cult of Impotence: Selling the Myth of Powerlessness in the Global Economy* (Toronto: Viking, 1998), and Janice Gross Stein, *The Cult of Efficiency* (Toronto: Anansi, 2001).

9. Jean Baudrillard, *Simulations*, trans. Paul Foos, Paul Patton, and Philip Beitchman (New York: Semiotext[e], 1983), p. 2; qtd. in Kenneth J. Saltman and David A. Gabbard, eds., *Education as Enforcement: The Militarization and Corporatization of Schools* (New York and London: RoutledgeFalmer, 2003), p. 280.

10. See Thomas S. Kuhn, *The Structure of Scientific Revolutions*, 3rd ed. (Chicago: University of Chicago Press, 1996).

11. See his "Communications, Culture, and Co-operatives: Liminal Organizations in a Liminal Age," paper presented at the conference Mapping Co-operative Studies in the New Millennium: A Joint Congress of the International Co-operative Alliance Research Committee and the Canadian Association for Studies in Co-operation, University of Victoria, 27–31 May 2003.

12. See Audre Lorde, *Sister Outsider: Essays and Speeches* (Trumansburg, New York: Crossing Press, 1984).

13. Quoted in *Report of the Royal Commission on Aboriginal Peoples (RCAP)*, vol. 1: *Looking Forward, Looking Back* (Ottawa: Minister of Supply and Services Canada, 1996), p. 335.

14. Graham Hingangaroa Smith, "Protecting and Respecting Indigenous Knowledge," in *Reclaiming Indigenous Voice and Vision*, ed. Marie Battiste (Vancouver: UBC Press, 2000), p. 211.

15. See, for example, J.M. Blaut, *The Colonizer's Model of the World: Geographical Diffusionism and Eurocentric History* (New York: Guilford Press, 1993), and Albert Memmi, *The Colonizer and the Colonized*, trans. Howard Greenfield (New York: Orion Press, 1965).

16. The terms "studied ignorance" and "privileged innocence" I owe to Sheila McIntyre, "Studied Ignorance and Privileged Innocence: Keeping Equity Academic," *Canadian Journal of Women and the Law* 12 (2000): pp. 147–96.

17. For a compelling mapping of the postcolonial, see the multicultural, multidisciplinary, and multivolume Diana Brydon, ed., *Postcolonialism: Critical Concepts in Literary and Cultural Studies*, 5 vols. (London and New York: Routledge, 2000).

18. See Linda Smith, *Decolonizing Methodologies: Research and Indigenous Peoples* (London: Zed Books, 1999).

19. Strategic Research and Analysis, and the Social Cohesion Network, *Holding the Centre: What We Know About Social Cohesion,* January 2001, posted at http://www.geog.queensu.ca/soco/pdf/sra-558-dck-e.pdf. And *The Report of the Royal Commission on Aboriginal Peoples (RCAP)* claimed that a staggering three hundred thousand new jobs would need to be created for Aboriginal people between 1991 and 2016 "to accommodate growth in the Aboriginal working-age population and to bring employment levels among Aboriginal people up to the Canadian standard" (vol. 2: *Restructuring the Relationship* [Ottawa: Minister of Supply and Services Canada, 1996], p. 775). Consider, too, the experience of visible minorities in Canada, whose educational attainment has increased while their participation in the workforce has decreased. See *Does a Rising Tide Lift All Boats?* a study by the Canadian Council on Social Development, February 2002: "The large gap between recent visible minority immigrants and other Canadians cannot be explained by inferior levels of formal education," the report claims. "The point system used for selecting immigrants brings many highly educated people to Canada." Part of the reason for the discrepancy, the report argues, is "racial discrimination" and the invisibility of immigrants' education and skills.

20. Gayatri Chakravorty Spivak, *Outside in the Teaching Machine* (New York: Routledge, 1993).

21. Inspired by the theory and practice of Maori scholars Graham and Linda Smith among others, those associated with the Indigenous humanities work and publish in a number of areas. See, for example, Marie Battiste and James (Sakej) Youngblood Henderson, *Protecting Indigenous Knowledge and Heritage: A Global Challenge* (Saskatoon: Purich, 2000); Battiste, ed., *Reclaiming Indigenous Voice and Vision;* Battiste, Lynne Bell, and L.M. Findlay, "Decolonizing Education in Canadian Universities: An Interdisciplinary, International, Indigenous Research Project," *Canadian Journal of Native Education* 26, no. 2 (2002): pp. 82–95; L.M. Findlay, "Always Indigenize! The Radical Humanities in the Postcolonial Canadian University," *ARIEL: A Review of International English Literature* 31, nos.1 and 2 (2000): pp. 307:26; J.Y. Henderson, Marjorie Benson, and Isobel M. Findlay, *Aboriginal Tenure in the Constitution of Canada* (Scarborough: Carswell, 2000); Isobel M. Findlay, "Working for Postcolonial Legal Studies: Working with the Indigenous Humanities," special issue on Postcolonial Legal Studies, *Law, Social Justice and Global Development,* ed. W. Wesley Pue, 2003–1, posted at http://elj.warwick.ac.uk/global/issue/2003-1/findlay.htm.

22. "Responding to the Needs of Aboriginal Peoples: A Workshop on Practical Strategies for Student Support," 20–22 June 2002, University of Saskatchewan. Interestingly, the title remained unchanged in a workshop on progress and priorities on 15 March 2003.

23. Similar patterns of (at best) add-on treatment of Aboriginal knowledge are registered in the K–12 system. See, for example, J. Tim Goddard, "Ethnoculturally Relevant Programming in Northern Schools," *Canadian Journal of Native Education* 26, no. 2 (2002): pp. 124 33, on the experience of Cree, Dene, and Métis in northern Saskatchewan and Alberta. School administrators report, "We follow the provincial curriculum here and don't see why we should change it" or "the students here have to write the provincial examinations like everyone else"

(130). Schooling remains "locked in the late modern period," where education is believed to be neutral and testing against dominant values remains central (128). In the process, ethno-cultural difference is produced and reproduced in binary patterns that characterize Indigenous knowledge as local, scattered, and political.

24. *RCAP,* vol. 2: *Restructuring the Relationship,* p. 780.

25. *Selections from the Prison Notebooks of Antonio Gramsci,* ed. and trans. Quinton Hoare and Geoffrey Nowell Smith (New York: International Publishers, 1971), p. 9.

26. On co-operative education, see Cheryl Turner, "Co-operative Learning, Citizenship and Current Adult Learning Policies," *Journal of Co-operative Studies* 35, no. 2 (2002): pp. 88–85; Ian MacPherson, "Encouraging Associative Intelligence: Co-operative Shared Learning and Responsible Citizenship: Plenary Presentation," *Journal of Co-operative Studies* 35, no. 2 (2002): pp. 86–89; and Elizabeth G. Cohen, "Co-operative Learning and the Equitable Classroom in a Multicultural Society," keynote for International Association for the Study of Co-operation conference, Manchester, England, June 2002, *Journal of Co-operative Studies* 35, no. 2 (2002): pp. 99–108.

MURRAY FULTON AND JULIE GIBBINGS

COGNITIVE PROCESSES AND CO-OPERATIVE BUSINESS STRATEGY

INTRODUCTION

SINCE THE LATE 1980S, co-operatives have faced a number of significant changes in the environments in which they operate. These changes include new technologies, new regulatory regimes, growing corporate concentration, and new social relations. In the agricultural sector, for instance, the introduction of genetically modified foods has changed production methods and altered consumer attitudes towards food.[1] Farm consolidation has resulted in increasingly commercialized farming operations and an increasingly diverse farm population, while new trade regimes have opened up markets that were traditionally separated.[2] Agri-business firms have responded to these changes with mergers and acquisitions, thus creating increasingly concentrated industries.[3]

Similar changes have occurred in other sectors where co-operatives operate. In the Canadian financial services sector, for example, a new regulatory regime has resulted in increased competition as foreign companies enter the Canadian market, and as insurance and trust companies provide more and more of the services that were previously provided by only banks and credit unions.[4] As well, consumers are increasingly demanding financial services that are available twenty-four hours a day, seven days a week. In response to these and other changes, the financial institutions have invested in new information technologies and have attempted a number of high-profile mergers. In the retail sector, changes include: new competitors such as WAL-MART; a growing centralization of purchasing; an increased demand by retailers for service, dependability, and quality assurance at the lowest possible price; increased corporate concentration; rapid product development; and rapidly shifting consumer purchasing habits.[5]

Co-operatives have adapted their business strategies in response to these changes. Like their non–co-operative counterparts, co-operatives have restructured their operations, invested in new technology, and undertaken mergers and acquisitions. Some of this adaptation appears to have been successful, including mergers and joint ventures by local retails to create the so-called super-locals, mergers by credit unions to create larger entities able to provide services more cost effectively, and the revamping of stores and the withdrawal from manufacturing undertaken by Federated Co-operatives Limited.

Not all the adaptation, however, has been successful. Prominent examples include: Agway and Farmland Industries in the United States, both of whom filed for Chapter 11 bankruptcy protection in 2002; Dairyworld, which was purchased by Saputo in 2001; Agricore, which merged with United Grain Growers in 2001; and Saskatchewan Wheat Pool, which has experienced extremely difficult financial times. In all these cases, the co-operatives in question had been long established in their respective sectors and held a significant market share.[6]

The purpose of this chapter is to explore why some co-operatives have been able to successfully adapt to a new environment while others have not. The chapter begins by laying out a framework for understanding why organizations (including co-operatives) might differ in their ability to adapt. The development of this framework requires an examination of cognitive processes and the implications of the manner in which knowledge is created for the decisions and strategies that organizations undertake. The framework is then used to examine unsuccessful adaptations by two co-operatives—Agway and Farmland Industries. The chapter concludes with some implications for co-operative business strategies during times of rapid change.

Cognitive Processes and Knowledge

Adaptation is of the utmost importance in a world of constant and rapid change. It requires decision making, which in turn demands knowledge of existing opportunities and challenges of the world as it is now and of how it might be in the future. It is difficult, however, to be sure of how the world appears today, and an even more complex task to determine what it may look like tomorrow. This lack of complete knowledge—whether of the past, the present, or the future—arises because of the way in which information is processed.

Cognitive Processes

Information is not knowledge, and to transform it into knowledge requires the interpretive resources of cognitive models or frameworks. Cognitive models are the mental structures that people impose on the world to make sense of it. These structures organize information from the environment in a meaningful way and represent the perceived essential qualities of an object or event.[7]

Cognitive models are made up of slots, or frames, which act as containers for specific information. Information is thus categorized into different frames according to perceived similarities with other objects or events, or on the basis of an explanatory structure. By classifying objects, events, actions, and people into a series of frames and containers, the world is made to appear as if it has a structure.[8] This structure is based on a series of rules that outline the relations between and among objects and events, although it is important to remember that both structure and rules are often based on idealized and/or abstract examples of these objects or events.

Cognitive models typically have a story that provides a way of ordering the sequence of events[9] and that guides expectations about the ordinary course of events, including the presumed actions of other actors. These narrative structures are often reflected in how past examples of these situations are remembered, with the possibility of selective and/or false memories being constructed in order to make past and current situations "fit" into an existing template.

The combination of categories and narratives that make up cognitive models provides the rules by which people are told—and tell—

what the world is like. They delimit what events and actions are thinkable, and what is not; they also point to the problems that need to be solved and the limits to acceptable solutions.[10] In short, these structures mark out where attention is to be focussed and what decisions are to be made. They also, of course, determine what escapes perception.

Cognitive Processes and Their Implications for Knowledge

The process by which information is sorted, ordered, and selected has important implications for the nature of knowledge. Specifically, the cognitive processes that individuals use and the limited cognitive capacities that people possess mean that knowledge is never complete—whether it is of the past, the present, or the future.

One reason that knowledge is never complete is that it is always partial and relative. The perspective people have of the world is shaped by history and culture, as well as by the relationships they have with each other and with the institutions that govern the economy and society (e.g., markets, regulatory regimes, social norms). These factors—culture, history, and relationships—make up a context, which provides the basis for the frames and the narrative that in turn form the foundation for knowledge. This connection between context and knowledge implies that knowledge is only partial, that it is relative to context, and that there is more than one way of knowing or understanding.

Second, knowledge is never complete because it is difficult for the production of knowledge to "keep pace" with new situations and new information in circumstances of rapid change. There is no necessary correlation between information and knowledge; instead, knowledge is produced only when information is sorted, processed, and selected by the cognitive processes described above. Moreover, the world is much too complex to fully comprehend. In complex situations, individuals and organizations are only able to focus attention on a certain number of activities at any given time, and adding new scenarios or information will result in decreased attention elsewhere. Thus, attention devoted to one area may impede notice of new information or scenarios in another. In addition, when situations are constantly undergoing change, individuals must spend more time readjusting their picture of the world. Combining these two factors—more information and more rapid change—suggests that people and organizations must constantly be reconceptualizing their knowledge of the world.

Third, knowledge is incomplete because it is impossible to know the future outcomes of current actions. If knowledge of the current world is partial and relative, it follows that knowledge of the future is, at the very least, uncertain. While it is true that predictions can be made about the future based on current actions, these predictions follow from incomplete knowledge of the current situation, and hence they, too, will be deficient. Further, the more rapid and profound the change, the more likely the deficiency of the predictions.

Fourth, knowledge is incomplete because it is not possible to know the current or future actions of other individuals. Since all knowledge is relative and partial, different people are likely to understand the world in different ways, and hence will not react to changes in the same way. Moreover, since the outcome of current actions can never be completely known, the future actions of others (and indeed of oneself) as they respond to these outcomes can equally never be known.

Economics literature makes a distinction between risk and uncertainty that neatly captures the incompleteness of knowledge. Risk describes situations in which the probability of all outcomes can be determined through analysis (e.g., deductive reasoning, empirical analysis). Risk, therefore, presumes complete knowledge, even though it may consist of probabilities. In contrast, uncertainty characterizes situations in which there is no method for determining probabilities. Uncertainty can also be extended to cover situations where it is impossible to even establish the set of possible outcomes that might arise.[11] Thus, uncertainty implies incomplete knowledge.

COGNITIVE PROCESSES AND ORGANIZATIONS

The nature of knowledge and the manner in which knowledge is created have significant implications for organizations and the way in which they operate. As Loasby argues,[12] organizations exist because of the lack of complete knowledge and because of the nature of how knowledge is created. If knowledge were complete, there would be little or no need for organizations. Everyone—including CEOs, managers, employees, and customers—would view the world in the same manner and would make the same decisions. While organizations might exist to formally structure the relationships among the various parties that are required for the production, distribution, and sales of goods and services, they would serve no other purpose.

The role of organizations changes fundamentally when it is recognized that knowledge is not complete and that different people view and understand the world in different ways. When information is incomplete and decisions are thus made under uncertainty and ignorance, organizations emerge as places where knowledge is created. Through the various functions that the organization carries out, it is able to generate information, and from it, knowledge. Since the creation of knowledge depends on context, on the nature of the people who undertake it, and on the relationships that exist among these people, organizations will differ in the knowledge they create.

This difference in knowledge, in turn, creates both opportunities and obstacles for an organization. If it is able to effectively create knowledge, the organization is more likely to succeed in whatever activity it is undertaking. If it is unable to create effective knowledge, however, it is more likely to be unsuccessful. Organizations thus become the vehicles by which various views of the world—whether knowledge frameworks or structures proposed by entrepreneurs, or traditional frameworks that have been used repeatedly—are created, tested, and implemented. In short, organizations are interpretative systems in which knowledge is created and assembled. By undertaking this role, organizations become the mechanisms by which society deals with complexity and change.

Organizations create and assemble knowledge by bringing a number of different perspectives and vantage points to bear on any given situation. Organizations allow people to specialize in certain areas, which is, of course, critical in the creation of knowledge, particularly given the complexity of most issues. In addition, organizations allow for variety, which is important because as noted above, knowledge is never complete. Because conceptual models both reflect and produce world views, people will have unique ways of approaching problem solving and knowledge gathering, although these different conceptual models are not necessarily incompatible. More often, when combined, different conceptual models offer a fuller and richer picture of the world and provide the basis for skilful decision making. Indeed, the greater the incompleteness of knowledge, the greater is the need for a variety of approaches to problem solving as a safeguard against poor solutions. By creating access to a number of different viewpoints and perspectives, organizations generate ideas for consideration and opportunities for individuals to learn from each other.

Thus, to be successful, organizations must have available the expertise and insights of a range of individuals. In addition, organizations must have some way of assembling the dispersed information and knowledge that has been created.[13] The manner in which this is carried out, however, will determine the organization's effectiveness. It is particularly important during times of rapid change, since it is during these periods that historical structures and processes are likely to be relatively ineffective at providing knowledge of how the system will operate and recognizing available opportunities. As a consequence, organizations that fail to adapt their knowledge creation processes are unlikely to fare well in the activities they undertake.

To recap, organizations arise as a vehicle for interpreting the events that occur in the world and for creating knowledge out of this interpretation. This knowledge can be used to provide benefits or advantages to the individuals and groups that created the organization. Indeed, it is the potential for advantage or benefit that causes organizations—be they for-profit businesses, co-operatives, or universities—to be created in the first place.

Organizations differ in their ability to create and assemble knowledge, both because of the different histories and contexts in which they developed, and because of the manner in which they are structured. During times of rapid change in the economy and society, the world view of an organization—and the manner in which it creates and assembles knowledge—will require modification or adaptation. Without this, an organization typically finds itself being "beaten to the punch" by organizations that have a world view or perspective that provides them with an advantage. Indeed, organizational adaptation is almost always about how the organization interprets the world and constructs knowledge. Changes in activities—e.g., in the products that are produced or the customers who are targeted—are invariably a reflection of a different perspective and understanding of events.

Co-operative Business Strategy

Like any organization, the success or failure of a co-operative depends on its ability to create and assemble knowledge—in short, to act as an effective interpretative system. The manner in which it organizes these activities affects its business decisions, and in turn, its performance. As outlined above, these decisions are invariably a reflection of how decision makers in a co-operative perceive and understand events.

To illustrate this connection between the perspective and understanding of events and the performance of the co-operative, this chapter will analyse two examples of unsuccessful co-ops—Agway and Farmland Industries Ltd. Both organizations had a long history in the agricultural industry and were significant players in their respective sectors. Farmland was the largest agricultural co-op in the US at the time it filed for bankruptcy, and was one of the largest firms in the livestock industry. Agway was the largest agricultural co-operative in the US for much of the 1970s and 1980s. In 2002, both filed for Chapter 11 bankruptcy protection. The discussion of Farmland is based on Randall Torgerson's presentation to the joint meetings of the American Agricultural Economics Society and the Rural Sociology Society in Montreal in August 2003. That of Agway is based on a case study written by Brett Fairbairn for the CARD II Leadership Development Forums in 2003, and on a paper written by Bruce Anderson and Brian Henehan shortly after Agway filed for bankruptcy protection.

Table 1 outlines a number of the factors that have been identified as contributing to the failure of the two co-operatives. These factors are similar across the two firms and have been grouped together to facilitate their analysis and comparison. While there are other ways of interpreting these factors (indeed, this was the essence of the discussion earlier), each of the groupings identified in Table 1 can be directly linked to the ability of these co-operatives to effectively create and assemble knowledge. The remainder of this section will explore these linkages.

Table 1: Factors Contributing to the Failure of Agway and Farmland Industries Ltd.

Agway	Farmland
Lack of Flexibility	
Heavily leveraged balance sheet that made co-op vulnerable when specific activities became unprofitable	Heavily leveraged balance sheet that reduced flexibility in economic downturns; subordinated investment made up significant portion of debt, leading to run on callable notes
Complex Organization	
Large conglomerate with interests in many sectors	Large conglomerate with interests in many sectors; loss of core competency
Perception by the management that they could run any business	
Overall goal was growth in sales, not profitability	
Concentration of Decision Making	
CEO was appointed member of the board in 2001, when it was clear that Agway was facing serious financial troubles	Lack of separation of management from the board of directors (CEO was, for a while, a member of the board)
Low turnover among board members	Board of directors ineffective in oversight role
Large board, with representation by districts (not all of which contributed equally to earnings)	
Loss of Member Commitment	
Equity write-downs due to operating losses left members with very little ownership in the co-op	Equity write-downs due to operating losses left members with very little ownership in the co-op
Involvement in nonagricultural operations (e.g., lease financing, insurance, energy) weakened sense of member ownership	Use of joint ventures had unintended consequence of distancing members from the organization
Changes in the agricultural economy were reducing number of members and causing members to interact with co-operative less and less (e.g., direct delivery of goods from warehouse to farm)	Growth in food marketing area through cross-subsidization

Inability to Deal with Structural Issues

Numerous attempts to restructure throughout the 1990s. Restructuring included a conversion to a centralized organization that dealt directly with members	Tensions in federated system between central and the large locals
With a few exceptions, Agway's agricultural services were losing money while their nonagricultural services were profitable	Serious attempts to consolidate with other regional co-operatives were unsuccessful
Nonagricultural services required more capital than Agway could provide	

Source: Agway—Fairbairn; Anderson and Henehan; Farmland—Torgerson.

Agway and Farmland were both highly leveraged by the time they filed for bankruptcy protection. While a co-operative's financial leverage may not directly affect its ability to create and assemble knowledge, it does affect a co-operative's ability to act on the knowledge it does create. As Loasby notes,[14] organizations faced with a highly uncertain future must develop flexibility so they can adapt to whatever outcome eventually occurs. Both Agway and Farmland clearly had not cultivated flexibility; the most visible evidence of this is the degree to which they were leveraged. While this lack of flexibility cannot provide conclusive evidence as to what cognitive processes were at work inside these organizations, the high debt load is consistent with a world view that the future is highly predictable and/or that management clearly believed they knew how the world was going to unfold.

In Agway, at least, there is additional evidence to support the latter contention. As Anderson and Henehan note, "There was a longstanding attitude at Agway, and predecessor organizations, that they could manage any type of business, even when other people could not."[15] The persistence of this attitude is consistent with Fairbairn's observation that Agway had a large board of directors with little turnover.

In both Agway and Farmland, there appears to be a lack of separation between management and board. In cognitive terms, the result is that there are fewer places in the organization where knowledge is created and assembled. The board's failure to perform an oversight role noted in the Farmland case is consistent with this lack of knowledge creation.

As discussed earlier, complex situations create circumstances in which attention devoted to one area may impede notice of new information or scenarios in another. Both Agway and Farmland were exceedingly complex organizations with a large number of business lines; they commonly entered into joint ventures with other co-operatives. This complexity suggests that the decision makers in both firms may have been unable to fully focus their attention on the changes underway in all their sectors and markets, and thus unable to entirely comprehend what changes were necessary to keep their co-operatives profitable.

As outlined in the introduction, there have been significant changes in the agricultural sector since the mid-1980s. In the case of Agway, for instance, these changes included a loss in farm numbers due to consolidation, a geographical shift in the dairy industry towards the southwestern US, a growing demand by farmers for highly specialized products and services, a shift in the manner in which farmers were provided with service, and the emergence of new competitors in traditional market areas (e.g., retail). These changes had the effect of significantly reducing the profitability of Agway's agricultural lines. Indeed, with a few exceptions, Agway's agricultural business operations were unprofitable.[16]

While Agway made numerous attempts to restructure its operations throughout the 1990s, no effort was made to deal with the fundamental structural issue that its nonagricultural ventures were generally profitable, while its agricultural business lines were not. As well, the nonagricultural ventures required more capital than Agway could provide, particularly since the agricultural businesses were a drain on capital.

One reason that this structural issue was so difficult to deal with may have been Agway's co-operative structure. The company's cross-subsidization of its agricultural businesses was attractive to its farmer members, who were represented on a regional basis that did not reflect the contribution to volumes and earnings. Thus farmers who were contributing very little to the financial health of the organization had an interest—as well as the ability through their voting rights—to continue cross-subsidization. Given this mismatch of interests, it is not surprising that the knowledge that would have been required to restructure the co-op was neither created nor acted upon.

Cross-subsidization was also an issue in Farmland, which invested in food processing using profits from activities in which farmers had a more direct connection—farm fuel supply. This cross-subsidization, along with a heavy reliance on joint ventures that allowed the company to move into new lines of business, reduced member commitment. In addition, the loss of member equity over the years meant that members had less and less of an ownership stake in the co-op, a dynamic that was also at play in Agway, where member commitment was on the decline as well.

This loss of member commitment may have had an impact on the cognitive processes at work in these two organizations. Specifically, with little to lose if the co-operatives failed, members had little incentive to try and conceptualize the problems that their businesses were facing. As well, the loss of member commitment and the attendant loss in business meant that members had fewer opportunities to provide input into the problems facing their organization, thus directly affecting the manner in which knowledge was created and assembled.

Discussion and Concluding Remarks

While additional research is clearly required, the discussion above suggests that the poor financial performance of Agway and Farmland Industries Ltd. can be linked at least in part to the cognitive processes at work in these co-operatives, which in turn can be linked to their co-operative structure. Put somewhat differently, their business strategies did not successfully position them in their respective industries, and this appears to be directly connected to their ability to fully understand and act upon the changes underway in their sectors.

The establishment of a link between a co-operative's financial performance and the manner in which it creates and assembles knowledge means that co-operatives have to pay much more attention to how they are conceptualizing and understanding the economic and social environment in which they are operating. In particular, the discussion above suggests that co-operatives should pay close attention to the role played by the board and management, as well as the knowledge possessed by its members.

At the risk of oversimplification, the problems facing both Farmland and Agway appear to stem from a lack of diversity in views and perspectives about how the agricultural industry might unfold and, closely related, from a sense that these co-ops could do no wrong—that they had the world figured out. While these perspectives and dynamics might serve an organization well during times of relative stability, they are antithetical to success when the economic and social environment is changing rapidly.

Given that the rapidity of change does not appear to be lessening, co-operatives must find mechanisms to ensure that effective knowledge is being created and assembled, that world views are challenged, and that new ideas are forthcoming. As suggested by the discussion here, these mechanisms are likely to involve governance structures that limit the power of management and more properly reflect the role played by members, as well as investment decisions that reduce cross-subsidization and create greater member commitment. Greater transparency in the co-operative, a concentration on core activities, and the creation of business units that can focus on a particular group of members are all consistent with making co-operatives more effective at fulfilling their key role—the interpretation of information and knowledge in a highly uncertain world.

Endnotes

1. M. Boehlje, *U.S. Agriculture in an Increasingly Competitive Global Market* (West Lafayette, IN: Purdue University, Department of Agricultural Economics Staff Paper #02–06, November 2002).
2. Rural Business—Cooperative Service, *Agricultural Cooperatives in the 21st Century* (Washington, DC: United States Department of Agriculture, Co-operative Information Report 60, November 2002).
3. J. MacDonald, "Agribusiness Concentration, Competition, and NAFTA," paper presented at the NAFTA Policy Dispute and Information Consortium's 7th Annual Workshop, 14–17 February 2001.
4. H. MacKay, *Change, Challenge, Opportunity* (Ottawa: Department of Finance,

report of the Task Force on the Future of the Canadian Financial Services Sector, 1998).

5. Rural Business—Cooperative Service.

6. For further details on these co-operatives, see B. Anderson and B. Henehan, "What Went Wrong at Agway?" (Ithaca, NY: Cornell University, Cornell University Cooperative Enterprise Program, extension paper, 2002); B. Fairbairn, "Losing Sight of the Goal: Agway," paper prepared for the CARD II Leadership Development Forums, Centre for the Study of Co-operatives, University of Saskatchewan, 2003; A. Ewins, "Special Report: Saskatchewan Wheat Pool," *Western Producer,* 9 May 2002, pp. 10–11; E. Goddard, "Factors Underlying the Evolution of Farm-Related Co-operatives in Alberta," principal paper, Canadian Agricultural Economics Association annual meeting, Calgary, 30 May–1 June 2002; and R. Torgerson, "Farmland Industries Limited," presentation to the annual meeting of the American Agricultural Economics Association and the Rural Sociological Society, Montreal, 27–30 July 2003.

7. F.C. Bartlett, *Remembering: A Study in Experimental and Social Psychology* (Cambridge: Cambridge University Press, 1932); J. Piaget, *The Child's Conception of Number* (New York: W.W. Norton, 1952); and R.C. Schank and R.P. Abelson, *Scripts, Plans, Goals and Understanding: An Inquiry into Human Knowledge and Structures* (Hillsdale, NJ: Lawrence Erlbaum Associates, 1977).

8. Martin Heidegger, "The Age of the World Picture," in *The Question Concerning Technology and Other Essays,* trans. William Lovitt (New York: Harper and Row, 1977), pp. 115–54.

9. Schank and Abelson.

10. Thomas Kuhn, *The Structures of Scientific Revolutions,* 2nd ed. (Chicago: University of Chicago Press, 1970).

11. B.J. Loasby, "Organisations as Interpretive Systems," *Revue d'Économie Industrielle* 97, no. 4 (2001): pp. 17–34.

12. Ibid.

13. Ibid.

14. B.J. Loasby, *Choice, Complexity and Ignorance: An Inquiry into Economic Theory and the Practice of Decision Making* (Cambridge: Cambridge University Press, 1976).

15. Anderson and Henehan, p. 2.

16. Fairbairn.

LESLIE BROWN

INNOVATIONS IN CO-OPERATIVE MARKETING AND COMMUNICATIONS

INTRODUCTION[1]

IT IS COMMONLY ASSERTED that co-operatives blend social and economic goals. Yet for many co-operatives this truth does not translate into distinctive and innovative "co-operative differences" in such areas as marketing, member relations, operational policies, and day-to-day business activities. In reality, the blend of social and economic is often experienced more as an uneasy relationship between "association" and "business" than as a dynamic strength of co-operatives. Beset by competition, lured by mainstream corporate structures and processes, co-operatives have often presumed that their associative side would take care of itself. Calls for elevating the associative side to a level equal to the business side have often fallen on deaf or over-worked ears.

With the changes wrought by the various strands of neo-liberal globalization, including the downsizing of governments and the upsizing of undemocratic, powerful international bodies such as transnational corporations, this issue takes on renewed relevance. What is the role of co-operatives in this playing field? How are co-operatives to respond to the challenges in local and international markets (e.g., mass but also fragmented, diverse, multiple customer and member types), and to changes in the nature of community (e.g., multiple forms, increased diversity, multifaceted and shifting identities, increased significance of the third sector)? Further, what are co-ops to make of the rise in consumerism, individualism, values of diversity and novelty, countervailed and paralleled by a search for meaning and identity beyond the material, for new forms of community, and for rootedness and social cohesion? How are co-operatives to understand and market themselves, and how are they to communicate with their various stakeholders, including member-owners, nonmember users, employees, and communities? How can the new technologies be used to advantage? One expert in the field of co-operatives asserts:

> As globalisation and market competition intensifies, we cannot continue with the old idea that a co-operative has a dual character, as an association of members and a business, and that what the managers and board of directors have to do is somehow to live with the tension between them. If co-ops and mutuals cannot fuse together the association and the business into something new that builds on the strength of membership to gain market advantages, then they will not be able to survive.[2]

From both academics and practitioners we hear calls for "Marketing the Co-operative Advantage" and "Reasserting the Co-operative Advantage."[3] Many analysts now believe that attention to the co-operative difference demonstrates forward-thinking leadership and a capacity for creative innovation.[4] It provides a basis for manifesting a clear co-operative identity and carving a significant place for co-ops in the contemporary world. As the United Kingdom's Co-operative Commission reports, "The co-operative movement needs to recapture its sense of mission, commitment and excitement ... and ... create a successful family of businesses that offer a clear co-operative advantage."[5]

This paper develops the thesis that to survive and thrive in the future, co-operatives will have to develop communications strategies, including marketing strategies, that explore and stress their advantages as co-operatives. It suggests a framework for integrating marketing into an overall communication strategy that is integrated and centred on the particular co-op's vision of the "co-operative difference."

THE CO-OPERATIVE DIFFERENCE

Rooted in co-operative values, the seven co-operative principles emphasize democracy, voluntarism, and community in the context of a business that serves member needs and in which member-owners invest.[6] Economics to serve people, not vice versa.[7] Amid analyses of the "crises" of co-operatives and calls for mergers, national and international branding, innovative business creation and acquisition, and marketing of the co-operative advantage, co-operative leaders and activists struggle to find points of agreement and to foster the needed momentum for change. While there is no agreement on what the essential co-operative differences are in operational and business terms, the literature reported here reveals some overlap regarding the key co-operative advantages.

The Reasserting the Co-operative Advantage Research Project in the UK identified where the co-operative advantage lies for consumer co-operatives in the contemporary business context, and pointed out existing examples of management and organizational development practices that implement these advantages.[8] Among the conclusions reached by the authors were the following: In general, the movement tends to be inward-looking and strategically reactive, unaware of the links between member relations and marketing, and unsure of how co-operative values and principles can be made integral to the core business of a co-operative. The research also revealed significant attitudinal and other barriers to changing organizational culture and behaviour. Further, there was generally a significant gap between the rhetoric of co-operation (in mission statements, etc.) and the actual workings of the co-operatives. UK co-operatives are, of course, not unique in this.

Key co-operative advantages identified by the UK project include: co-operative values, trust, unique ownership structures, and community rootedness. The authors point to co-operatives exemplifying best practice in capitalizing on these, and they conclude that the key co-operative advantages must be realized if co-operatives are to flourish in the current economic and social context. The following quote from Commission Chair John Monks illustrates the tone of the report:

> Today's co-operative movement has many strengths. Its ethos can tap into the public's disillusionment with corporate greed

and lack of ethical standards displayed by parts of the private sector, but the structures and the ways in which co-operative principles are implemented need to be brought up to date in order to deliver those values in today's fiercely competitive world.[9]

In honour of International Co-operative Day, July 2001, the International Co-operative Alliance released a message identifying co-op values, principles, ethics, and business competence as constituting the co-operative advantage.[10] The message points out that the social dimension differentiates co-operatives from other business enterprises, but asks "What makes the co-operative approach to business development different and what are the different ways in which employment is created through co-operatives?"[11]

Johnston Birchall, past editor of the *Journal of Co-operative Studies,* agrees about the centrality of the social dimension and has developed a powerful analysis of co-operative values and principles. He emphasizes that a grounding in these helps co-operatives deal with what Alexander Laidlaw identified as the ideological crisis of co-operatives—What is the purpose of co-operatives and are they fulfilling a distinct role as a different kind of enterprise?[12]

Birchall's work complements that of co-operative management theorist Daniel Côté, who distills the co-operative difference down to three main aspects: the double identity of ownership and usership, democratic control and orientation, and the redistribution of surplus based on the transactions between the members and the co-operative. While he adds that these differences are often not recognized by members in large, mature co-operatives and suggests why this is the case, he emphasizes that co-operatives are suited by their very nature to address the major issues facing organizations of the future: loyalty, the search for meaning and legitimacy, mobilization through values, and finding ways to be a learning organization.[13]

Co-operative activist and consultant Tom Webb is also concerned with helping co-operatives meet their potential. His focus is specifically on marketing the idea of co-operation in the global economy.[14] He notes that co-operatives have a unique area of vulnerability—they are especially vulnerable to attacks that they lack integrity. On the other hand, they have two "Unique Selling Points"—their ownership structure and the values they hold. Webb has been part of the development of a program called Marketing the Co-operative Advantage (MOCA), which is receiving considerable attention from co-operatives. MOCA aims to help co-operatives market their unique selling points effectively and with integrity.

Richard Radtke, author of *The Power of Business Ethics,* notes that the claims of co-operatives to be ethical and principled organizations, focussed on "people helping people," fall on receptive ears in this era. Marketing, for co-operatives, should not be the same beast as it is for other enterprises. Co-ops are led by their principles and values to favour equity over efficiency, needs over wants, the whole of society over the affluent, common interest over self-interest. People are citizens of the co-op as well as customers, a fact co-operatives are positioned to emphasize. Any effort to market this claim, however, will be put to the test—are co-operatives really doing what they claim to be doing? As Radtke puts it, "They bear a special obligation to the people and communities they serve to live up to their words and philosophy with deeds and actions to match."[15]

In North America, co-ops are themselves exploring their co-operative differences, trying to become more explicit regarding their organizations in the contemporary context. In 2002, for example, the Canadian Co-operative Association (CCA) fielded a national community-contribution survey to more than seven thousand nonfinancial co-operatives in order to better understand the type and extent of these contributions, and to identify whether co-op participation is different from that of other businesses.[16] Another objective of the survey was to gather data that could be used for member or employee orientation, and marketing and promotion initiatives. Responses came in from more than eight hundred co-operatives across ten provinces and one territory. Of these responding, more than 60 percent believed that co-operatives do contribute in ways different from conventional firms, but 31.5 percent did not answer this question and 7.4 percent believed that co-operatives are not different. Somewhat surprisingly, more than half do not consult with employees and their communities to determine community needs. The publication of the detailed results of this survey should help generate discussion on the co-operative difference.

Also in 2002, the CCA published on-line a Social Audit Toolkit designed to help co-operatives that want to explore the degree to which their social commitments and their behaviour are in line, and the degree to which they are meeting the priorities of their stakeholders.

The work of the Credit Union National Association (CUNA) in the US provides a second example of co-operative explorations of their co-operative difference. CUNA has developed a Project Differentiation Strategy, which asks credit union boards to consider and publicize their social commitments and activities in six areas, and to develop a commitment statement for their members.[17] While more than nine hundred credit unions have completed the commitment statement, those who organized this project recognize that at some point credit unions will need to go further than merely listing their commitments and activities. Why should people believe their claims about themselves? Questions of credibility and legitimacy arise.

LEGITIMACY OF KEY STRUCTURES AND INSTITUTIONS IS IN QUESTION

The context for co-operatives today is one in which public cynicism and disenchantment with institutions both public and private is pervasive. Even the erstwhile powerful rallying cry of "Democracy for the people!" is not particularly effective these days. Perhaps as part of the overall reduced trust in authority evidenced in public opinion polls in Canada and the US, political cynicism is quite high.[18] In addition, the Canadian Democracy and Corporate Accountability Commission reports that while recognizing the legitimacy of the pursuit of profits, 72 percent of Canadians want companies to broaden their sense of accountability beyond the bottom line.[19] Issues of corporate governance are in the headlines these days, and demands for accountability and transparency are mounting. These are perhaps related to concerns about the present forms and paths of globalization, especially concern about corporate influence on elected governments, corporate social responsibility, and the degradation of the environment. There is, however, limited awareness of alternatives such as co-operatives. It is difficult to build trust in organizations claiming to represent the collective good, and people tend to take refuge in legal definitions of individual rights as consumers and clients.

In consequence, worldwide, corporations of various kinds (for profit, nonprofit, co-operative) are becoming interested in, or are being pushed towards, demonstrating social responsibility in a credible way.[20] In order to make headway in such a climate of opinion, co-operatives need to be accountable for their social and financial commitments. Indeed, many argue that the two are linked. As self-styled democratic and socially responsible organizations, transparency and accountability are extremely important, with the concomitant necessity of being seen to be transparent, accountable, democratic, and socially responsible. Practices of social and ethical accounting, auditing, and reporting (SEAAR) are developing both within the co-operative and corporate sectors.[21] As many co-operatives and credit unions are again beginning to emphasize, the natural competitive advantage of co-operatives derives from their social values.

This, then, is the context in which credit unions and co-operatives are considering their social commitments, community involvements, and overall priorities. Reinvigorating membership commitment and loyalty to their co-ops is one challenge; building and maintaining trust and trustworthiness is another. Especially as the scale of co-operatives enlarges, co-op leaders often feel out of touch with members and their perceptions of actual and potential membership advantages. As well, there is still a perception in the general population that co-ops are good institutions, but for the needy, or for niches the market is not already adequately serving. Co-operatives are not often seen as the institutions of choice, despite the increasing cynicism and distrust of private, and even public, institutions.

Co-operative Communications in Overview

Co-operatives now find that while communications of various types are more important than ever, the world is all but saturated with "information" and "communications." Every forum chosen, especially outgoing unsolicited messages (e.g., advertising, newsletters, e-mail), must be used judiciously and to best advantage. This offers one strong argument for developing an overall framework for the various types and venues of communication. A second argument is that, vulnerable as they are to accusations of inconsistency or lack of integrity, co-operatives need to make sure that the messages they are communicating, whether directly or indirectly, are consistent and fit with the co-operative's claims about itself. A likely framework for a communications strategy is provided by a focus on the co-operative difference, the advantages of co-operation.

As seen in the above discussion, these advantages centre around the values and principles of co-operatives, which encourage them to develop a clear ethical stance and to emphasize meeting people's needs over maximizing profits for shareholders. In so doing, co-operatives work within democratic structures, which provide opportunities for input and involvement for key stakeholders (e.g., member-owners, management, employees, community), and which necessitate emphasis on transparency and accountability.

To communicate effectively, and to encourage multidirectional communication, co-operatives must also maintain close connections to their stakeholders, which will give them the opportunity to educate palates for democracy, environmental sustainability, ethical commitments, and so on. Stakeholders develop their knowledge, commitments, and identities through a variety of ways. Members develop identities through participation in informal groups and/or not-for-profit organizations, for example, not just through their identities as consumers of goods and services. A co-op can reach them in multiple ways, not just by appealing to their identities as consumers/clients. In co-operatives, individual and collective interests must be balanced, and so too must the identities of member-owners as clients and members.[22] Similarly, employees can be reached on multiple levels, both material and nonmaterial.[23] The most effective way to reach employees is to show them that in the co-operative they have not only an excellent work environment, but also the satisfaction that comes from working for an organization that contributes positively to society in a variety of ways. As Reichheld reminds us, it is not possible to build a loyal client base without loyal employees.[24]

To do all this successfully, individual co-operatives need to be very clear about what they are, and what they are trying to accomplish. They must also consider the ways in which they communicate with stakeholders. It is common, for example, to establish four separate organizational functions dealing with various aspects of communications: marketing, public relations, human resources, and member relations. In all four areas, though to varying degrees, there is discussion of education, training, recruitment, increasing awareness of what a co-operative is, publicizing and informing, and so on. To a significant degree, these four organizational functions need to be reconceptualized and aligned. While different communications will necessarily have different emphases, they must exhibit an overall consistency and compatibility. Stakeholders may well be aware of inconsistencies in the messages sent by the co-operative, most especially the employees who do this work. Inconsistencies can undermine trust and credibility.

Further, it is imperative that communication not be considered a one-way street—simply something "done" to stakeholders. It must be multidirectional, communicating both within and beyond the co-op itself. People can be encouraged to voice (praise, get involved, criticize) rather than exit (leave the organization). The various incentive structures and strategies in place for the different elements of the co-operative need to reinforce the priorities of the communications strategies developed.

Figure 1 (overleaf) presents one possible approach to conceptualizing an integrated communication strategy. At the core are the key features of the co-operative advantage as seen in the literature reviewed above. These are the reference points for co-operative communications with stakeholders.

Marketing

All communications and actions in a co-op must be consistent in their message and rooted in the principles and values of co-operation. This may require a managerial revolution, suggests Côté, as managers (both boards of directors and paid managers) rethink their strategies. As both Webb and Côté emphasize,[25] the process of unquestioningly importing management standards and approaches developed for other types of firms has hurt co-operatives and created divisions within them. Consider, for example, the classic tension between member relations and marketing in many co-operatives. In North America, co-operatives are abolishing member relations functions altogether, or situating member relations within marketing departments, without

Figure 1: An Integrated Communications Strategy*

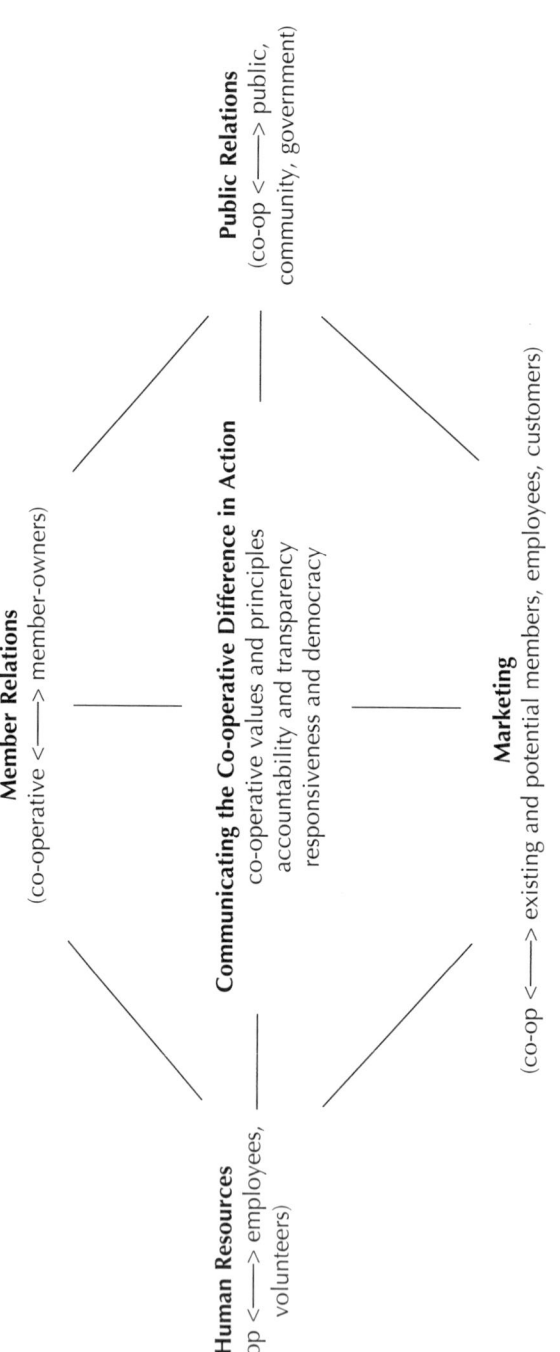

* The stakeholders can also communicate with one another, as they or the co-op communication strategists consider appropriate. This is important if mutual respect, understanding, and good decision making are to be fostered. The stakeholder groups are themselves diverse along a variety of dimensions.

changing the way marketing is conceptualized and executed. Similarly, many co-operatives that once had employees charged with member education have blended education with marketing, or erased it altogether. Unfortunately, marketing in co-operatives has tended to look just like marketing in other companies. But what does this say to members and customers/clients? Co-op marketing needs to be developed in line with co-operative values and beliefs, avoiding the manipulation often associated with its mainstream counterpart.[26]

In the schema proposed above, marketing functions are not given their customary pre-eminence, nor are they the arbiters of strategies of communication with the outside. Instead, communications for the purpose of marketing are closely aligned with all forms (and contents) of communication engaged in by the particular co-operative, whether labelled education, community involvement, member relations, recruitment of members and employees, or employee and volunteer training. This is important, writes Roger Spear of England's Open University: "Unless co-operative values are replicated through the way in which consumers transact with the co-operative, then the essence of co-operation has no future."[27]

Benander and Webb[28] suggest *character marketing* and *relationship marketing* as two proactive strategies that are consistent with a nonmanipulative focus on the co-operative advantage. Unlike the more familiar image marketing, character marketing flows from what the business actually is—its values and principles, its products, actions, and commitments. Focussed on meeting people's needs rather than on the competition, character marketing has a distinct emphasis: "We are who we say we are, we do what we say we'll do! And for those times when we fall short, let us know and we can improve!"

Henry Mintzberg, a prominent management theorist and consultant, has proposed that co-operatives play an integral role as one of four types of organizations required in any balanced economy: private, co-operative, non-owned, and public/state.[29] Co-ops can take advantage of being located conceptually in their own special category as an integral part of a balanced economy, and can use this in their character marketing. While promotion of a co-operative commonwealth is not heard these days, the ideas that the economy is out of balance, that private corporations are too powerful, and that realistic antidotes are needed resonate with many people—the more so in a globalizing world. Co-operatives speak to these concerns, and this needs to be communicated and improved with input from stakeholders.

Relationship marketing refers to the process of developing an ongoing relationship with stakeholders, individually and collectively. Often used these days by conventional businesses (e.g., marketing club memberships), it can be adapted to fit co-operatives too. While keeping privacy issues firmly in mind, a co-operative can focus on such things as, for example, an owner's manual for co-op members, or ongoing relationships with other publicly minded organizations in the community and abroad. Again, the essence of co-operatives is that they can deliver in ways that conventional businesses cannot. This approach can also point to the rights, privileges, and obligations of "citizenship" in the co-operative—requiring an emphasis on education—and rewards for those who put these into practice. The rewards can be as simple as being heard and responded to, receiving a dividend, or having input into the products and services of the co-operative. Webb[30] stresses a co-operative strength in this area—without becoming a co-operative, no other business can enjoy the relationships that co-operatives have. In no other business are democratic ownership and participation rights so fundamental, in no other business is the raison d'être to meet the needs of the members and to serve the communities in which the business is located.

A third marketing strategy, *cause-related marketing,* is also being advocated in Canada.[31] This type of marketing sees businesses and charities forming partnerships to serve their mutual benefit. While so far primarily pitched in the traditional language of image and corporate profit/fund-raising objectives, it is possible that such a strategy could establish one venue for stakeholder involvement in the activities of the co-op. For example, when the Co-operative Bank first produced its Partnership Report, it sought input from various stakeholders regarding the priorities of social issues.[32] Lindee David mentions the following as pros of cause-related marketing: image enhancement, hidden benefits, rewarding stakeholders, and customer loyalty. Co-operatives would presumably recognize similar pros, though the focus would be substance rather than image.

David sees the cons as: measuring return on investment, challenges of informing consumers, responding to consumer cynicism, and finding a unique and popular niche cause. Co-operatives should experience few of these, since keeping stakeholders informed should be part of an overall communications strategy; consumers are less likely to be cynical, at least initially; and the identification of a cause can be done by stakeholder groups themselves. The main con for co-operatives would be that it is easy for cause-related marketing to degenerate into gimmickry and image management—the death knell for trust, loyalty, and character marketing.

A significant recent development mentioned above is that more and more co-operatives are taking into their own hands various tools and procedures for demonstrating transparency, accountability, and responsibility. The application of social and ethical accounting and auditing tools is resulting in reports that often use the services of external auditors to provide independent verification.[33] Stakeholders are consulted as part of the process and are also invited to read and respond to the reports. These methods are useful in assessing marketing and other communication strategies in relation to co-operative (and stakeholder) aims and objectives, and in light of co-operative values and principles. This type of check is an essential part of maintaining integrity in co-operative marketing and communications. Indeed, Peter Rogan of the Co-operative Union's Social and Co-operative Performance Working Group asserts that the commercial success of co-operatives "will increasingly depend on building trust based on transparent social reporting practices."[34] The report itself can be a useful communication tool in marketing, public relations, member relations, and human resources, palpably demonstrating a commitment to continuous improvement in social, ethical, and environmental obligations, and responsiveness to stakeholders' concerns. It will also help stakeholders to maintain realistic expectations of their co-operative as changes are phased in and reported on.

SUMMARY

Communication strategies are best when tailored to the specific contexts in which they are to be used. That said, however, this paper suggests that co-operatives eschew their current tendency to look to conventional business strategies when developing their marketing and other communications endeavours. Instead, they can fruitfully work with a framework such as that presented here, which takes a more wholistic approach to communications and marketing, and emphasizes that the approach must have at its core a vision of the co-operative advantage and a consistent application of the characteristics that constitute this advantage in all aspects of the communications strategy. The future of co-operatives lies in the distinctive contributions they can make to people and their communities. Their communications strategies must recognize and reflect this.

ENDNOTES

1. Throughout this paper, "co-operatives" refers to all co-operatives, including credit unions.
2. Johnston Birchall, "Editorial," *Journal of Co-operative Studies* 33, no. 2 (August 2000): p. 93.
3. See the report of the Co-operative Advantage Research Team, *Journal of Co-operative Studies* 33, no. 2 (August 2000), as well as J.G. Craig, *The Nature of Co-operation* (Montreal: Black Rose Books, 1993), and Tom Webb, "Marketing the Co-operative Advantage," *Journal of Co-operative Studies* 87, no. 2 (1996): pp. 10–15.
4. Leslie Brown, "Organizations for the 21st Century: Co-operatives and 'New' Forms of Organization," *Canadian Journal of Sociology* 22, no. 1 (1997): pp. 65–94; Daniel Côté, "Co-operatives and the New Millennium: The Emergence of a New Paradigm," in *Canadian Co-operatives in the Year 2000: Memory, Mutual Aid, and the Millennium,* eds. Brett Fairbairn, Ian MacPherson, and Nora Russell (Saskatoon: Centre for the Study of Co-operatives, University of Saskatchewan, 2000), pp. 250–66; Ralph Mintzberg discussed in Brett Fairbairn, "Balancing Act," posted at http://www.usaskstudies.coop/publications/pdfpubs.html; Professor Janice Gross Stein's "Assets and Challenges for the Co-operative Sector," posted at http://www.coopcca.com/NewsLetter/InterSector/summer 2001.
5. United Kingdom, *Report of the Co-operative Commission,* 2001, posted at http://www.co-opcommission.org.uk.
6. The values are: self-help, self-responsibility, democracy, equality, equity, and solidarity. The principles are: voluntary and open membership, democratic member control, member economic participation, autonomy and independence, education, training, and information, co-operation among co-operatives, and concern for community (Ian MacPherson, "The ICA Statement on the Co-operative Identity," in *Co-operative Principles for the 21st Century* (Geneva: The International Co-operative Alliance, 1995), p. 1.
7. For a valuable discussion on this idea, see Hermann E. Daly and John B. Cobb,

Jr., *For the Common Good: Redirecting the Economy Toward Community, the Environment, and a Sustainable Future* (Boston: Beacon Press, 1989).

8. See the reports in the *Journal of Co-operative Studies* 33, no. 2.
9. The Co-operative Commission.
10. See http://www.coop.org/ica/ica/coopday.enmessage2001.html, November 2001.
11. See http://www.copacgva.org/idc/ilo-idc2001.htm, October 2002.
12. Johnston Birchall, "Co-operative Values and Principles: A Commentary," posted at http://www.co-opstudies.org.
13. Côté, p. 255.
14. Tom Webb, "Marketing Co-operation in the Global Economy," posted at http://www.wisc.edu/uwcc/icic/orgs/ica/pubs/review/ICA-Review
15. Richard Radtke, *The Power of Business Ethics: Credit Unions in the Real World* (Dubuque, Iowa: CUNA & Affiliates, Kendall/Hunt, 2001), p. vii.
16. See http://www.coopscanada.coop/newsletter/CSR/index.html.
17. These are: service to members; member education; involvement/governance; diversity; commitment to the credit union movement and other co-operative activities; public service/corporate citizenship. See http://www.cuna.org/data/cu/different/pd_front.html.
18. See the report on attitudes towards government institutions posted at http://www.environicsinternational.com.
19. See http://www.corporate-accountability.ca. This seems to be part of a larger pattern, as reported by Environics International's survey of twenty thousand people in twenty developed countries, 2001 (as reported in the Corporate Social Responsibility Monitor, http://www.bsdglobal.com/issues/sr_csrm.asp). They report that 26 percent of share owners in Canada take into account a company's social performance when purchasing and trading shares; in developed countries, social responsibility makes a greater contribution to corporate reputation (49 percent of image) than brand image (35 percent). Increasing numbers of people will "punish" a company perceived to be irresponsible (42 percent of North Americans, including 29 percent of Canadians, up from 20 percent the year before). Opinion leaders are 50 percent more likely to boycott poor performers, and have higher expectations of companies. North American consumers are the most demanding worldwide. Canadians are demanding more than profits from companies—74 percent of them agree that "business executives have a responsibility to take into account the impact their business has on employees, local communities, and the country, as well as making profits."
20. Even the Conference Board of Canada has responded to such concerns, establishing the Canadian Centre for Business in the Community. Also, note the rise in institutes and academic programs addressing ethical, environmental, and corporate social responsibility concerns.
21. See Jack Quarter, Laurie Mook, and Betty Jane Richmond, *What Counts: Social Accounting for Non-profits and Co-operatives* (Toronto: Prentice Hall, 2002); and Leslie Brown, "The Co-operative Difference? Social Auditing in Canadian Credit

Unions," *Journal of Rural Co-operation* 28, no. 2 (2002): pp. 87–100.

22. See examples of innovations in marketing ownership in Leslie Brown and Moira Clancey, "Marketing Ownership as a Co-operative Brand," *Concern for Community Newsletter* 2003 (December), posted at http://www.coopscanada.coop/newsletter/csr/december2003/index.html.

23. See the report on what Canadians look for in jobs at the website http://www.jobquality.ca.

24. As discussed in Côté, p. 256. As seen from VanCity Savings Credit Union's annual Social Reports, employees can be very proud indeed to work for a credit union. See http://www.vancity.com.

25. See notes 4 and 14.

26. See Webb, p. 272.

27. Roger Spear, "Membership Strategy for Co-operative Advantage," *Journal of Co-operative Studies* 33, no. 299 (2000): pp. 102–23.

28. See Lynn Benander and Tom Webb, "Adding Value to Membership: The Co-operative Challenge for the New Millennium," address to the ICA Congress and General Assembly, 1999, posted at http://www.coop.org/ica/ica/icaevents/congress1999. See this source as well for cases of co-ops that use these strategies.

29. See Fairbairn, "Balancing Act," and Leslie Brown, "Co-operatives and Social Cohesion: The Co-operative Way," posted at http://www.agr.gc.ca/policy/coop/publi_e.html, 31 December 2002.

30. See note 14.

31. See the website http://causemarketing.brunico.com/2002/sessions.html.

32. See http://www.co-operativebank.co.uk.

33. See Brown, "The Co-operative Difference?" for a discussion of social and ethical accounting, auditing, and reporting, and for an examination of three credit unions engaged in social auditing.

34. See http://www.co-opstudies.org/Conference/Conf_02/Peter_Rogan.htm.

CRISTINE de CLERCY

LEADERSHIP AND REPRESENTATIONAL DIVERSITY
THEORY, OPERATIONALIZATION, AND MEASUREMENT

BOARD MEMBERS are central to the function of any co-operative. There are many studies concluding that without excellent board-level leadership, organizations perform well below their capabilities.[1] People holding board offices often possess much experience and insight into the co-op, its community context, and business or service objectives. The efforts of board members to steer the co-op and to help define and achieve overarching policy goals constitute a key leadership contribution. Board members are valuable in another area, however—one that is too often ignored—and that is their ability to represent their membership. This is also referred to as their representative function.

Owing to the democratic structure of co-operatives, the constituency of the board is the larger membership. Effective board directors represent the interests of their constituents within executive-level, decision-making processes. Often, this representative function is carried out consciously as well as unconsciously. This is to say that board members may actively consult co-op members on a particular decision, such as opening a new branch or service location. At the same time, however, board members also help to represent the membership via their unique sets of personal experiences and social characteristics.

Although this unconscious or latent representation function is easy to overlook, it is nevertheless important. This essay discusses the connection between effective board leadership and representational diversity. Many analysts are calling for increased diversity in co-op governance, but there seems to be much confusion about how to approach the issue.[2] The main objective here is to demystify the concept of diversity. First, the discussion below considers why the goal of diversity is often difficult to achieve, and reviews some key theoretical propositions about its importance. Then, we consider how to "operationalize" the concept of diversity, or ground its abstract ideals in the real world. Finally, we provide some strategies for measuring and enhancing a board's level of representational diversity.

Leadership, Diversity, and Democratic Representation

The principle of member representation is given much lip service within the literature on co-operative governance, and many people may assume that representative leadership occurs simply as a function of the democratic process. There is not necessarily a connection, however, between organizational democracy and representational diversity. Several recent studies suggest that considerable deliberate planning and effort is required to create and sustain a representative leadership body.[3] Indeed, within the co-op sector as well as Canadian society generally, representational diversity increasingly is identified as a central, but elusive, governance objective.

The demographic composition of Canadian society is changing dramatically in response to trends in the birthrate, the ageing of the baby-boomer generation, and demands for skilled workers. Measured in terms of immigrants per capita, no other country in the world relies so heavily on the arrival of new citizens as does Canada. The federal and provincial governments continue to carefully track changes in the composition of Canada's population because they must anticipate how these changes will influence public policy. These same trends and pressures influence groups and organizations within Canadian society. Many firms, nonprofit groups, and voluntary associations monitor societal change for the purpose of estimating the future effects of current trends. It is interesting to note, however, that most co-operatives do not regularly track changes in the composition of their membership. Curiously, and with the exception of credit unions, the co-op sector generally lags behind other sectors in terms of collecting sectoral, organizational, and membership statistics.[4]

In part, this reluctance may owe much to the tenets of the traditional co-op model. Here, the democratic method of board elections ideally carries with it the potential for diverse interests to be represented in executive decision making. It is assumed that because members own the co-op and govern themselves, and because they select their own leaders, the characteristics of members and leaders are coincident, if not identical. Certainly, this model has many merits, and still may function relatively well within smaller co-operatives, where the ratio of board members to co-op members is rather low. The scale of co-operative membership has exploded in several areas, however, over the last twenty years. Mountain Equipment Co-operative, for example, is a consumer co-op with more than 1.5 million members, and operations in most major Canadian cities. As its business grows, soon one in five adult Canadians may hold an MEC membership.[5] Can we expect the traditional ten-person-board model to represent the social diversity inherent in a few million people? As the scale of co-op membership increases owing to factors such as success in the marketplace or co-op mergers, boards face many large challenges in representing their increasingly diverse memberships.

The discussion in the preceding paragraph suggests that the representational diversity found in smaller-scale, traditional co-operatives may be diminishing as co-ops change, grow, and adapt to new market environments and realities. However, there are many examples of traditional co-operatives that have lacked, and continue to lack, representational diversity among board members. At this point, it is useful to pause and consider briefly why representational diversity is a difficult goal to achieve. Why do so many boards fail to resemble the composition of their memberships?

This question is a variant of a general inquiry that has been posed many times concerning the nature of elites. Studies of social elites and organizational leaders confirm that most human organizations are susceptible to a common phenomenon known as elite capture. Over time, the mechanisms of governance become dominated by leaders who share certain values, characteristics, and traits, and lack others. The phenomenon has other labels. In the field of women's studies, for example, this is known as the rule of "the higher, the fewer." Here, as one reviews an organization's hierarchy, positions with more status, power, prestige, or benefits are populated by few women. In the field of political science, this is referred to as Putnam's Law. In administrative and sociological studies, another expression is found in Michel's Iron Law of Organization, where "he who says organization, says oligarchy." Any organized group, necessarily, is "ruled" by a select few. The phenomenon of elite capture seems to permeate most sorts of human institutions, even those designed specifically to avoid this problem.

In and of itself, this phenomenon is not necessarily problematical. In the corporate world, for example, it is quite normal for people holding senior management jobs to share certain attitudes, interests, educational credentials, and even recreational hobbies such as golf or tennis. Elite capture does not necessarily imply the organization's demise. Indeed, many sorts of organizations have functioned for a very long time without highly representative leadership. For example, the membership of Canada's central chamber of democracy—the House of Commons—only slowly has changed to encompass representatives of the many diverse groups present in the polity. Even today, numerically large groups such as women voters remain underrepresented in Parliament. While the House continues to function fairly well, however, there is little doubt that its legitimacy increasingly is being questioned. It is interesting to note, for example, that many of those citizens pressing to change Canada's electoral system to a proportional representation regime argue that change is necessary because the House fails to represent the interests of minority parties and minority factions within parties. Similarly, many new governments in provinces such as British Columbia, Prince Edward Island, and Québec are seriously considering changing their voting systems because of widespread concern that the broad range of political preferences are not being adequately represented.

Although we can easily identify several sorts of democratic organizations where elite capture clearly exists without apparent harm or dysfunction, the two concepts, in fact, are intrinsically incompatible. Elite capture is a significant problem in democratic organizations because elite homogeneity contradicts the idea of democratic self-rule and the pluralistic notions embodied within the ideal of democratic representation. Beyond theoretical incompatibility, we can find many examples in the real world, as discussed above, of elite capture within democratic organizations. The point here, however, is that such cases are dysfunctional. While the costs may be hidden or ignored, they do exist and are revealed in many ways, such as when concerns are expressed about organizational legitimacy and democratic representation, or where membership begins to decline dramatically. Comparing highly representative boards with less representative organizations helps to illustrate some of the tangible benefits of diversity in governance.[6]

Many scholars have noted that certain structural factors seem to produce elite capture, or help to ensure its continuation. There is a large literature, for example, on how certain sorts of occupations enhance one's potential to be a board leader, while other job roles seem less conducive to board-level participation. As well, many studies suggest that other factors, such as one's educational attainment, age, or degree of family responsibility, correlate with low levels of leadership participation. In addition, a co-operative's particular organizational culture simply may send clear signals that certain sorts of people are not welcome or valued.[7] Finally, potential board members may be discouraged from seeking board election because they do not believe they have the necessary experience and qualifications.[8]

While one could go on at length about how the representational gap is created and how this implies large performance inefficiencies and unnecessary membership dissatisfaction, it is sufficient for the purposes of this paper to say that a lack of diversity on boards of governance seems to be inherent in most human organizations. It is reified by structural factors and it varies in severity, depending on the specific organization under study. This point leads to other questions, such as how, in reality, do we know when a particular board is unduly representative? How do we define diversity and recognize its presence or absence? These are good questions, partly because they require us to define diversity and to operationalize this abstract concept, or ground it in the real world. These tasks are addressed in the next section.

Defining Diversity

We can think about diversity in terms of *social diversity*.[9] Complex, heterogenous societies comprise millions of individuals who differ in terms of key characteristics such as culture, ethnicity, religion, gender, sexual orientation, language, age, sex, income level, and education. As microcosms of such societies, co-operatives reflect these multiple social characteristics within their memberships. So, social diversity may be defined as the breadth of social characteristics carried by the individual members of a group.

We may conceptualize social diversity in terms of two distinct categories: demographic diversity and functional diversity. The concept of *demographic diversity* refers to the descriptive categories commonly employed to describe an individual's social characteristics—one's ethnicity or sex or level of educational attainment, for example. The idea of demographic diversity assumes that simply incorporating more heterogeneity into a group's composition necessarily broadens the content of its decisions. Increasing the number of women from one to five on a ten-person board, for example, will produce better representation of women's interests and therefore more representative policy decisions.

On the one hand, this view makes sense because broadening the number of social characteristics represented in a group necessarily implies a reduction in elite homogeneity. On the other hand, it assumes that the presence of diverse demographic characteristics necessarily implies the overt representation of these interests. This assumption may be fallacious. The concept of demographic diversity assumes that it is sufficient to simply ensure the presence of overt social diversity. In other words, ensuring there are diverse "inputs" to board decision making ought to produce diversity in the board's "outputs."

The concept of demographic diversity is appealing because it is relatively easy to measure and understand. However, it has been criticized as an insufficient approach to the complexities of diversity. Simply being a woman, for example, does not mean one is able to represent the interests of all women. In addition, it is quite possible for a group of leaders to represent a heterogeneous set of social characteristics yet share homogenous perspectives. For example, a board with representatives from several ethnic groups and age cohorts may share the same middle-class, professional viewpoint on key issues such as tax redistribution. So, while demographic diversity is important, there is another, more substantive, category: *functional diversity*. As the name suggests, the emphasis here moves beyond the appearance of diversity to ensure that board decisions reflect multiple perspectives. Towards securing functional diversity, a co-operative's governance processes and policymaking functions are designed to maximize the incorporation of diverse voices, interests, and perspectives.[10] The focus shifts towards ensuring that social diversity is represented in the output of board decisions, as well as among the inputs to decision making.

OPERATIONALIZING DIVERSITY

Having reviewed the theoretical arguments for more socially diverse boards, and having defined diversity in two ways, the next step is to operationalize these concepts, or develop real-world indicators for theoretical abstractions and then identify means to measure their presence (or absence). Although there are many sorts of specific strategies, the focus here is on a few commonly used means for measuring board diversity.

Most authors agree that the first step in operationalizing the concept of board diversity is to adopt a definition or definitions. As noted above, this article recognizes two types of diversity: demographic and functional. Now we must define the context. To be useful in the real world, abstract statements about whether there is more or less diversity must be grounded in reference to a specific group. The composition of a group supplies the context necessary for the investigation. As well, it is worth noting that a theoretical statement such as "boards ought to have more diverse social representation than they do" contains a latent comparative reference. This is to say that most efforts to enhance board diversity are based on an inherent comparison between what is and what ought to be. Recognizing this comparative dimension helps us to study the issue, because it permits us to locate or identify a model or standard against which to measure a board's current level of diversity.

The group comprising the co-operative's membership supplies the starting point for judging whether the goal of adequate social diversity in board representation has been achieved. This is a sensible starting point both theoretically and practically. Theoretically, the idea of diversity implies the presence of multiple characteristics and identities within a community, so to begin to grasp the diversity inherent in a community, we must focus on the community or group that is of interest to us. Second, in the real world, co-operators concerned with board diversity issues normally have a specific co-operative in mind. Recognizing the sorts of identities currently present and absent among the membership allows us to compare whether, and to what degree, the board is representative of the membership.

How do we determine the representational characteristics of a co-op's key constituencies? Although this may appear to be an easy task, John Carver notes that identifying the stakeholders may be difficult as well as controversial.[11] While some may argue that one ought to survey all those who use a co-op's services or buy its goods, surely most people will agree that persons holding a membership constitute the core group at the centre of any co-operative. To understand this group's characteristics, in smaller co-ops such as those with memberships of less than one hundred people, it may be possible to collect data from the entire group, perhaps through a short survey administered at an annual general meeting. Alternatively, the information may be obtained by distributing a mail-in survey form. In the case of larger memberships, surveying all the members probably will be impossible. Here, if the resources are available, employing a survey research firm to collect the necessary information may be the most reliable and economically efficient method. Using probability sampling techniques, most survey firms are capable of lending insight into the membership's characteristics based on the responses of three or four hundred people.

In the case of both small and large co-op memberships, survey questions ought to collect information that reflects how the concept of diversity has been defined. For example, if one is interested in probing a membership's demographic diversity, a proper questionnaire ought to give respondents a full range of options in key categories such as age, cultural background, and economic level. At the same time, it is worth mentioning that surveys with rigid response parameters may not be sufficiently flexible. It is difficult to anticipate all the possible demographic characteristics that respondents recognize as part of their individual identities. One method for overcoming such limitations is to employ questions with open-ended response options to encourage respondents to indicate the presence of important identity characteristics. For reasons such as marriage or adoption, for example, some people may have strong ties to a group outside their own specific background. Asking respondents, "Do you identify with any other cultural or ethnic group beyond your parent's main cultural background?" may help to reveal this subscription. If diversity has been defined as more than simply the overt appearance of difference, more complex questions testing underlying attitudes and perceptions are likely required. For example, questions about whether members believe that their co-op operates in ways that serve the interests of minority groups may be as important as whether the member actually belongs to an underrepresented group.

Once basic information about the composition of the co-op's membership has been collected, the same sort of information is required with respect to the board. Surveys may be administered by interviewers or self-administered by the board members. Precisely because it is up to most boards to initiate change aimed at remedying the overrepresentation of certain groups, it is worth asking board respondents directly about their views on enhanced diversity. It may be that change will only proceed once board members recognize their own limitations as well as the presence of attitudinal barriers to change.

Finally, the results for the two groups are compared. Deficiencies ought to be easily apparent as the characteristics of the co-op's membership are set against those of the board. It is worth repeating that there is much merit in treating information about the membership's composition as the baseline for assessing the level of diversity. This baseline provides the real-world model for efforts to increase diversity. Moreover, critics of enhanced diversity strategies have difficulty arguing that a board should *not* reflect the composition of its membership. The concept of representative democracy legitimates using the make-up of the membership as the model for the board. Although it is normally not possible to represent all the characteristics of the membership within a board, modelling the board in view of the membership's main attributes is a rational and defensible strategy.

One final note concerns addressing the issue of functional diversity. In this case, ensuring that the board's overt characteristics reflect those of the membership is a necessary condition, but not a sufficient one. Because functional diversity focusses on the representation of multiple interests in the creation of board decisions as well as on the actual decisions taken, other indicators are necessary. One method for measuring the level of functional diversity is to probe the level of interest fragmentation and conflict in board discussions. Disagreement and conflict are not necessarily bad. In fact, authors who sing the praises of functional diversity suggest that healthy boards do not necessarily agree on key issues precisely because multiple perspectives are being articulated in board discussions.[12] Efforts to measure a board's functional diversity may have to move beyond survey techniques to examine the structure of interests on the board, the tenacity of particular voting patterns, and whether certain coalitions of board members always dominate key discussions and votes.

Positive Remedies

This discussion aims at explaining why increasing board diversity is beneficial, and how we may think about diversity both abstractly and in the real world. It is beyond the scope of this article to review the many strategies for expanding representational diversity in concrete terms. To point readers towards such useful strategies, however, this last section briefly reviews three options recommended by many leading authors.

Once deficiencies in board representation have been identified, solutions must be found and implemented. One widely supported strategy is to recruit candidates from underrepresented groups. Karen Hughes suggests that many female board members are recruited through informal personal networks by sitting board members or the CEO. Another useful approach is to address structural barriers to board participation. Say, for example, that a co-op board lacks representation from a certain geographic area owing to a large distance between the head office and the branch operation. In this case, rotating meetings between the two locations may offer a way to minimize the time and travel costs imposed on potential board participants. A third strategy to improve board diversity is to concentrate on creating a change-oriented environment. Making small changes designed at increasing inclusiveness can have large effects in the board environment. Moving to gender-neutral language, for example, or inviting speakers to give presentations on key issues such as new Aboriginal economic development strategies may accomplish much in terms of making board members feel comfortable. Such changes are also important in terms of signalling a strong commitment to increased diversity to the membership, staff, and stakeholders.

Conclusion

The call for increased diversity in board governance is heard frequently among co-operators. To many people, however, the concept seems vague or intangible, and there is some consternation as to how to answer this call. In an effort to demystify the notion of diversity, this essay reviewed the theoretical connection between effective board leadership and representational diversity. We considered how to "operationalize" the concept, or ground its abstract ideals in the real world. Finally, we provided some strategies for measuring and enhancing a board's level of representational diversity. In conclusion, it may be comforting to know that there is no one "right way" to understand diversity or facilitate its presence. Particularly in the case of co-operatives, enhancing board diversity is a goal with considerable democratic and economic merit. Studying the characteristics of the membership supplies insight into what sorts of groups and interests ought to be represented, and there are several solid, tested strategies for addressing representative deficiencies.

Endnotes

1. R.D. Herman and D.O. Renz, "Thesis on Nonprofit Organizational Effectiveness," *Nonprofit Voluntary Sector Quarterly* 28 (1999): pp. 107–25; John Carver, *Boards That Make a Difference: A New Design for Leadership in Nonprofit and Public Organizations* (San Francisco: Jossey-Bass, 1997).
2. For example, see Muriel Draaisma, "Electing a Balanced Board," *Credit Union*

Way (July/August 1998): p. 18; Jamie Swedburg, "The Board Balancing Act," *Credit Union Management* (September 2002): pp. 42–45.

3. See, for example, Karen D. Hughes, *Women and Corporate Directorships in Canada: Trends and Issues* (Ottawa: Canadian Policy Research Networks, Discussion Paper no. CPRN/01, September 2000); Heather Berthoud and Robert D. Greene, "A Multifaceted Look at Diversity: Why Outreach Is Not Enough," *The Journal of Volunteer Administration* 19, no. 2 (Spring 2001): pp. 2–10; L. Jacques Menard, "Une saine gouvernance pour preserver nos avoirs collectifs," *Policy Options* 24, no. 3 (Nov 2003): pp. 40–45.

4. Angela Wagner, Carol Shepstone, and Cristine de Clercy, "A Compendium of Co-operative Statistical Collections in Canada and the United States" (Saskatoon: Centre for the Study of Co-operatives, forthcoming).

5. Membership information posted on the Mountain Equipment Co-operative website, 1 September 2003, at http://www.mec.ca/Main/content_text.jsp?FOLDER%3C%3Efolder_id=619583&bmUID=1063660527685.

6. For example, see David A.H. Brown, Debra L. Brown, and Vanessa Anastasopoulos, *Women on Boards: Not Just the Right Thing, But the "Bright" Thing* (Ottawa: The Conference Board of Canada, 2002).

7. For further information about other factors related to why some groups are underrepresented on boards, see Conseil Canadien de la Coopération, *A Boon for the Future: The Participation of Women in Co-operative Democracy* (Ottawa: Conseil Canadien de la Coopération/Canadian Co-operative Association, 1996); Hughes; Lou Hammond Ketilson and Leona Theis, *Research for Action: Women in Co-operatives* (Saskatoon: Centre for the Study of Co-operatives, 1994).

8. Hughes, pp. 8–9.

9. John Michael Daley and Flavio Francisco Marsiglia, "Social Diversity Within Non-Profit Boards: Members' Views on Status and Issues," *Journal of the Community Development Society* 32, no. 2 (2001): p. 291.

10. Ibid.

11. See Carver.

12. See Daley and Marsiglia, also William A. Brown, "Inclusive Governance Practices in Nonprofit Organizations and Implications for Practice," *Nonprofit Management and Leadership* 14, no. 2 (Summer 2002): pp. 369–85.

REFERENCES NOT APPEARING IN THE ENDNOTES

Rogers, Diane. "Women Still Scarce in Board Rooms." *The Western Producer*, 17 October 2002, p. 91.

WARREN WEIR AND WANDA WUTTUNEE

RESPECTFUL RESEARCH IN ABORIGINAL COMMUNITIES AND INSTITUTIONS IN CANADA

INTRODUCTION

IN HER BOOK *Decolonizing Methodologies: Research and Indigenous Peoples,* Linda Tuhiwai Smith states "The word itself, 'research,' is probably one of the dirtiest words in the Indigenous world's vocabulary."[1] In Canada, Aboriginal peoples describe themselves as "the most researched peoples in the world." They believe that they have been "researched to death" and that nothing good has ever come from the research activities in which they have been involved.

It is no secret why research is viewed in such a negative light in so many Indigenous communities across Canada and around the world. Academic scholars have used it to legitimize and further their own careers without acknowledging or giving credit to the people or communities involved. Government departments intent on categorizing, marginalizing, and/or assimilating Indigenous citizens have sponsored research in an effort to further their colonial policies. Corporations have exploited Indigenous communities in an attempt to profit from their resources and knowledge. In extreme cases, corporate interests have funded "bio-pirates" to "steal" Indigenous biological and environmental knowledge. Fortunately, approaches for research on Aboriginal peoples are undergoing positive change.

A growing number of Indigenous communities are starting to control and conduct their own research activities. In addition, Aboriginal institutions are beginning to manage research activities in their communities through the development of research codes, protocol agreements, or legislation. At the same time, other institutions such as universities and governments are developing policies specifically designed to guide and direct ethical research involving Aboriginal peoples and communities. Researchers are making efforts to learn about the Aboriginal communities in which they work or plan to work, and are also creating new approaches to research that situate the Aboriginal community as an active participant in the process. This trend includes an acknowledgement of the centrality of local Indigenous peoples and the value of their knowledge and ideas.

Despite their concerns, not all Aboriginal communities or institutions have developed their own unique approach to research, researchers, and research activities. And due to a lack of connection and opportunities, some researchers have been unable to apply their newfound knowledge of Indigenous peoples and participatory research methods. Nor have all research institutions been successful in developing effective and mutually beneficial relationships in and with Aboriginal communities.

While researchers, institutions, and Indigenous communities are developing guidelines and approaches that promote *respectful* research methodologies, it is not altogether clear what this means *in practice*. We feel that these methodologies are beginning to emerge, and that the challenge now is to further their evolution through the development and maintenance of research *relationships*—partnerships based on negotiated and mutually agreed upon terms of reference. Clearly defined relationships will help to ensure that the emerging ethical research guidelines are applied in ways that are agreeable and useful to everyone concerned.

This paper acknowledges and applauds those institutions, researchers, and Aboriginal communities—in Canada and around the world—that are developing research relationships and finding ways to make research in, with, and for Aboriginal communities more respectful, ethical, transparent, and relevant. The paper will:

- identify ways in which researchers, research institutions, and Indigenous and other institutions and communities are developing ways to make research work for Aboriginal communities;
- describe participatory research approaches that are well suited to be respectful to and thoughtful of the Aboriginal communities and all participants involved;
- describe key examples where respectful research relationships are being built; and
- suggest that lessons emerging from research practices in Aboriginal communities can inform how research is approached in Aboriginal institutions, including co-operatives.

The paper concludes with thoughts and observations on the practice of respectful research in Aboriginal communities and institutions in Canada. In our experience, respectful research relationships must acknowledge and tend to the needs of everyone involved, including the researcher, the research institution, and the community. Definitions of respectful research will become more clear through negotiation, ongoing communication, and consideration of evolving participant needs. If these relationships are to be nurtured and sustained, the idea of respect must be specifically and operationally defined, which will, in turn, enhance the quality of research being undertaken.

Researchers, Research Institutions, and the Aboriginal Community

In the past, research concerning Aboriginal peoples has usually been initiated outside the Aboriginal community and carried out by non-Aboriginal personnel. Aboriginal people have had almost no opportunity to correct misinformation or to challenge ethnocentric and racist interpretations.
—Royal Commission on Aboriginal Peoples, 1996

Residents in Canadian Aboriginal communities tend to talk about and view research in both negative and positive ways. On the one hand, describing themselves as "the most researched peoples in the world" and believing that they have been "researched to death," they feel that research has afforded no positive outcomes for them or their communities, and are tired of being defined and described by outside agents who refer to them in merely statistical terms. On the other hand, a growing number of Aboriginal people, including leaders and community economic development officers, believe that information derived from research is essential to making the timely and effective decisions required for self-governance and economic self-sufficiency. On the whole, Indigenous peoples are supporting research they believe will inform and enhance their ability to make decisions and plan for the future of their communities. They realize that the creation of knowledge, when done in respectful ways, can be enhanced through clearly defined partnerships with noncommunity institutions and researchers, and that these relationships can lead to the improvement of research capacities within the community.

Across Canada and around the world, a number of groups are discussing, developing, clarifying, and promoting ideas about respectful research methods in Aboriginal communities. First, many Indigenous communities and institutions are developing guidelines, codes, and/or legislation in an effort to promote, control, and enhance the benefits research can bring to their peoples and communities. Second, mainstream institutions—primarily universities, interest groups, and government agencies—are developing policies specifically designed to guide and direct ethical research involving Aboriginal people. Third, researchers are learning how to be informed partners in Aboriginal research initiatives. Using Canadian and international examples, the following sections highlight some of the activities of these three groups.

Indigenous Community-Based Initiatives

Not all Indigenous communities in Canada are ready, willing, or able to lead their own research activities. Some believe that outside researchers and institutions still need to play a critical role in this work. Hence, a growing number of Aboriginal communities and organizations continue to partner with and employ individuals and academic institutions to assist them in their community-based research endeavours.

Some communities have developed or are in the process of developing strategies to conduct their own research activities, such as gathering and analysing data, interpreting what the data means to them, and disseminating knowledge to their citizens and other interested parties. Many of these communities partner with experts to develop their research capacity. Others are sending their students to college or university to learn about research methods, the analysis of data, and the informational requirements of policy development.

Other Indigenous communities look to research guidelines that have been developed and promoted through bodies such as the International Indian Treaty Council, an organization of Indigenous peoples from North, Central, and South America, and the Pacific. With support from the World Health Organization,[2] the council is in the process of developing participatory research management guidelines for Indigenous peoples and institutions undertaking collaborative health research.

National Aboriginal organizations do the same for research in Aboriginal communities in Canada. *Negotiating Research Relationships: A Guide for Communities*,[3] an oft-cited working paper by the Nunavut Research Institute and the National Inuit Tapirisat of Canada (now the Inuit Tapiriit Kanatami), for example, includes the following twelve principles developed through consultation with members of the Inuit community:

1. Informed consent should be obtained from the community and from any individuals involved in research.
2. In seeking informed consent, the researcher should at least explain the purpose of the research, sponsors of research, the person in charge, potential benefits and possible problems associated with the research for people and the environment, research methodology, participation of or contact with residents of the community.
3. Anonymity and confidentiality must be offered and, if accepted, guaranteed, except where this is legally precluded.

4. Ongoing communication of research objectives, methods, findings, and interpretation from inception to completion of project should occur.
5. If, during the research, the community decides the research is unacceptable, the research should be suspended.
6. Serious efforts must be made to include local and traditional knowledge in all stages of research, including problem identification.
7. Research design should endeavour to anticipate and provide meaningful training of Aboriginal researchers.
8. Research must avoid social disruption.
9. Research must respect the privacy, dignity, cultures, traditions, and rights of Aboriginal people.
10. Written information should be available in the appropriate language(s).
11. The peer review process must be communicated to the communities, and their advice and/or participation sought in the process.
12. Aboriginal people should have access to research data, not just receive summaries and research reports. The extent of data accessibility that participants/communities can expect should be clearly stated and agreed upon as part of any approval process.

Today, most community and institutional research guidelines reflect similar themes promoted through these twelve basic principles.[4]

Other national and regional Aboriginal organizations assist with research at the local level. A number of Manitoba First Nation communities, for example, get direction on research in which they are becoming involved through the guidance of the Assembly of Manitoba Chiefs.

In the United States, the American Indian Law Center has developed a tribally-based legislative approach to research in Indigenous communities in their *Model Tribal Research Code,* which is based on the views that:

> Over the years, research has produced many good things for our society in general and for Indian people in particular.

Many, if not most, researchers are sincere and dedicated professionals who want to help Indian communities solve their health and social problems and preserve their cultural heritage, and in the process to be sensitive to the legitimate needs of the individuals and communities with which they work. But governments, unfortunately, cannot assume that everyone will act according to the highest standards. Legislation is necessary where there are, or might be, problems affecting society in an important way. In order to look at tribal legislation regulating research on Indian reservations, then, we must look at the worst-case situations resulting from research and determine whether the tribal government should act.... Some of these issues are matters of professional ethics among the various research professions and, at the very least, matters of common courtesy and basic respect for human dignity.... In fairness to researchers, the expectations of the Indian community may not always be clear to them, and a published set of tribal standards embodied in a regulatory process may be helpful.[5]

Materials in the American Indian Law Center publication—which includes a research checklist—have been designed to provide Indian tribes (and other Indigenous communities) "both a framework within which the tribe's expectations will be clearly articulated to would-be researchers, governments, and other funding agencies, and a clear process for compliance."[6]

Local Indigenous communities across Canada are developing their own approach to research that takes into account their local histories, political structures, stories, traditions, language, and cultural practices. The Central Region Nuu-chah-nulth First Nations, for example, have developed a community-based "Template Letter of Informed Consent" for research involving their peoples, their knowledge, and Nuu-chah-nulth land and resources.[7]

Of course, principles, guidelines, and codes of conduct are not necessarily enforceable in courts of law. As Brascoupé and Endemann argue, with respect to traditional knowledge:

Guidelines should reflect how a community wishes to use and control its traditional knowledge [and research in the Indigenous community]. For example, obtaining informed consent from the Aboriginal community when traditional knowledge is shared with others, or when Aboriginal symbols or photographs of Aboriginal people are used in advertising. Guidelines may raise awareness and define expectations of Aboriginal people with respect to the sharing of traditional knowledge. As guidelines [and codes of conduct] are not enforceable in court, however, they can only be enforced through sanctions within an Aboriginal community or be used as principles of conduct.[8]

Guidelines and codes of conduct provide guidance to those truly committed to respectful and meaningful research in Aboriginal communities. If the information is important and valuable, and the Aboriginal leaders are justifiably concerned about the way in which the research will proceed, the community may want to utilize a legal contract to spell out its rights with respect to the research process and the use of the findings. Many argue, however, that the contract should be broad and flexible in order to be tailored to suit the needs of every research request that seems viable.[9]

Institutional Initiatives

While Aboriginal communities are discussing and developing their own community-based legislation and research protocols, institutions concerned about this type of work in Aboriginal communities are developing research and ethics guidelines of their own. The Royal Commission on Aboriginal Peoples,[10] for example, developed and implemented guidelines for ethical research in advance of work done by or for the commission. MiningWatch Canada,[11] a pan-Canadian initiative supported by environmental, social justice, Aboriginal, and labour organizations across the country, has developed a framework for capacity-building research. The Wildlife Management Advisory Council[12] makes use of a research guide that meets requirements set out in the Inuvialuit Final Agreement, and the International Development Research Centre has a guide for individuals researching Indigenous knowledge.[13]

Institutions developing guidelines for research in Aboriginal communities are doing this not only out of self-interest or in reaction to the protocols beginning to emerge in Aboriginal communities. Many of these institutions are sincerely interested in proving that they can conduct their work in ways that are respectful and promote the shared creation of knowledge and understanding.

Very few, if any, universities in Canada have overarching institutional guidelines and binding protocols for research in Aboriginal communities,[14] although there appears to be a growing recognition of the need. The office of the vice-president academic presented a "Conceptual Framework for Aboriginal Initiatives" to its University of Saskatchewan Council in late 2001, which recommended, in part, the development of a research protocol on Aboriginal topics.[15] Universities and colleges in Canada often talk about relations with Indigenous peoples in their strategic plans or presidential addresses, but to date the activities surrounding education and research relationships with Aboriginal communities usually take place within specific departments with little institutional direction, control, or support.

A number of international universities are beginning to establish and utilize formal institutional guidelines that promote the conduct of culturally appropriate, respectful, and nonexploitive research. The University of Otago in New Zealand, for example, in its Policy for Research Consultation with Maori, states a "commitment to partnership with Maori consistent with the Treaty of Waitangi and the University's stated objectives."[16] The research office of the University of Canterbury, also in New Zealand, clarifies the importance of the Treaty of Waitangi, stating in one of its five guiding principles:

> In order to give effect to the University's obligations under the Treaty of Waitangi, researchers whose projects raise ethnic issues involving a significant proportion of Maori participants should pay particular attention to the following:
>
> (i) the need to consult with an appropriate Maori body and, if necessary, to obtain permission for access to participants and to carry out the research,
>
> (ii) the need to recognize Maori attitudes to ownership of information that they supply, and

(iii) the desirability of obtaining advice from, for example, a member of the University's Maori community at an early stage of planning a project that is intended to involve a significant number of Maori participants.[17]

The institutional work in Canada also takes place through educational associations and research alliances that often include corporate and government representation and input. Much of the discussion in this regard has taken place within the Association of Canadian Universities for Northern Studies (ACUNS),[18] a voluntary association of thirty-five Canadian universities and colleges with northern programs and interests, which adopted a statement of "Ethical Principles for the Conduct of Research in the North" in 1982 (revised in 1997). Participants believed that "guidelines, or principles, are needed to provide a foundation for and to foster a mutual understanding of community and researcher needs and goals and to ensure that research is carried out with the least friction and social disruption and the most co-operation and support."[19] The twenty ACUNS ethical principles "are intended to encourage the development of co-operation and mutual respect between researchers and the people of the North. They are also intended to encourage partnerships between northern peoples and researchers that will, in turn, promote and enhance northern scholarship."[20]

Many northern communities have established research institutes with specific protocols that aim to rectify the imbalance between researchers and the communities by requiring community input, guidance, and approval. In addition to ACUNS, other examples include the Science Institute of Northwest Territories, the Nunavut Research Institute, and the Yukon Science Institute.

Canadian federal, provincial, and municipal governments are also developing policy and guidelines that facilitate ethical research in Aboriginal communities. Indian and Northern Affairs Canada (INAC) recently commissioned "A Community Guide to Protecting Indigenous Knowledge." Written by Brascoupé and Mann, the guide was developed "to empower communities to recognize, protect, preserve and share their [Indigenous] knowledge in keeping with their goals and traditions."[21] It outlines in accessible language the ways in which communities might organize, among other things, to gather and assess information. With useful tips on issues to consider and items to be included, the guide also touches on the importance of "written documents that are developed by the community to guide researchers inside and outside the community on what is expected of them."[22]

The Social Sciences and Humanities Research Council (SSHRC) recently initiated the development of program and policy considerations regarding Aboriginal research. In 2002, SSHRC's board of directors made Aboriginal research a priority and set about to gather advice from "over 500 individuals from a wide variety of Aboriginal, academic, government and nongovernmental organizations" in its "Opportunities in Aboriginal Research: Results of SSHRC's Dialogue on Research and Aboriginal Peoples."[23] The dialogue provides an excellent example of a thoughtful and collaborative effort to both promote "knowledge opportunities" while envisioning a "set of measures designed to correct situations in which positive and full development of the research potential represented by Aboriginal researchers and their respective knowledge traditions is impeded."[24] One of the impediments listed is the "lack of respect for Aboriginal peoples and their knowledge traditions."[25]

Researcher Initiatives

Of course, researchers continue to conduct studies in Aboriginal communities and organizations. Many researchers—like us—have an ongoing interest in better understanding the Aboriginal world that exists in Canada. We fulfil this role as partners, colleagues, and as members of Aboriginal communities and organizations.

Individuals new to Aboriginal research are preparing to engage the communities by learning about their peoples, cultures, and histories through university courses or by participating in relationship-building activities within Aboriginal organizations and communities. Experienced research consultants and academics typically visit the community in advance of the research taking place to learn as much as possible about the peoples and communities involved.

Researchers utilize existing guides and ideas developed and presented by other researchers with similar experiences. Piquemal,[26] for example, outlines four principles to guide research with Aboriginal peoples, while Davis and Reid[27] explore the impact of historical concerns with research in American Indian communities on attempts to promote respectful research in those communities today.

Increasingly, Indigenous researchers are presenting models that reflect the concerns aired by their communities.[28] They gather to discuss the issues at meetings such as the Aboriginal Strategies Conference[29] and the forum Indigenous Research: What's It About?[30] Aboriginal and other researchers are also publishing materials on Indigenous issues and communities, which act as guides to further research in and with Aboriginal peoples.[31]

More and more frequently, researchers are taking part in collaborative research practices using participatory methods that promote a respectful approach to research in Aboriginal communities. These methods are examined in the following section.

RESEARCH METHODS THAT WORK FOR ABORIGINAL COMMUNITIES

Science is becoming very important in the North, and the Inuit must become involved in all levels of research or be left even further behind. This includes carrying out our own studies; working more co-operatively with scientists from the south; developing training programs and school curriculums in science; and collecting and utilizing our own knowledge and understanding of our culture and environment. It must also include the political aspects of science so that Inuit can gain a stronger voice in controlling the type of problems that are to be studied, determining the best way to do these studies, and to make sure that Inuit receive a fair share of research funds.

—Daniel Weetaluktuk,[32] Inuit scientist and researcher

Participatory and collaborative research methods allow researchers and communities a process that, at least in theory, minimizes the problems associated with the research of the past while accentuating the positive possibilities of research in Aboriginal communities. Appropriate participatory methodologies create an environment that acknowledges and values the needs of both the community and researcher. Participatory methods define research as a two-way street that offers ways of incorporating the researchers' understanding of the community while acknowledging the critical role of community members. Participatory research makes room for oral tradition, unique world views, and perspectives that might otherwise be lost or considered meaningless. It would be difficult today, in fact, for anyone to propose research in an Aboriginal community that did not promote community participation and collaboration.

Researchers select participative methodologies because they are not overly theoretical, but support instead a practical approach that is culturally sensitive, seeks to include community members, and values their voices. A set of research methods generally defined as Participatory Action Research (PAR) is becoming more acceptable to Aboriginal communities as individual residents become skilled and capable researchers through training incorporated into the research plan. Communities approve of this approach because they "own" the research questions and the results,[33] maintaining shared ownership of, and playing an integral part in, the research process. Research results are not the goal, but rather provide the tools for the community to meet its own research and community development goals.[34]

A pragmatic and useful approach within the PAR framework— Community Participation (CP) research—proactively includes the community within the parameters of the project being undertaken. According to Ryan and Robinson:

> CP is a method of community-based research that involves an outside facilitator or trainer and a small group of community people in a focussed project of short duration, usually from three to six months. It is distinguished from PAR in that it involves less training, less institutional development, less political change, and less cost.... CP projects have a marked practical orientation, and they often result in the negotiation of co-management agreements, investment plans, or rapid program evaluations.[35]

CP has been used successfully in a number of land-use and -occupancy studies that have helped Aboriginal communities direct their strategies for developing natural resources in a way that is consistent with community values and not solely influenced by corporate bottom lines.[36] In the end, relationships between researchers and a community seek a *balance* that is different from the imbalance maintained in the dominant research paradigm. As Hall argues:

> The fundamental question is "Who has the right to create knowledge?" The vast majority of all social science research done is characterized by methods which limit analysis, and hence the ability to create knowledge, is left to persons working and living for the most part in isolation from the social realities they describe.[37]

Many believe that Aboriginal researchers are better equipped to lead research in their own communities. Debates around creating knowledge lie within the purview of mainstream researchers, while the main debates for Aboriginal researchers following a traditional path are to give thanks for the gift of understanding from the Creator. Hall's account is an accurate description of a social reality that grants little or no weight or validity to traditional knowledge, Elders, Aboriginal women, and in general, the wisdom that is the responsibility of Aboriginal society. Voices are effectively silenced. Examples include researchers who operate in areas occupied by Aboriginal peoples but who do not involve the residents. There is little, if any, communication. Community approval is not sought, nor are the research results shared.

> In some cases, these activities have led Aboriginal communities to charge individual investigators with unethical practice. And it is not uncommon to hear social scientists being accused of exploiting Aboriginal peoples by illegally trading in their artefacts, stealing their stories and experiences, and ultimately appropriating their right to present, promote, and benefit from their living legacy.

Questioning old precepts and attitudes creates ripples of discord within academic disciplines and may influence the work of some researchers. The impact of the unrest is often felt in the communities affected by the research. Within anthropology, for example, scientific humanism's purpose has been to deliver a message that "the ways of our society or of any given society are not the only imaginable or acceptable ones."[38] Validating diversity of experience necessitates a re-examination of the way in which researchers explore individuals and communities.

Most northern Aboriginal communities located in Nunavut, the Yukon, and the Northwest Territories support this re-examination, since the customary methods of conducting research about them, their communities, and their environment are becoming less and less acceptable. It is a challenge for academic disciplines to re-examine "claims of exclusive possession of specialized professional expertise and knowledge."[39] Postpositivist methodologies, such as Participatory Action Research and Community Participation research, are collaborative, empowering, and acknowledge the rights of the research subjects. In this scenario, research subjects develop and influence dialogue and information exchange that shapes knowledge and may help them to develop skills to complete the research themselves.[40] An inclusive research methodology, with room for both researcher and community members, breaks down the walls of academic obfuscation. Accuracy and clarity promote understanding for researcher and community alike. Inclusive methodologies "demystify," thus strengthening and validating research results for all those involved and affected.[41] Cultural, historical, and practical realities now have a place in negotiating what is mutually defined as "true" knowledge, and measurement standards become more broadly defined and more meaningful to both communities and academia. Measures of "success" in economic development, for example, can integrate crosscultural perspectives with Western social science and incorporate pluralist world views to "engender a shift in the direction of the pursuit of knowledge."[42]

Participatory Action Research methodologies not only provide ways and means to include the community in the research process; they also promote a change process whereby communities identify and solve their own problems with the assistance of researchers. These methodologies offer a number of advantages: the right for diverse voices to be heard; input into the research process; skill development in designing research, collecting data, and analysing the results; and the ultimate right to "control" the process and "own" the results.

Building Respectful Research

When Indigenous peoples become the researchers we move towards control over our futures. We begin to harness effective mechanisms by which communities themselves determine their own priorities and needs. In other words, this is an essential part of our own self-governance.

—Lionel Quartermaine,
keynote address opening the Indigenous Researchers' Forum,
Canberra, Australia, 2003[43]

People we talk to are not sure if respectful research with Aboriginal communities exists. We feel that respectful practices are starting to emerge, but that the key challenge now is in the development of respectful research *relationships*—partnerships based on negotiated and mutually-agreed-upon terms of reference that empower everyone involved, particularly those whose communities and practices are the subjects of the research. Clearly defined relationships that connect research institutions, researchers, Aboriginal communities, and other communities and interests in meaningful ways must be developed and maintained in order to ensure that the research approaches highlighted in guides are applied in ways that are agreeable and useful to all.

These types of partnerships are emerging on a case-by-case basis. As institutions and researchers contemplate the possibility of research opportunities in Aboriginal communities, negotiated agreements are developing that take into account Aboriginal concerns, legislation, and protocols, as well as generic, non-Aboriginal, institutional policies and ethical guidelines.

The following sections profile three examples of research partnerships currently at work in Aboriginal communities in Canada.

Understanding the Strengths of Indigenous Communities Project (USIC)

With the support of a federal government grant, a team of researchers and community-based people is working to identify the strengths of Aboriginal communities across Canada, studying eight examples that have unique aspects to offer the project.[44] Lead investigator Dr.

Cynthia Chataway, based at York University, heads a committee drawn from government, economic development, academia, and health to oversee the project. Although the research process is community based and participative, it is supported and reviewed by individuals representing academic, Aboriginal, government, and business interests at national, regional, and local levels through the National Project Oversight Committee, a Community Oversight Team, a University Support Committee, and a Community Research Team.

The eight communities have been involved in the research through focus groups, surveys, and several exercises in which they identified important community strengths and positive initiatives. In the process, citizens teach each other and build clarity about their community. The final products incorporate many opinions that have been developed by experienced and trained community members. This community-based approach will generate leading-edge policy recommendations and leave a lasting legacy for those involved.

The Clayoquot Alliance for Research, Education, and Training

The Clayoquot Alliance is a partnership of the University of Victoria and the First Nations and non–First Nations communities of the Clayoquot Sound Biosphere Reserve region, supported through the Clayoquot Biosphere Trust. The region is on the west coast of Vancouver Island near Pacific Rim National Park and Long Beach. One of the first tasks was the creation of a Protocols Project, the purpose of which was "to develop consensus on protocols/guidelines for community-based research in the Clayoquot Sound Biosphere Reserve region."[45] The Aboriginal partners include members of the five Central Region Nuu-chah-nulth Nations.

The Protocols Project "Standard of Conduct for Research in Northern Barkley and Clayoquot Sound Communities" was designed "to encourage mutually-beneficial research collaborations between local communities and researchers in ways that maximize benefits, share burdens fairly, minimize risks, support local participation, and make research results more locally meaningful."[46] Further, as its cornerstone for the collective effort, it highlights "respect for the well-being and interconnectedness of individuals, communities and ecosystems... [a] concept [that] is consistent with the Nuu-chah-nulth principles of

Iisaak (Living respect) and *Hishuk ish ts'awalk (Everything is one, or everything is connected)*."[47] The document is more than a set of guidelines; it is structured to facilitate research by providing prospective researchers contact information for inquiries and orientating them to Nuu-chah-nulth peoples and their territory, including the Pacific Rim National Park.

The authors conclude by reminding researchers "that whenever you are conducting your research, you are in someone's community or a First Nations territory. If you show patience, respect, and appreciation for the people, creatures, and places in whose communities you are a guest, your experience will be fulfilling and you and future researchers will continue to be welcomed back."[48] In effect, the "Standard of Conduct" relates respectful research to sustainable research practices.

Kahnawake Schools Diabetes Prevention Project

Officials initiated the Kahnawake Schools Diabetes Prevention Project (KSDPP) after a significant number of people in the area were diagnosed with Type II diabetes. With interventions clearly required to curb the high rate of the disease, education and activities targeting change began in schools with young Mohawk community members. The KSDPP focussed not only on the short-term objectives of increasing physical activity and healthy eating, but also sought to promote community capacity building and ownership while respecting Mohawk traditions and cultural ways. These objectives, along with support for "the respect for the scientific and social integrity of the project," facilitated the creation of a KSDPP Code of Research Ethics,[49] which outlines, among other things, the obligations of the academic researchers, community researchers, and the community partner.

Potvin et al.[50] evaluated the KSDPP once it was completed and used the experience to develop four principles for an implementation model for community-based programs:

1. the integration of community people and researchers as equal partners in every phase of the project;
2. the structural and functional integration of the intervention and evaluation research components;

3. the development of a flexible agenda responsive to demands from the broader environment; and
4. the creation of a project that represents learning for all those involved.

While these principles sound similar to guidelines discussed earlier in this chapter, the major difference is that they have been developed in relation to the lessons learned from a specific project that involved a community, researchers, and institutional partners. Perhaps even more significant is the authors' conclusion:

> The research component [of the project] was never conceived of as the project's driving force. Researchers were there to observe, and learn from, the experience this community was sometimes willing, and sometimes less willing, to have submitted to the reflexive process of research. This was partly responsible for creating an environment that was highly responsive to the synergy that emerged from the co-presence of both research and intervention components. Capitalising on this synergy allowed the programme to be responsive to the various and evolving needs of the partners. Because each partner's voice was heard and respected, constructive negotiation occurred allowing transformations in the programme in a way that did not threaten its identity. On the contrary, these transformations were seen as creating new opportunities for the programme to help the community develop its own vision of health.

In this case, research was not the driving force. It was an important, although seemingly secondary, task for those involved in the project. More important were the relationship building, negotiation, and intervention.

RESPECTFUL RESEARCH AND ABORIGINAL INSTITUTIONS IN CANADA

The Understanding the Strengths of Indigenous Communities project has been well received within our community. One of the main reasons is the fact that Aboriginal people have been involved in the creation of the research model, and community members continue to be involved in the research and analysis of the findings. An additional positive component has been the ongoing participation of our political leadership. Political interest in any project is key to forming partnerships with those who are seeking the information that will lead to the improvement of social and community development. Finally, members of our community have been formally trained in research protocol and conduct, matters of confidentiality, conducting qualitative surveys, facilitating focus groups, website design and development, and detailed analysis of research data. The training and education alone have set the project apart from so many others.

—Patrick Derocher, Flying Dust First Nation

The Aboriginal institution is an emerging participant in the discussions on the theoretical approach and practical application of respectful research in Aboriginal communities. There are thousands of Aboriginal organizations in Canada, representing a new and interesting area of research and field of inquiry. These organizations are owned, managed, and staffed by status and nonstatus Indian, Inuit, Métis, and non-Aboriginal peoples. They exist in every region in the country, where they perform profit, not-for-profit, and governmental tasks and functions. Research in these institutions may benefit from the discussion of collaborative and respectful research currently taking place in Aboriginal communities.

Frideres and Gadacz acknowledge that while research on Aboriginal organizations is gaining in importance as they have had "both a political and social impact on Canadian society…, little has been written about these organizations and the role they have played in the development of Canada."[51] Even less consideration has been given to research *within* Aboriginal institutions and organizations. Many argue that more research in and with Aboriginal organizations is required. Ketilson and MacPherson, in fact, mention research and the need to share information in eight of the nine major recommendations highlighted in their report, proposing an inclusive research process that is respectful of Aboriginal peoples, communities, and organizations.[52]

Although Indigenous organizations have existed for thousands of years, contemporary Aboriginal organizations in Canada have grown exponentially over the past forty years. In the mid-1980s, there were an estimated three thousand of them in Canada. This number had doubled by the early 1990s, with numbers now (2004) standing at about twenty-three thousand. There has been a tremendous growth in business and for-profit organizations in particular. In the early 1990s, 50 percent of the six thousand organizations were not-for-profit and governmental, while the other 50 percent were businesses. Today, about three thousand organizations continue to provide not-for-profit and governmental services to Aboriginal peoples and communities, while the number of businesses now stands at an astounding twenty thousand plus.[53]

Large organizations act at international, national, regional, and local levels, while smaller ones attend primarily to community needs and demands. Most important, many of these organizations are playing an increasingly active role in supporting movements by Aboriginal peoples in regaining control and authority over their own economic, social, and political affairs. This includes recovering, managing, and governing land and resources, defining and pursuing sustainable economic and social development, and promoting varied business and entrepreneurial activities. Ketilson and MacPherson, for example, found that there are more than 130 Aboriginal co-operatives operating in Canada.[54]

There is a great deal about Aboriginal organizations that is not generally known. Many questions have yet to be answered regarding location, size, growth, and type. Further analysis is necessary to examine issues related to human resource management, organizational goals and objectives, power, service and product types, funding, control, and larger questions of organizational efficiency and effectiveness. There is also a need to address the importance of tradition and Aboriginal values, consensus decision making, community participation and direction, and the effect and influence that Elders and hereditary leaders have on the organizing process.

Since Aboriginal organizations are different from those in the mainstream, it is essential that researchers approach the study of them in ways that respect and take into account such differences. Even within Aboriginal organizations located in urban settings, there are often implicit and influential cultural values and traditional norms and protocols at work.

Questions and concerns related to respectful research within and about Aboriginal organizations are fairly similar to those currently facing Aboriginal communities. There are differences, however, primarily related to the role Aboriginal communities should play when research is being entertained in their own, often fairly autonomous, institutions. If an individual is considering research on or in an Aboriginal organization, should they discuss the research process with the larger community first, or could they go straight to the organization and begin a research relationship? Would a researcher be bound to community research guidelines and protocols if the organization were located outside the Aboriginal community that created it?

The answers to these and other questions will probably differ from organization to organization and community to community depending, for example, on the role that the organization plays in the realization of larger community goals and objectives, the legitimate connection between the organization and the community (if any), and the ability of the organization to control research in accordance with larger community guidelines, protocols, and practices.

Research in Aboriginal Co-operatives

Research in Aboriginal co-operatives is a specific subset of respectful research in Aboriginal communities and institutions. The research relationship between co-ops and academics and institutions is generally acknowledged and clarified through the International Co-operative Alliance's thematic Committee on Co-operative Research. Formed in 1957, the members of the committee form a growing network of individual researchers from more than twenty countries in Europe, Australia, Asia, America, and Latin America. According to ICA materials, "The Committee is a bridge between academic research and the co-operative world. It aims at strengthening activities and making the work of researchers more visible, particularly to ordinary managers and co-operators. Questions concerning education, social audit, co-op principles, developing co-operative advantage and the emergence of new wave co-operatives have all been reviewed from both a practical and theoretical stance."[55]

Research on Aboriginal co-operatives in Canada will require a similar approach. Researchers and institutions as well as Aboriginal communities and co-op managers will have to work together to develop protocols and approaches that offer advantages to everyone concerned. Co-operative literature will benefit from the addition of knowledge and experience involving Aboriginal co-ops, and Aboriginal communities will gain a clearer understanding of the value of a co-operative approach in the development of their economic and political systems.

Colleagues working in Aboriginal economic development are already asking us questions about the viability of a co-operative approach in their communities. They see the value of research in determining whether this is a strategy they would want to consider. Approaches include canvassing community members for their opinions, determining community and political support, sharing stories of successful Aboriginal co-operatives, and learning about the trials and tribulations of starting and operating a co-op in an Aboriginal community. Researchers can assist with this initial work and can gain a deeper understanding of the "Aboriginal" aspects of co-operative activities in Indigenous communities, including the importance of Indigenous knowledge and values, the political aspects of owning and operating a business in an Aboriginal community, and developing a sense of community and co-op member identity within the Aboriginal context.

Conclusion

Aboriginal peoples have distinctive perspectives and understandings, deriving from their cultures and histories and embodied in Aboriginal languages. Research that has Aboriginal experience as its subject matter must reflect these perspectives and understandings.
—Royal Commission on Aboriginal Peoples, 1996

Although research is viewed in rather negative ways within many Aboriginal communities in Canada, its reputation is changing for the better as researchers and institutions are trying to make research in and for Aboriginal communities not only effective but also more respectful, thoughtful, and meaningful. It is the hope of the authors that respectful practices grow and mature as research relationships are created, developed, and managed. As some groups claim, however, it is one thing to create a solid research-based relationship that includes institutional representatives, researchers, and Aboriginal community partners who have done their work in understanding what a more meaningful and respectful approach to research is *in theory*. It is quite another to work together over time in ways that are respectful and meaningful to all involved *in practice*.

Informed researchers are learning that they can play an active role in minimizing the negative aspects of research in Aboriginal communities by thoughtfully utilizing participative and collaborative approaches. At the same time, Aboriginal communities that have experienced collaborative research that is thoughtful and respectful are finding that the experience not only provides the community with useful information, but that it also leads to capacity building within communities and for individual community members. Approaching research in respectful and thoughtful ways creates new, valid, and useful knowledge; sharing the process can also assist in rebuilding and strengthening healthy relationships both within Aboriginal communities and between Aboriginal and Canadian communities and institutions.

Challenges remain for communities, researchers, and institutions attempting to develop respectful partnerships that work. These relationships must acknowledge and tend to the needs of everyone involved, including the researcher, the research institution, and the community. Negotiation, ongoing communication, and maintaining the balance of evolving participant needs will nurture respectful research relationships and enhance the quality of the work being undertaken.

We have worked in and with Aboriginal communities and institutions for more than fifteen years, during which time we have interviewed hundreds of Indigenous managers, leaders, Elders, educators, and community economic development practitioners.[56] Over the past two years we have had the opportunity to focus on and share our thoughts and experiences about developing and utilizing respectful and thoughtful research in Aboriginal communities with dozens of other researchers and community practitioners. These discussions, which form the basis of this chapter, were inevitably enthusiastic and engaging, as individuals involved or planning on being involved have many questions about collaborative research methods and how to make them more respectful and meaningful.

Most of the researchers we talked to—particularly those connected to academic institutions—were aware of the literature on collaborative research and the guidelines and protocols about working in Aboriginal communities being developed by community and other groups. Community participants were often aware that such references existed, but were curious about where to find them and which ones we might recommend they look at first.

Key questions remain, however, particularly with regard to respectful research in Aboriginal communities *in practice*. Many researchers continue to struggle with questions such as: Does it matter if I am Aboriginal or not? How do I get fully accepted as a researcher in Aboriginal communities? How do I make contact with those individuals in the community who will help me start my research, and where do I begin? How can I get a response on my proposal?—If I don't get feedback soon, my funding will run out.

Many researchers comment on difficulties they have experienced when navigating institutional ethics procedures and community protocols in the name of respectful research. One Aboriginal student doing research for her degree took an entire year to work through all of the community and academic requirements necessary to earn the permission to proceed. This takes patience, time, and commitment on behalf of the researcher. Not everyone would be willing to undertake such a process.

Other researchers share stories about difficulties receiving feedback on interim reports. One person actually lost his funding because he could not get a response from the community in time to meet the date his funding agency had set. The research was important to the community and it promoted a participatory process, but the community partners simply did not act quickly enough to satisfy all of the other requirements.

Representatives from Aboriginal communities engaged in participatory research have also come to us looking for answers to pressing questions. One leader asked us how they might best handle researchers in their communities on a day-to-day basis. Specifically, she felt that while the research was important, the community had not thought about the organizational structure that should be in place to facilitate informed and timely research requirements and decisions.

Many community representatives displayed disappointment with the way in which work had proceeded in their community once the research partnership had been struck. Some felt certain researchers did not act in ways that reflected mutually agreed upon principles and guidelines. Others felt that they were not given enough opportunity to properly understand the research process or the outcomes. One person felt that, while the research was interesting and the researchers were respectful to the community, not much research know-how had been passed on to residents once the project was finished.

It is our belief, despite continuing questions and concerns, that research in and with Aboriginal communities and institutions, when done in respectful ways, can be facilitated through clearly defined, community-based partnerships and alliances with outside researchers, research institutions, government organizations, other community groups, and funding agencies. Meaningful research partnerships enhance a community's ability to develop and improve strong governments and effective community-based economic, cultural, and social systems.

Those of us who wish to work in this area need to thoughtfully analyse and evaluate respectful research in practice in Aboriginal communities, as well as the ways in which research partnerships and agreements are negotiated and maintained. We must also attempt to grasp a better understanding of how effective research alliances are determined. Further, we must critically examine the use of mainstream quantitative research tools and techniques in the creation, gathering, and analysis of Indigenous knowledge.

Continuing conversations that review and revisit the meaning of respect in the research context will strengthen future research practices and relationships. Although the word respect is used freely in discussions related to Aboriginal and Indigenous communities, issues, and initiatives, it is rarely defined in specific and operational terms, and this is important if research in Aboriginal communities is to be done in ways that are respectful in practice. This is the challenge for those engaged in research relationships with Aboriginal communities and institutions in Canada.

Endnotes

1. L. Smith, *Decolonizing Methodologies: Research and Indigenous Peoples* (London and New York: Zed Books, 1999).
2. World Health Organization, *Participatory Research Management Guidelines for Indigenous Peoples and Research Institutions Undertaking Collaborative Health Research* (Ste. Anne de Bellevue, PQ: WHO Department of Health and Development, 2002, document prepared by K. Fediuk and H.V. Kuhnlein of the Centre for Indigenous Peoples' Nutrition and Environment). Posted at http://www.treatycouncil.org/about11.htm.
3. Nunavut Research Institute and Inuit Tapirisat of Canada, *Negotiating Research Relationships: A Guide for Communities* (Ottawa: Inuit Tapirisat of Canada, 1998).
4. See, for example, *Mi'kmaq Ethics Watch: Principles and Guidelines for Researchers Conducting Research with and/or among Mi'kmaq People* (Sydney, NS: Mi'kmaq College Institute, University College of Cape Breton, 1999). Posted at http://www.stfx.ca/campus/service/academic_funding_and_research/Mi'kmaqEthicsProcedures1.doc.
5. American Indian Law Center, Inc., *Model Tribal Research Code: With Materials for Tribal Regulation for Research and Checklist for Indian Health Boards*, 3rd ed. 1999, pp. 1–2. Posted at http://www.ihs.gov/MedicalPrograms/Research/pdf_files/mdl-code.pdf.
6. Ibid., p. 2.
7. See Appendix F, "Central Region Nuu-chah-nulth First Nations [DRAFT*] Template Letter of Informed Consent" (pp. 27–29), in the Clayoquot Alliance for Research, Education, and Training (CLARET) document, "Standard of Conduct for Research in Northern Barkley and Clayoquot Sound Communities," (June 2003). Developed through the CLARET's Protocols Project; posted at http://www.clayoquotalliance.uvic.ca/PDFs/CLARETStdConV1Jun03.pdf.
8. S. Brascoupé and K. Endemann, *Intellectual Property and Aboriginal People: A Working Paper* (Ottawa: Minister of Public Works and Government Services Canada, Research and Analysis Directorate, Indian and Northern Affairs Canada, 1999). Posted at http://www.ainc-inac.gc.ca/pr/ra/intpro/intpro_e.html.
9. S. Brascoupé and H. Mann, *A Community Guide to Protecting Indigenous Knowledge* (Ottawa: Minister of Public Works and Government Services Canada, Research and Analysis Directorate, Indian and Northern Affairs Canada, 2001). Posted at http://www.ainc-inac.gc.ca/pr/ra/ind/gui_e.html.

10. Royal Commission on Aboriginal Peoples, *Ethical Guidelines for Research,* vol. 5, app. E (Ottawa: Minister of Supplies and Services Canada, 1996). Posted at http://www.ainc-inac.gc.ca/ch/rcap/sg/sgmm_e.html.

11. MiningWatch Canada, *On the Ground Research: A Research Agenda for Communities Affected by Large-Scale Mining Activity* (Ottawa: International Development Research Centre (submitted), 2000). Posted at http://www.miningwatch.ca/publications/Research_agenda.html.

12. Wildlife Management Advisory Council (North Slope), *Yukon North Slope Research Guide, 2001.* Posted at http://www.taiga.net/wmac/researchplan/researchguide.pdf.

13. L. Grenier, *Working with Indigenous Knowledge: A Guide for Researchers* (Ottawa: International Development Research Centre, 1998).

14. University of Victoria, *Protocols and Principles for Conducting Research in an Indigenous Context* (Victoria: University of Victoria, Faculty of Human and Social Development, 2003). Posted at http://web.uvic.ca/igov/programs/masters/igov_598/protocol.pdf.

15. University of Saskatchewan, *Responding to the Needs of Aboriginal Peoples: A Conceptual Framework* (Saskatoon: University of Saskatchewan, presented to University Council, 2001). Posted at http://www.usask.ca/vpacademic/programs/aboriginal/UofS-ConceptPlan2001_Council.ppt.

16. University of Otago, "Policy for Research Consultation with Maori," (n.d.). Posted at http://www.otago.ac.nz/research/maoriconsultation/policy.html.

17. University of Canterbury, "Human Ethics Committee: Principles and Guidelines," (August 2001). Posted at http://www.research.canterbury.ac.nz/ethics.htm.

18. Posted at http://www.cyberus.ca/~acuns/.

19. "Ethical Principles for the Conduct of Research in the North," posted at http://www.cyberus.ca/~acuns/EN/n_res_02.html (1998).

20. Ibid.

21. Brascoupé and Mann, p. 2.

22. Ibid., p. 32.

23. C. McNaughton and D. Rock, "Opportunities in Aboriginal Research: Results of SSHRC's Dialogue on Research and Aboriginal Peoples," posted at http://www.sshrc.ca/web/apply/background/aboriginal_backgrounder_e.pdf.

24. Ibid., pp. 3–4.

25. Ibid., p. 4.

26. N. Piquemal, "Four Principles to Guide Research with Aboriginals," *Policy Options* (December 2000): pp. 49–51.

27. S.M. Davis and R. Reid, "Practicing Participatory Research in American Indian Communities," *American Journal of Clinical Nutrition* 69 (1999): pp. 7558–98.

28. See L. Rigney, "Internationalisation of an Indigenous Anti-Colonial Cultural Critique of Research Methodologies: A Guide to Indigenist Research Methodology and Its Principles," in HERDSA Annual International Conference

Proceedings, *Research and Development in Higher Education: Advancing International Perspectives* 20 (1997): pp. 629–36; L. Smith, *Decolonizing Methodologies;* and G. Smith, "Protecting and Respecting Indigenous Knowledge," in *Reclaiming Indigenous Voice and Vision,* ed. Marie Battiste (Vancouver: UBC Press, 2000), pp. 209–24.

29. Statistics Canada, 2003 Aboriginal Strategies Conference, posted at http://www.aboriginalstrategies.ca/.

30. See Australian Institute of Aboriginal and Torres Strait Islander Studies; and L. Quartermaine, keynote address to open the Indigenous Researchers' Forum 2003, Indigenous Research: What's It About? Australian Institute of Aboriginal and Torres Strait Islander Studies, 2003. Posted at http://www.abc.net.au/message/news/stories/s957650.htm.

31. D. Newhouse and E. Peters, *Not Strangers in These Parts: Urban Aboriginal Peoples* (Ottawa: Privy Council Office, Policy Research Initiative, 2003); and J.P. White, P.S. Maxim, and D. Beavon, *Aboriginal Conditions: Research as a Foundation for Public Policy* (Vancouver: UBC Press, 2003).

32. Inuit Tapiriit Kanatami, "Daniel Weetaluktuk: Inuit and Science," (n.d.), posted at ftp://209.195.99.10/pub/environment/enviro_tek03.pdf.

33. J. Barnsley and D. Ellis, *Research for Change: Participatory Action Research for Community Groups* (Vancouver: The Women's Research Centre, 1992).

34. Ibid, p. 11.

35. J. Ryan and M. Robinson, "Community Participatory Research: Two Views from Arctic Institute Practitioners," *Practicing Anthropology* 18, no. 4 (1996): p. 10.

36. T. Garvin, G. Hodgson, and M. Robinson, *Mapping How We Use Our Land: Using Participatory Action Research* (Calgary: Arctic Institute of North America, 1994 and 1996); and T. Garvin, F. MacDonald, and M. Robinson, *There Is Still Survival Out There* (Calgary: Arctic Institute of North America 1994 and 1996).

37. B. Hall, "Participatory Research: Expanding the Base of Analysis," *International Development Review* XIX (1997): p. 24.

38. M. Richardson, "Anthropologist: The Myth Teller," *American Ethnologist* 2, no. 3 (1975): pp. 517–33.

39. N. Dyck and J. Waldrum, "Anthropology, Public Policy, and Native Peoples: An Introduction to the Issues," in *Anthropology, Public Policy, and Native Peoples in Canada,* eds. N. Dyck and J. Waldrum (Montreal: McGill-Queen's University Press, 1993), p. 15.

40. Ibid.

41. G. Reimer, "Community Participation in Research and Development: A Case Study from Pangnirtung, Northwest Territories" (Ph.D. diss., McMaster University, 1994), p. 26.

42. Ibid., pp. 27–28.

43. Address posted at http://www.abc.net.au/message/news/stories/s957650.htm.

44. "Understanding the Strengths of Indigenous Communities," (n.d.), posted at http://www.usic.ca/.

45. University of Victoria, "Protocols Project of the Clayoquot Alliance for Research, Education, and Training," (n.d.), posted at http://web.uvic.ca/~scishops/protocols.htm.
46. Posted at http://www.clayoquotalliance.uvic.ca/PDFs/CLARETStdConV1Jun03.pdf, p. 4.
47. Ibid.
48. Ibid., p. 12.
49. Kahnawake Schools Diabetes Prevention Project (KSDPP), "KSDPP Code of Ethics," (1997). Posted at http://www.ksdpp.org/code.html.
50. L. Potvin, M. Cargo, A.M. McComber, T. Delormier, and A.C. Macaulay, "Implementing Participatory Intervention and Research in Communities: Lessons from the Kahnawake Schools Diabetes Prevention Project in Canada," *Social Science and Medicine* 56 (2003): pp. 1295–1305.
51. J. Frideres and R. Gadacz, *Aboriginal Peoples in Canada: Contemporary Conflicts*, 6th ed. (Toronto: Prentice Hall, 2001), p. 296.
52. L. Hammond Ketilson and I. MacPherson, *A Report on Aboriginal Co-operatives in Canada: Current Situation and Potential for Growth* (Saskatoon: Centre for the Study of Co-operatives, University of Saskatchewan, 2001).
53. Aboriginal Business Canada, *Aboriginal Entrepreneurs in Canada—Progress and Prospects* (Ottawa: Industry Canada, n.d.). Posted at http://strategis.ic.gc.ca/pics/ab/440_ref_rep001_e.pdf.
54. Ibid.
55. Posted at http://www.ica.coop/ica/ica/sb/research.html.
56. See W. Wuttunee, "Partnering among Aboriginal Communities: Tribal Councils Investment Group," *Journal of Aboriginal Economic Development* 3, no. 1 (2000): pp. 9–17; and *In Business for Ourselves: Northern Entrepreneurs* (Calgary: The Arctic Institute of North America and University of Calgary Faculty of Management, and Montreal: McGill-Queen's University Press, 1992). See also W. Weir, "Economic Development and the Nisga'a Treaty: An interview with Dr. Joseph Gosnell," *Journal of Aboriginal Economic Development* 1, no. 2 (2000): pp. 7–13; and "David Newhouse: On Describing Aboriginal Organizations and Management, and Understanding the Role These Organizations Can Play in the Re-Traditionalization of Aboriginal Communities." Posted at http://www.uleth.ca/man-bess/case/david_newhouse.htm. See also W. Wuttunee and W. Weir, "CANDO Aboriginal Economic Development Recognition Awards," *Journal of Aboriginal Economic Development* 2, no. 2 (2002): pp. 8–12.

PART TWO: CASES

NEW DIRECTIONS IN RESEARCH AND PRACTICE

*Four researchers offer case studies
on co-operatives in the dairy and forestry
industries and the solidarity co-operatives
of Québec.*

DANIEL CÔTÉ

THE ISSUES AND CHALLENGES FACING A CO-OPERATIVE IN SEARCH OF NEW COHESION
THE CASE OF AGROPUR

A BRIEF HISTORY[1]
Agropur—A Strategy Developed over Several Decades

EIGHTY-SIX FARMERS came together in 1938 to create La Société coopérative agriocole du Canton de Granby, renamed Agropur in 1979. It began as a mill, and it was only in 1941 that the co-operative became active in milk processing with butter production. Successful from the beginning, the organization underwent rapid development. Dynamism has been a constant throughout the history of this co-operative, and a simple reading of the chronological events that have marked its sixty-year existence illustrates this observation.

It ensured its development through *multiple strategic approaches*. Whether through consolidation, market penetration, new market or product development, or diversification strategies, Agropur has progressed year after year, decade after decade. These various strategies were implemented as much through internal sources as by way of acquisitions, joint development, and alliances.

In the years between 1950 and 1970, more than 150 local co-operatives joined Agropur, during which time the company also acquired a hundred or so private businesses. Initially local enterprises, they rapidly became regional and then provincial. Although acquisitions outside of Québec began in the late 1960s, it was not until the mid-1990s that this aspect of Agropur's strategy really took off. After having set up distribution centres in Ontario in the mid-1980s, Agropur made various acquisitions in the fluid milk sector in 1997 and 1998, and in the cheese-making sector in 1998.

After having built and consolidated its position in the niches of cheese, butter, and milk powder during the 1950s and 1960s, Agropur diversified its activities during the 1970–90 period. The company made its first incursion into the fluid milk sector in 1971, with the acquisition of several dairies grouped within Québec-Lait following in 1973, thereby forming the base of what would become Natrel in 1990. It was also in 1971 that it signed a first agreement with Sodima to become a Yoplait® franchiser for the entire Canadian market. In 1978, Agropur entered the fancy cheese market sector. This diversification occurred through multiple acquisitions and alliance strategies. At the same time, the organization withdrew from its involvement with certain other products such as pâtés, juices, and farm supplies.[2] The recentring of its strategic activities took place between the late 1980s and the early 1990s.

Very early on, a concern for quality led to the construction of a permanent research and control laboratory. In the early 1950s, Agropur became involved in the manufacturing of refrigeration tanks to improve milk conservation on the farm. From the mid-1980s on, it has been active in innovation with products such as UHT creams, Yop (a yoghurt drink), Rivella (a whey-based soft drink), Purifruit, Miko (frozen desserts), double cream Brie, Mingo (fresh desserts), Yoplait-tube, and Moustache (long-life conserved milk).

In the early 1990s, Agropur confirmed its leadership position in the Canadian market by developing its operations from sea to sea. At present, it is the Canadian leader in the cheese (industrial and fancy) and yoghurt markets, and in the fluid milk market, it is the Québec leader and a major player in Ontario.[3]

The following table shows the main quantified benchmarks in the evolution of this co-operative over its sixty-year history.[4]

Year	Consolidated sales ($)	Milk volume (litres)	Number of members
1942	168,696	2,200,000	109
1950	4,422,741	33,883,882	972
1960	19,289,748	167,349,547	3,812
1970	95,200,000	735,643,162	8,279
1980	453,280,000	992,314,475	8,186
1990[5]	496,100,000	707,100,000	4,620
1997	1,293,800,000	1,323,300,000	4,738
1998	1,445,000,000	1,400,000,000	4,832
1999	1,470,900,000	1,433,200,000	4,914
2000	1,542,100,000	1,478,600,000	4,891
2001	1,850,100,000	1,776,100,000	4,732

AGROPUR AND THE DEVELOPMENT OF ASSOCIATION

A Network of Amateurs

The founders of the Granby Co-operative were infused by a democratic spirit. They held two annual meetings instead of only one, as required by law. These meetings became information forums and were quite successful, although the growth of the membership and the complexity of the subject-matter made these exchanges increasingly difficult. By the mid-1940s, the directors had implemented a series of measures intended to ensure the transmission of information and the professional training of farmers. In 1949, they created a network of facilitators,[6] which became the pillar of Agropur's democratic structure. In 1953, they created the Co-operative Action and Education Service, which became the Member Relations Service in 1972. This service is responsible for promoting the development of the co-operative, and educating and training facilitators.

Throughout Agropur's history, its directors have insisted strongly on the importance of co-operative education, and a substantial and ongoing effort is devoted to this end. Year after year, on behalf of their members, directors allot more than six thousand person days to associative life. These activities include education, participation in the various regional and general meetings, and facilitator meetings. Particular attention is paid to training the facilitators, who are responsible for informing and consulting all the members. The network of facilitators, each of whom is responsible for seven members, makes it possible to maintain a vibrancy in the associative structure.[7]

Agropur's Democratic Structure

Agropur's democratic structure has three complementary dimensions: consultation, decision making, and education and information.

The *Solidarity Committee* is the first element of the consultative structure. Created in the 1940s, it now consists of all fifteen members of the board of directors. Although its membership is identical to the board, this committee only concerns itself with associative issues, and its overall mandate is to plan the co-operative's associative life. During its four annual meetings, the members discuss the annual general meeting, the regional meetings, and the co-operative's social role.

One of the major responsibilities of the Solidarity Committee is overseeing the network of facilitators. It sets the schedule of their meetings, the program content, and topics of discussion. Facilitators are chosen on the strength of their contacts and credibility in their environment, with selection criteria based on leadership skills, involvement in the co-operative and the community, and geographic distribution. The network's goal is to ensure good circulation of information, both internal and external, between the members and the administrators, which is integral to maintaining democratic values across a vast territory. The facilitators are the members' main contacts, not only keeping them informed, but also transmitting member questions and comments to the administrators. The facilitators also play an important role in member recruitment, with outreach activities consisting of various forms of involvement in other agricultural, co-operative, and community structures.

There are four meetings between the facilitators and the administrators. A single meeting, in the summer, brings together all the facilitators to present the semi-annual financial report and to discuss all appropriate issues with the administrators. The other three meetings are held locally.

The *regional general meetings* initiate the decision-making process. Twenty general meetings are held annually in the fifteen administrative regions, with certain regions being large enough to justify two meetings per year. During these meetings, to which all members are invited, the participants elect delegates (one for every ten members) to the co-operative's annual general meeting. The great majority of these delegates are facilitators. The regional meetings enable the members to learn about and discuss the quarterly financial results as well as other issues pertaining to the co-operative's activities.

Participation in decision making is most obviously apparent during the *annual general meeting*, in which 40–50 percent of the delegates participate. It is during this meeting that the members approve the financial statements and elect the fifteen members of the board of directors. The AGM also serves as an occasion to learn about and approve major projects such as mergers and acquisitions. This is made possible by the fact that the projects are usually discussed in meetings with the facilitators throughout the year.

Each year, the three-year terms of five administrators come up for renewal, which ensures a healthy turnover while also maintaining continuity. The executive committee is made up of five elected officials (president, vice-president, and three administrators) and senior management personnel (executive director, corporate secretary, and treasurer). The member participation rate at Agropur's various regional meetings is around 40 percent.

The first *team of co-operative consultants*, all of whom are Agropur employees, appeared in 1963. At present, eight consultants cover the co-operative's various administrative regions. Essentially, they co-ordinate the co-op's activities in their respective territories and collaborate in presenting dossiers to members at the co-operative's meetings. The members refer to them for all questions regarding such items as membership, capital portfolio, and production planning. The consultants also provide support to the facilitators, and together, they organize local member meetings.

Co-operative education at Agropur is an essential element in the democratic structure. As mentioned above, Agropur annually devotes more than six thousand person days to associative life for its members. In addition to educating and informing members, these different sessions are intended to bring people together, develop leadership, and serve as springboards for action. The Solidarity Committee supervises the content of these sessions, which last from two to four days. Topics can range from the distinct nature of the co-operative to its democratic framework, its history, the role of each member of the co-operative, and its strategic actions. The two annual sessions intended for the facilitators focus on their role, the importance of the democratic dimension, the acquisition of knowledge about the sector, the development of autonomous thinking and analysis and leadership abilities, and the relevance of the co-operative organizational style in the context of globalization.

Both the content and the dissemination of the sessions are handled for the most part by the Member Relations Service.

The results of these educational activities are felt throughout the organization. Education has an impact on the democratic structure, in that participants can discuss "hot" issues pertaining to the co-operative. They can thus develop their vision with regard to certain issues because they are both informed and educated, which enables the organization to take strategic shifts that would otherwise be more difficult. The people appropriate the decisions because they understand the issues facing the co-operative. In addition, since the facilitator network is a kind of breeding ground for the administrative level, the facilitators are under a certain amount of pressure. The young members understand how the structure works and many hope to become administrators one day. As such, all levels must perform well. Education creates a powerful feeling of belonging and motivation among the members.

The Current Context

A Petition Signed by Three Thousand Members

Despite a successful history marked by many high points, Agropur began the twenty-first century faced with challenges at the level of both associative life and strategic orientation. Roughly three thousand of its members recently presented the co-operative with a petition, an expression of dissatisfaction orchestrated by the UPA, a farm union, in reaction to a Farm Market Board[8] decision to recognize Agropur's right to develop its own co-operative export channel. This decision gave Agropur the authority to solicit members interested in producing milk for export. Once contracts were signed with international buyers, the co-operative committed itself to marketing its members' milk, and in doing so, created an obligation on its members for a small portion of their product.

Very quickly, the federation of milk producers saw this decision as a threat to its monopoly in the marketing of milk produced in Québec. It also feared that the production of milk intended for export (at a price that differs from the Canadian price[9]) would fuel the viewpoint of (international) opponents of the Canadian dairy system. Why take this kind of risk when the export market is only marginal? Why risk weakening the political position of producers in their own Canadian market?

This petition forced the hand of the Québec government, which, via its Ministry of Agriculture, rescinded the Farm Market Board's decision.

Relations between the co-operative world and the union world have been complicated since the creation of joint plans in the mid-1950s. This tension reached a peak in the mid-1980s with the imposition of a milk marketing agreement between the federation of milk producers and milk buyers. According to this agreement, dairy co-operatives were lumped into the same category of buyers as private processors.

This 1985 decision by the Farm Market Board created a precedent and engendered a rupture in the link between milk producers and their co-operative. According to the terms of its decision, whether they were members of a co-operative or not, milk producers were obliged to send all of their milk to the federation, which then sold it in line with the marketing and supply agreement with the dairy processors. Thus, since 1985, Agropur has found itself in the paradoxical position of no longer receiving milk produced by its own members.

Although it was triggered by the export strategy, the petition signed by three thousand members reflects an important tension in Agropur's membership. On the one hand, there is a group of Agropur members with strong union ties, while on the other, there are members who view themselves as co-operators. This tension has only been accentuated in the past fifteen years, exacerbated by conflicts between the federation and the co-operative.

This difficult political context has led many producers to question the relevance of the co-operative model for the dairy industry. For some, the federation is the main actor with respect to the price accorded to producers. In this view, Agropur's role should be a congruent one, limited to dividends and price complements. For others, the co-operative continues to play a strategic role. It is the producers' window on the processing world, and represents the possibility of influencing the behaviour of industry actors.

The co-operative is thus faced with questions about its place and role vis-à-vis both its members and the dairy industry. In concrete terms, however, it is treated by the federation as just another milk buyer.

The Competitive Environment

Adding concern to this difficult political context is the evolution of the competitive environment in the Canadian dairy industry. A trend towards concentration considerably modified the industry's structure throughout the 1990s.[10] Today (2004), there are three dominant dairy processing businesses in Canada—Parmalat, Saputo, and Agropur. In addition to this intense concentration in processing is an equivalent concentration in food distribution throughout the country. Loblaws and Sobeys dominate the industry, with an almost 50 percent share of the Canadian market. In Québec, it is even more intense, with Loblaws, Métro, and Sobeys controlling 80 percent of the market. These statistics are also reflected at the international level, with giants such as Nestlé, Dean Foods, Danone, and Parmalat dominating the processing sector, and WAL-MART, Carrefour, and Métro Ag developing global strategic positions in the distribution sector. It is anticipated that planetary concentration efforts will only continue in the coming years.

This international trend affects the Canadian dairy industry as well as the food products distribution industry. The strong presence of Parmalat following the acquisition of Ault Food and Béatrice Food illustrates well how Canada is responding to this international situation, and Saputo's investments in the United States follow the same logic. Of the three leaders in the Canadian dairy industry, Agropur[11] alone has only a Canadian strategic position. The two other dominant players have an international (Parmalat) or continental (Saputo) presence.

Above and beyond the structural changes transforming the landscape, we are also witnessing a change in milk and dairy product consumption habits. The Canadian market has matured. Moreover, it is now the dairy ingredients sector that is developing, and there is a sharp increase in imported dairy products, despite international trade barriers that protect the Canadian market. At the same time, Canadian exports have developed in an uneven manner and are still a residual market, which makes it difficult to develop and control stable international markets.[12] There are also strong political pressures from the international community that seek to eliminate barriers to free trade.

Agropur's members are thus faced with complex and highly strategic issues with regard to the future of their co-operative. What is the co-operative's role and place now that the usage link has been ruptured? How can cohesion be reconstructed among a membership torn between a union allegiance and a co-operative allegiance? Is it possible to have a dual allegiance? What are the future strategic prospects for Agropur in light of the fact that its failed merger attempt with Agrifoods was followed by the latter's bankruptcy and the fact that Saputo took advantage of the situation to stage a strong return on the Canadian market? In the long term, the pressure on the rules regulating the industry will only intensify. Despite the fact that the Canadian dairy industry management system seems to have several lives, it is no less true that this system contradicts the currently dominant free trade rules. Can these protectionist rules resist the ongoing and possibly endless assaults by the World Trade Organization rounds of talks?

It was in this context that Agropur's board of directors began to plan a broad consultation with its members.

Consultation

The board submitted a strategic consultation proposal with regard to the co-operative's future at the February 2002 annual general meeting, the salient features of which were published in the February edition of Agropur's newsletter, *Intercom*.

The proposal contained the following elements:[13]

1. The premises of the discussion:
   - the co-operative seeks the well-being of its members
   - it seeks to reaffirm its co-operative status
   - it recognizes the key role of the supply management system
   - it seeks harmonious cohabitation with farm unionism

2. The rules of a constructive consultation:
   - transparency, openness, and democracy as the guiding principles of the discussion

3. The major issues to be debated by the members:
   - the development of the "business" relationship between the members and their co-operative
   - the members' vision of the future of the Québec and Canadian dairy industry
   - the strategic role they see for Agropur in both the current and the future industry
   - the development of a strategy for finding the resources necessary to meet Agropur's financial needs, to ensure its development
   - the actions that need to be taken to ensure the viability and future of the members and their co-operative

To ensure the success of this consultation, the board of directors chose to conduct it in several steps over a twelve-month period, which would lead to the proposal's submission to the AGM the following year, in February 2003. The various steps were planned as follows:

Phase A (March 2002)

The aim of the first phase was to come into contact with the greatest number of members possible, to initiate discussions, and to allow members to express their points of view. The members were invited to one or another of the forty-five meetings held across the province over a three-week period, with each meeting bringing together no more than a hundred people. Three administrators were to participate in each of the meetings. Their role consisted of presenting a few elements of the context,[14] in the most neutral terms possible, and in listening to the opinions expressed by the members. Questions seeking clarification could be asked, but the administrators' answers were not to raise the strategic issues at the heart of the consultation.

Eight hundred members attended these forty-five meetings. Their opinions were systematically noted and summarized before being circulated to all Agropur members.

Phase B (April and May 2002)
The second phase was intended to develop an understanding of the opinions expressed during the first phase, and took the form of focus groups lasting an entire day. To ensure a broad representation of members, it was decided that they would be invited to participate in the focus groups after having participated in one of the Phase A meetings. Recruitment was thus on a voluntary basis. More than 120 individuals signed up and more than 70 of them participated in one of the six focus groups held in different places throughout the province. The groups were chaired by an outside expert.

Although the focus-group discussions were similar to those in the first phase, the objective was different, in that it sought to draw out the underlying logic and coherence of the members' opinions. At this stage, no effort was made to find answers to the questions posed. Rather, the goal was to identify the different positions within Agropur's membership. As in the first phase, opinions were systematically recorded at each meeting.

At this point, around eight hundred people had participated in the consultation. Their opinions yielded more than five hundred pages of comments grouped as a function of the strategic questions retained by the board of directors.

As a follow-up, in the summer of 2002, the board arranged to have a summarizing document produced and circulated among the entire membership. As was the case with the Phase A and B meetings, this document was meant to be neutral, its only purpose to express the various tendencies manifested by the members. Accompanying this document, written by a consultant hired to assist the board of directors throughout the consultation, were three question-and-answer sections, which were intended to provide answers to the questions asked in the first two phases.

Phase C

During the September regional general meetings, to which all members were invited, an effort was made to evaluate the importance of the various tendencies. To this end, members were grouped into roundtables, with about ten people per table, to discuss the strategic questions at the heart of the consultation. The objective was to quantify the relative importance of the opinions expressed in the preceding phases, with the summary document serving to identify the main tendencies in the answers to the strategic questions. Around fifteen hundred people participated in 160 roundtable discussions during this phase.

The Last Leg of the Consultation[15]

At this point, members of Agropur's board of directors have met with around two thousand members involved in the consultation phases initiated at the February 2002 annual general meeting. They know that "the ball is in their court"; they now have to digest all this information and formulate a proposal to submit to the members at special regional meetings in December 2002 and to the February 2003 AGM. This proposal must meet the expectations and opinions expressed by the members throughout the year. It also has to be a convincing platform to deal with the many short-, medium-, and long-term challenges.

With these many concerns in mind, the administrators prepare themselves for the meeting at Lac à l'épaule. In anticipation of this important meeting of the Solidarity Committee,[16] they consult the summary of the opinions expressed by the members. They are all conscious, however, of already having accomplished a great deal. The tensions between the members and the elected officials, which everyone felt, have been considerably attenuated, and the administrators feel the prevailing positive climate.

For their part, members were surprised by the approach adopted throughout the consultation process. They were gratified by the extent to which the administrators listened, and they appreciated being able to express their ideas. It was thus with a feeling of confidence that each participant prepared for this important meeting.

This confidence was amplified by the co-operative's excellent financial results. At the February 2002 AGM, the directors showed record results, with before-dividend surpluses of $64 million for the 2001 financial year. This resulted in nearly $43 million in dividends being paid out to members. The cash flow went from $20 million in 2000 to $84 million in 2001, while the long-term debt increased from $118 million to $156 million. Finally, member assets rose from $188 million to $253 million. Member equity has continued to increase over the past five years, rising from 32 percent to 39 percent of total assets. The midyear results presented to the members during the summer meetings indicated another exceptional year in 2002.

Results:[17] In Search of a New Membership Cohesion

In preparing for the meeting at Lac à l'épaule, the administrators review the events of the preceding year. The summary document sent to the membership is important inasmuch as it expresses the various opinions of the members. The essential features of this summary come back to them. Let us see what they contain.

The majority of the members would like Agropur to continue its *development at the continental level.* The members understand that:

- consumption in Canada has reached a ceiling[18]
- the rate of change is accelerating
- we have to take our place; otherwise we will disappear
- Agropur is essential

The members thus wish for Agropur to develop. They want their co-operative *to take its place, to seize opportunities, to forge ahead ... but to do so in a harmonious and profitable manner.*

While in favour of continental development, the members have some reservations.

- we have to remain profitable

- we should move ahead with caution
- continental development should not be done to the detriment of producers
- we also have to avoid "empire building" … otherwise we might lose some things
- this development should, therefore, be an add-on—that is, in line with our means and capacities

With regard to the issue of *co-operative status,* the opinions display a strong majority in favour of keeping the co-operative status.

- keep this status so as to be less subject to blackmail
- it is a model that has proven itself
- examples of demutualization in the West have been failures
- the co-operative status allows us to have our say
- it is indispensable
- it gives us control over change
- it thus enables us to discipline the market

The members also acknowledge, however, the need to adapt the model and the need to remain competitive while there are still financing difficulties.

The idea of demutualization has no appeal whatsoever to the members.

- we will be had afterwards, and will lose out in the long run
- it is the value of our farms that is at stake
- this value is linked to our ability to market our milk under decent conditions
- it is thus important to maintain control over the change
- at present we are well positioned
- in addition, "supply management" might disappear
- the co-operative is a heritage, an important part of our identity

On the issue of their *business relations* with the co-operative, the members feel that:

- we have to talk more in terms of participation than of the usage link
- the true usage link is capital

- we have to live with two systems—union and co-operative
- although the tensions are constant
- producers find themselves pulled in two directions
- however, we need the efforts of both of them
- we hope that they move in the same direction

The *hybrid model* is a strategic choice that a majority do not want to bring into question, feeling that:
- the current system gets the best for the producers
- it is a viable compromise with which they are comfortable, to the extent that the base and the top talk to one another
- this system does not inhibit Agropur's development
- the members need two strong organizations
- in the future, however, producers are going to draw nearer to their co-operative

Members also raised the issue of the *associative structure,* expressing the following opinions:
- we want to be heard more
- we also want more explanations of the decisions made
- we would like an increase in member participation
- the facilitator structure could be reviewed to make it better known, to reconsider its role and usefulness

In other words, they expressed the need for tightening the democratic process, greater transparency, reinvigorating various structures, and a better balance between information and consultation.

Members commented as follows on the *avenues envisaged* to support Agropur's development:
- we must first prioritize our current markets and products
- and find ways to develop consumption (in-store tasting, brands, etc.)
- then come up with innovative products; hence the need to accord considerable importance to R&D
- export markets, however, are a source of fear for members:
  – what would be the effects on quotas?
  – is it profitable?
  – should we go further than temporary efforts?

- perhaps we should target niche markets
- but with reasonable prices for producers
- even though they are expanding markets

- capitalization is, to be sure, a source of concern for members:
  - some prefer keeping dividends
  - others feel that the co-op should finance its activities via the members, but that it should be profitable ... and why not pay out a return?
  - in any event, it has to be done gradually (if there is an increase in share capital)
  - why not consider creating a development fund?

- with regard to the membership issue, the members have differing points of view:
  - since the addition of new members would only dilute dividends, the idea is not a good one
  - however, co-operation has a philosophy of adherence
  - and new members are the future
  - therefore, we need them for our development, especially since our membership continues to decline

During Phase B, the members expressed their *vision of the industry*. The recurring ideas in the various focus groups were as follows:

- we are witnessing the break-up and opening up of our markets
- like it or not, globalization is at our doorstep
- and producers are losing power
- while there is a concentration of the secondary and tertiary sectors
- we therefore have to adapt ourselves and reconsider our ways of doing things

Which Proposal Will Meet the Members' Expectations? Dealing with Short- and Long-Term Issues

It is thus with the significant contribution made by members during this consultation process in mind that the administrators ready themselves for their two-day meeting, during which they hope to formulate a series of proposals to meet member expectations.

The following issues also have to be taken into account:

1. Will the co-operative model be viable in the long term, given that the usage link with member-producers has been broken?
2. Will it be possible to rebuild strong member cohesion, given the often conflicting allegiances of unionists and co-operators?
3. How should business relations with members be reconfigured, given the issues and challenges facing the Canadian dairy industry? The members clearly expressed their fears about seeing the current system continuing to break up in the medium term.
4. What is the place and role of the co-operative in this context of change?
5. To be sure, the members expect concrete proposals with regard to the various issues raised during the year-long consultation.

It is not an easy task that lies ahead. What is the best way of tackling the proposal to be submitted to the members? And just what proposal should we submit?

Endnotes

1. This chapter was originally a case study prepared within the framework of the Canadian Adaptation and Rural Development Project, Phase II (CARD II), sponsored by the Canadian Co-operative Association. This section of the case study is taken from D. Côté, "Agropur, coopérative agro-alimentaire: la forme *holding* au service des sociétaires," dans *Holding coopératifs,* ed. D. Côté (Bruxelles, Belgique: De Boeck université, 2000).
2. Farm-supply activity was the reason for creating the co-operative, which ventured into the juice, cold meat, etc., sectors in the 1980s.
3. The fluid milk market is largely regional in nature, and the players have to position themselves in the various markets.
4. The brief history presented in this section, as well as the figures given in the table, were taken from an internal Agropur document produced on the occasion of its sixtieth birthday celebrations.
5. The figures for 1990 show a drop both in sales and in milk volume because Agropur grouped this volume in its subsidiary Natrel, over which it did not acquire majority control until 1991. It was only at this point that it integrated Natrel's activities into its consolidated statement.

6. This network is made up exclusively of members of the co-operative.
7. This responsibility is not direct, however, since it is a ratio or an average. The Solidarity Committee maintains this average of one facilitator for seven members by designating them without assigning them to particular members.
8. *Régie des marchés agricoles.*
9. International prices fluctuate as a function of supply and demand, whereas the Canadian price is set at around $56 per hectolitre. At the time of the consultation with Agropur members, international prices hovered at around $15 to $20 per hectolitre.
10. The leaders of the Canadian dairy industry in the 1990s were Ault Food, Béatrice Food, Agropur, Saputo, Agrifoods, and Lactel. Only two of these businesses, Agropur and Saputo, remain at the beginning of the twenty-first century.
11. Agropur recently announced the acquisition of a small company in the United States.
12. The WTO's recent decision severely limits possibilities for dairy exports. Canadian producers are now confined to the Canadian market to sell their production.
13. Agropur, « Vision : une perspective d'avenir, » *Intercom* (le bulletin d'Agropur), février 2002.
14. The presented contextual elements concerned the changes to the industry (primary, secondary, as well as tertiary), the evolution of the domestic market, etc.
15. Although inspired by reality, this part of the case study is fictional and seeks essentially to place the participant in the situation of the board of directors at a crucial step in the consultation process. Our goal here is pedagogical. In reality, Agropur completed its consultation and submitted a proposal to the delegates present at the February 2003 annual general meeting.
16. Throughout the consultation process, the administrators met to discuss it as members of the Solidarity Committee, which is responsible for associative affairs.
17. This section is intended as a brief summary of the opinions expressed by the members during the first three phases. It is informed by the summary produced by the consultant, Daniel Côté, and was sent to the members during the summer of 2002. This document was entitled *Strategic Reflection: A Summary of Phases A, B, and C of the Consultation of the Members in March, April, and May 2002.*
18. The sentences formatted as bullets reflect the sense of the opinions expressed by the members. To be sure, they are snapshots of the comments made.

REFERENCES NOT APPEARING IN THE ENDNOTES

Côté, D. « L'avenir de la coopération agricole au Canada : diagnostic et pistes de développement. » Report written in September 2000 for the CARD project as support material for the exchanges and discussions during the regional meetings (fall 2000) and the national symposium (winter 2001).

Côté, D., et al. « Agropur et la formation coopérative. » Montréal : Centre de gestion des coopératives, Cahier du Centre, 1993.

———. « L'industrie laitière de demain : les défis de l'internationalisation. » Montréal : Centre de gestion agroalimentaire, HEC, Cahier du Centre, 1995.

Côté, D., et M. Vézina. « Mutation de l'entreprise coopérative : le cas de l'industrie laitière québécoise. » Montréal : Centre de gestion des coopératives, Cahier du Centre, 1989.

MARIO CARRIER

Translated from the French by Wayne Hudson

FORESTRY CO-OPERATIVES IN QUÉBEC
SOCIAL COHESION AND ECONOMIC TIES

HISTORICAL OVERVIEW

SINCE 1985, forestry co-operatives in Québec[1] have been members of an association, the Conférence des cooperatives forestières du Québec (CCFQ). In 2000, the CCFQ had forty-two members, which represents the vast majority of Québec's forestry co-operatives. The CCFQ's members were in control of 95 percent of the total turnover of forestry co-operatives—excluding minority participation—which represented approximately $420 million and employed some 5,700 people. They are worker co-operatives whose principal goal is to provide work for their members. Of the 154 worker co-ops listed in Québec in 2000, forty-eight were forestry co-operatives.

According to the CCFQ's philosophy, a forestry co-op is a deep-rooted local enterprise that is a factor in the economic and social development of Québec regions. Table 1 shows the principal activities of forestry co-operatives in 2000.

Although Québec's first forestry co-operative was created in 1938 in Gaspésie, it was only in the late 1970s, as a result of government policy on development, that these organizations acquired the importance that they have today. The Québec government aimed to have an operational forestry co-operative on every management unit of public forest land. This policy also recognized the major role of forestry co-operatives in the development and training of a forestry workforce, which would be important for the future. Further to these goals, between 1980 and 1985 the Québec government made it possible for forestry co-operatives to negotiate directly with the ministry responsible for forestry resources to carry out up to 50 percent of each public forest management unit's development work. This measure, in favour of co-operatives, was renewed for the period 1985 to 1990. In the mid-1980s, the Québec government set up an important reforestation program. Building on the expertise they had acquired in the area, forestry co-operatives took advantage of the program, becoming significant producers of seedlings and strengthening their position in the forestry business. These new directions were in addition to their main activity, which remains the timber harvest. Since the early 1990s, government policies have changed; the measures taken in the 1980s, however, allowed co-operatives to become and to remain the principal contractors on public forest land.

Table 1: Principle activities, forestry co-operatives, 2000

Seedling production	31 million seedlings
Reforestation	44.5 million hectares
Forestry works	83,970 hectares
Forest roads	1,258 km
Timber harvest	5.89 million m^3
Lumber production	412 million bd. ft.*

*bd. ft.: board foot. One thousand board feet is equivalent to about 5m^3 of wood.
Source: CCFQ and Ministry of Industry, Commerce, Science and Technology, 2000.

The 1990s brought diversification to the activities of the forestry co-operatives. While consolidating their presence in the harvest sector, some co-operatives invested progressively in the area of wood conversion. Thus, several co-operatives are building sawmills, modernizing their existing mills, and acquiring others with industrial and co-operative forestry partners. From 1990 to 1998, lumber production coming from plants owned entirely or in part by forestry co-operatives rose from 170 million to 500 million board feet (bd. ft.). Meanwhile, other co-ops began working in second- and third-stage wood conversion based on the added value of wood products. Finally, new areas of expertise have emerged, with co-operatives entering forest planning, multiresource management, and forestry development management at the international level. This diversification, however, affects only a minority of forestry co-operatives. The majority remain exclusively in traditional fields of work: commercial logging, forest management, and seedling production in greenhouses and nurseries.

In this brief historical overview of Québec forestry co-operatives, the key points are the following:

- there was rationalization and consolidation in the organization of forestry co-operatives that were begun in the late 1970s;
- the trigger to this reorganization was state intervention, which set up a policy of forestry co-operative development in 1977;
- forestry co-operatives formed a representative association in 1985 known as the Conférence des cooperatives forestières du Québec (CCFQ);
- growth in the turnover of forestry co-operatives in the 1980s and 1990s was linked to government measures that aided their integration into the forestry industry;
- a tendency towards diversification emerged in the 1990s, principally in lumber production, but also, for example, in second- and third-stage wood conversion and multiresource management linked to the concept of "inhabited forest"; this diversification occurred in only a minority of the forty-eight co-operatives listed in Québec in the year 2000; and
- in the early 2000s, forestry co-operatives played a significant role in the Québec forestry industry, acting mainly in the areas of timber harvesting and forestry.

THE CHALLENGES OF DIVERSIFICATION AND INNOVATION: THE CASE OF THE COOPÉRATIVE FORESTIÈRE DE GIRARDVILLE[2]

The majority of forestry co-operatives have strong local roots and partly or totally ensure the survival of a village. Most of them confine themselves to subcontracting to big business in the areas of forestry and timber harvesting, and they carry out these activities within their own region.

In job creation, as well as in consolidation of their financial assets, the challenges of diversification and innovation are turning out to be pertinent ways to develop forestry co-operatives. These challenges do, however, bring their share of risks. In order to better understand a forestry co-operative's progress through challenges to its development, this paper will present the preliminary results of a case study of a forestry co-operative that has experienced significant development in its activities for almost twenty-five years, and which has opted for diversification of its activities, particularly since the 1990s.

The Coopérative Forestière de Girardville was created in 1979 in the village of the same name, north of the Lac-Saint-Jean region of Québec. The village has an area of seventy-six square kilometres. In 1996, with its fourteen hundred inhabitants, it made up one of the fourteen municipalities of the Regional County Municipality (RCM) of Maria Chapdelaine, which counted twenty-nine thousand residents that same year. The population is concentrated in 5 percent of the RCM's 40,000 square kilometres, which is 84 percent covered with public forest land, of which 85 percent is coniferous. The total potential forest in the RCM's territory is equivalent to almost half of that in all the Saguenay-Lac-Saint-Jean region.[3]

In the early years, the co-operative worked exclusively with the needles and branches of black spruce, this forest residue being used for the extraction of essential oils. After a slow start in the early 1980s, the co-operative entered progressively into all kinds of forestry work. As the data in Table 2 indicate, activities linked to reforestation, the production of forest seedlings, and the supply of timber have always been its principal functions, and in 2000–2001, reforestation work and coniferous and broad-leaved timber supply were still by far the dominant activities. From 1991 to 1997, the co-operative put in a bid for a sawmill in partnership with a large forestry firm that was also its principal customer in the areas of forestry and timber harvesting. It abandoned this venture into the first-stage wood conversion sector in 1997, selling its share to its partner. In 2000–2001, with a membership of 253, the co-operative reached a total wage bill of $8 million, providing 620 jobs with a turnover of $27.7 million.

Table 2: Coopérative Forestière de Girardville and its subsidiaries—achievements 1985–2001

	1985–86	1988–89	1991–92	1994–95	1997–98	2000–01	Total (16 yrs)*
Reforestation (seedlings)	2,264,487	4,883,923	14,276,535	7,357,615	14,112,982	16,482,761	161,059,832
Trenching (ha)	3,293	7,800	9,400	9,600	8,196	8,604	127,016
Clearing (ha)	25	300	1,720	735	768	1,285	13,854
Seedling production		5,000,000	5,000,000	5,000,000	1,500,000	500,000	53,004,227
Supply							
- conifers (m^3)	100,000	127,378	126,000	190,000	183,350	223,834	2,513,590
- broad leaf (m^3)				90,000	67,245	118,584	722,770
Wood conversion (million bd. ft.)			2,000	7,537			49,340
Total salaries ($)	900,395	1,798,066	3,908,395	3,882,044	4,831,423	8,000,000	61,780,654
Employees	193	451	585	419	474	620	7,432
Members	50	74	184	196	142	253	
Turnover ($)	3,540,268	5,758,012	11,528,127	14,609,614	13,975,886	27,695,000	201,204,698

* Please note that although the final column indicates totals for all sixteen years, because of spatial considerations, data from only representative years is shown.

As well as taking advantage of the same government measures concerning development work and reforestation during the 1980s as other Québec forestry co-operatives, the Coopérative Forestière de Girardville benefited from an arrangement that took the form of a government order on 17 July 1985 (decree 1486–85). This order concerned the supply from the Domtar Inc. sawmill situated at Mistassini in the electoral district of Lac-Saint-Jean. The supply agreement between the Québec government and the Domtar corporation defines the following obligation under subsection "f" of the order and reads as follows: "To grant to the Coopérative Forestière de Girardville the right of first lease ("premier preneur") at market value for the exploitation of coniferous timber for the use of the Beneficiary in the Crown Forest Reserves of Saint-Félicien and for the work of management and forestry that would be its responsibility."[4]

This agreement, which grants the Coopérative Forestière de Girardville the right to harvest one hundred thousand cubic metres of conifers in the Crown Forest Reserves of Saint-Félicien and to carry out development work in this territory, was renewed twice, once in 1994 and again in 2001, at the time of the sale of the beneficiary company to other businesses, as stipulated in the order.

Since the late 1990s, however, the Coopérative Forestière de Girardville has invested its assets into second-, third-, and fourth-stage wood conversion. These activities are carried out by a wholly owned subsidiary company named Coopérative Forestière Girardville Amérique (CFG Amérique), a value-added business specializing in the kiln drying of broad-leaved timber, whose offices are situated in the industrial park in the city of Saguenay. The kiln-dried timber is sent to third- and fourth-stage wood conversion factories and to the workshops of cabinet-makers and local artisans. In fact, CFG Amérique's activities are structured around three operations: kiln drying, wood conversion, and brokerage.

The business owns three timber kiln-drying units, each with a capacity of sixty thousand board feet (25 m^3), which generate an annual capacity of 10 million board feet (4,250 m^3). For its wood conversion operations, CFG Amérique owns a twenty-four-thousand-square-foot factory that generates an annual production capacity of 8 million board feet (3,400 m^3). The factory, which began operations in the autumn of 2001, manufactures products such as mouldings, jointed wood, sheathing and siding, cut-to-size materials for staircases and windows, glued pieces, various wood components, and panels. Finally, brokerage and product marketing are handled by Filière Bois Feuillu, a division of the Coopérative Forestière de Girardville. The timber is bought at sawmills from Jonquière and Québec, then kiln dried and resold. The wood is from broad-leaved varieties from southern Québec and the northeastern United States, as well as from regional varieties in the Saguenay-Lac-Saint-Jean region, in particular the white aspen, which has become CFG Amérique's speciality.

Since the late 1990s, the Coopérative Forestière de Girardville has also multiplied its business partnerships. At the international level, for example, the firm established a partnership in 1999 with the Alta Verapaz Co-operative Federation (Fedecovera) in Guatemala, which is managed by Quichua Aboriginals. Together they have created Forestal Maya Guatemala S.A. to implement the marketing, commerce, and exporting of exotic species from Central America. The firm's head office is situated in Coban, in the Alta Verapaz region. In the year 2000, the forestry co-operative became majority shareholder (81.43 percent) in the Domicilex firm, a builder of prefabricated homes situated in the city of Saguenay. Its business partner in this case is the previous owner of the firm, the Coopérative des Batisseurs du Saguenay (Saguenay Builders' Co-operative).

In 2001, the co-operative became a shareholder in an industrial firm specializing in the wood conversion of aspen. It is also a 50 percent shareholder in the co-operative firm of Serres et Pépinières Girardville, Inc. (Girardville Greenhouses and Nurseries). Among its other activities, it is worth noting that it owns sixty-four acres of blueberry production, and, staying faithful to its roots, continues to produce and market essential oils. Finally, we should note that in addition to its head office in Girardville, the co-operative has offices at Roberval in Lac-Saint-Jean, in Québec, and in Montréal, as well as in Saguenay, where the offices and factories of its subsidiaries CFG Amérique and Domicilex are located.

Theoretical Perspective

The case of the Coopérative Forestière de Girardville helps us to understand how, in the context of globalization, economic activity is interwoven into multiple institutional bonds. It is also an interesting case for examining how co-operatives can conserve their values and their identity, while adapting to the new conditions for economic development imposed by globalization.

This research on Québec forestry co-operatives, based mainly on one case study, is part of a wider program of research on co-operative membership.[5] The program's general objective is to analyse how, in the context of globalization, co-operatives can enter into market relationships while at the same time acting as agents of social cohesion.

While we share the objectives and general hypotheses of the project, we present here a theoretical perspective that, at this stage of the research, can serve as a guide for our case study. It is based on a collected work edited by J.R. Hollingsworth and R. Boyer,[6] which focusses on defining the different processes of economic co-ordination in contemporary capitalism. In the introductory chapter, the editors present a typology of these processes. It is constructed around two axes—power distribution and action motive. The market and hierarchy are opposed along the axis of power distribution, while self-interest is opposed to the principles of reciprocity and obligation along the axis of action motive. Starting with these two axes, the editors identify several forms of co-ordination, including the market and communities on the horizontal axis and private and public hierarchies on the vertical. Associations and networks are presented as hybrid forms of co-ordination.

According to the editors, there are four levels in society where these different kinds of economic co-ordination are exercised: the regional, the national, the transnational, and the global. The analyst's work consists of specifying how institutions act to co-ordinate economic actors within these four levels of society. For Hollingsworth and Boyer, enterprises fit into complex environments from which social systems of production emerge that consequently exercise constraints on their behaviour. These systems are of major significance for understanding the behaviour and economic performance of businesses. The question is how the state and the different co-ordination processes are linked to the different social systems of production.

As we have seen from the information gathered on the Coopérative Forestière de Girardville, this firm fits into the social system of production that is the forestry industry. The co-operative's development, which we have briefly described, cannot be dissociated from its links with the different co-ordination processes that include not only the state and the large private forestry firms, but also its associations, networks, and home communities.

Methodology

As a methodological framework, we will use the case study, and more generally, the qualitative method principles outlined by Anne LaPerrière.[7] According to the research objectives and our general theoretical perspective, we think that the case study model offers an appropriate method for performing a deep analysis of the phenomenon in question. The following criteria will serve as signposts to ensure that the case study responds to the goals of the research.

A Diversified Theoretical Sample

The variables and indicators detailed below will orient us towards the aspects of the phenomenon that will allow us to clarify our analytical categories and to verify our hypotheses. For now, we have chosen to make a diachronic study of the following aspects of the Coopérative Forestière de Girardville: its market strategies, including the evolution of its products, services, technology, and geographical markets; its management strategies regarding employees, members, and home communities; its strategies for locating its factories and business offices; its networking and partnership strategies; and its financial strategies.

Data Saturation

This principle consists of pursuing the research until no further observation will enrich the analysis.

Rigour

This criterion aims to establish solid links between theoretical interpretations and empirical data.

Triangulation

Triangulation allows the achievement of a greater objectivity and accuracy by looking at different sources of data from different angles, and concerning both the subjects of the study and the researchers. The information and the techniques used to obtain it are as follows:

- interviews and discussion groups with the following categories of people: administrators, members, and employees of the co-operative; representatives of the CCFQ and the various public bodies concerned; members and representatives of the co-operative's home communities; and business partners; and
- documentary research on the co-operative, the various agencies concerned, and the researchers.

Generalization—Representativeness—External Validity

Inspired by LaPerrière's discussion of grounded theory,[8] the aim of the contextualized description of the Girardville case will be to shed light on the fundamental social processes, using the case as a concrete example (process representativeness). As such, the case study can have wider significance.

ENDNOTES

1. Information on Québec forestry co-operatives contained in this text was provided by the Conférence des cooperatives forestières du Québec and was obtained at a meeting with a representative of the organization in autumn 2002.
2. Information on the Girardville forestry co-operative contained in this text came from meetings held with representatives of that co-operative between December 2000 and June 2001.
3. Jean Désy, Myriam Duplain, et Martin Truchon, *Girardville, 49e parallèle : haut lieu forestier du Lac-Saint-Jean* (Chicoutimi: Université du Québec à Chicoutimi, Groupe de recherche et d'intervention régionales, juin 1999).
4. *Gazette officielle du Québec*, 7 August 1985, year 117, number 36, section 2, p. 5352.

5. Co-operative Membership and Globalization: Creating Social Cohesion through Market Relations, a study funded by the Social Sciences and Humanities Research Council of Canada, and based at the Centre for the Study of Co-operatives at the University of Saskatchewan.

6. J. Rogers Hollingsworth and Robert Boyer, "Co-ordination of Economic Actors and Social Systems of Production," in *Contemporary Capitalism. The Embeddedness of Institutions*, eds. J. Rogers Hollingsworth and Robert Boyer (Cambridge: Cambridge University Press, 1997), pp. 1–47.

7. Anne LaPerrière, « Les critères de scientificité des méthodes qualitatives, » dans *La recherche qualitative : Enjeux épistémologiques et méthodologiques,* par Jean Poupart et al. (Boucherville : Gaëtan Morin, 1997a), pp. 365–89.

8. Anne LaPerrière, « La théorisation ancrée (grounded theory) : démarche analytique et comparaison avec d'autres approches apparentées, » dans Poupart et al., 1997b, pp. 309–40.

JEAN-PIERRE GIRARD AND PATRICK DE BORTOLI

Translated from the French by Nancy Senior

The Solidarity Co-operative in Québec and Social Cohesion
Measuring and Understanding the Impact

Since 1997, Québec legislation allows for the creation of multistakeholder co-operatives called coopératives de solidarité (solidarity co-operatives). The law recognizes three categories of members: users of the services provided by the co-op, workers in the co-op, and any other person or organization that has an economic or social interest in the goal of the co-op. This last category is called membre de soutien or sustaining member.[1]

Within five years, more than a hundred of these co-operatives had been created. They work in a great variety of areas, but particularly the area of personal and home services. Many of these co-ops are innovative in the products and services they offer, as well as in their system of governance.

By their nature as associations, solidarity co-ops have the potential to offer new kinds of partnership and governance among civil society, parapublic organizations, and various local actors in seeking solutions to needs that are not met or not met sufficiently. Joining workers and users in the same organization allows mutual balance of supply and demand. This structure is also a new way to use volunteer and activist resources, which reinforces the values of altruism and reciprocity. Like social co-operatives in Italy, solidarity co-ops are an original way of reconstructing the link between the economic and the social spheres.[2]

These few remarks show the value of trying to understand the impact of this kind of co-operative on social cohesion. The solidarity co-op is an original way of mobilizing various actors; it is a customized response to unmet needs; and it can serve as a unifying force.

As part of the research project titled Co-operative Membership and Globalization: Creating Social Cohesion through Market Relations, the Centre de recherche sur les innovations sociales dans l'économie sociale, les entreprises et les syndicats (CRISES) of the Université du Québec à Montréal (UQAM) will undertake a series of studies and analyses that will be carried out between 2002 and 2005. This article outlines the parameters of this research. It is divided into two parts, the first of which describes briefly the state of development of solidarity co-ops in terms of their spheres of activities, membership, and localization. The second part presents the main concepts that will be used for later work, including case studies.

Solidarity Co-operatives: An Overview

In June 1997, as the result of strong pressure by the Québec co-operative movement[3] and a commitment by the Québec government to explore new ways to respond to needs that are not met or not adequately met,[4] the Québec Assemblée Nationale adopted amendments to the law on co-operatives. It thus provided a legal basis for allowing the expression and the balancing of interests of the various actors concerned by the activity of these new co-ops. This serves the interests of users who wish to meet their needs for cost or quality of goods or services; it serves the interests of workers in terms of work conditions and salaries; and it serves the interests of organizations and individuals who, while not directly involved in supplying services, share the goals of the organization.

These new amendments to the law will soon have a significant impact, being immediately taken up by promoters of the new co-operatives. As shown in Table 1, some 146 solidarity co-operatives were formed between June 1997 and December 2001.

Table 1: Growth in number of constitutions of solidarity co-operatives in Québec: June 1997 to December 2001

Period	Number
5 June 1997 to 31 March 1998	13
1 April 1998 to 31 March 1999	41
1 April 1999 to 31 March 2000	47
1 April 2000 to 31 December 2001	45
Total	146

Source: Direction des coopératives, Government of Québec

From the constitutional point of view, the great majority of these solidarity co-ops are new creations; a few are the result of not-for-profit organizations changing their legal statutes to that of solidarity co-ops; and five other co-operatives of another kind also changing their statutes to this form. This rather rapid development of the solidarity co-operative had the advantage of support from various government programs. In addition to co-ops in the sectors of personal and home service and child care, several others have taken advantage of the program of financial support for the development of co-operatives provided by a government agency, Investissement-Québec. This program mainly offers loan guarantees. Another program developed by the Ministry for Regions offers subsidies to set up what are called social economy enterprises. It is used for start-up funding. This program, administered by local organizations called local development centres (LDCs), which also have resources to help start up social economy enterprises, has significantly stimulated the development of solidarity co-operatives.

Solidarity co-operatives are present in about ten sectors, especially in the category of personal and home services. This is not surprising considering the resources allocated since 1997 to helping develop this kind of organization.[5] In the category of leisure and entertainment, there are co-ops made up of consumers and workers who run a ski centre, or who own and operate an open-air centre that is not considered profitable from a financial point of view, but which is socially profitable from the point of view of usage. In the categories of groceries/food and restaurants/catering, solidarity co-operatives have made it possible for villages to keep a minimum of services, where social value is again considered more important than profit. Table 2 shows the state of the situation as of December 2001.

Table 2: Sectors of activities of solidarity co-operatives in Québec (December 2001)

Sector of activity	Number of co-operatives
Personal and home services	29
Professional and business services	18
Leisure and entertainment	16
Daycare centres	6
Groceries/food	8
Restaurants/catering	6
Agricultural	8
Garbage and recycling	3
Social services	12
Other	40
Total	**146**

Source: Direction des coopératives, Government of Québec

According to the data in Table 3, which are limited and up-to-date only to December 2000,[6] the average membership of a solidarity co-operative is 237, consisting of 160 user members, 21 worker members, and the rest in sustaining members. Of the latter, the corporate category is made up mainly of LDCs, public health clinics (CLSCs in Québec), local community service centres, financial service co-operatives,[7] and other local organizations.

Although financial data are still limited, a sample of about sixty co-operatives in December 2000 had an average annual turnover of $354,000, with assets of $221,000 and a nonrenewable, or start-up subsidy level, of about $144,000. Although there are other means of financing, such as preferred shares and participating shares, these resources do not seem to be much used.

Table 3: Solidarity co-operatives in Québec, partial results (61 co-ops) (December 2000)

Number of user members	10,678
Number of worker members	1,158
Number of sustaining members	261
Total number of members	12,097

Source: Direction des coopératives, Government of Québec

So far there is no solidarity co-ops federation, as is the case for social co-ops in Italy. While there are co-ops in a multitude of sectors, they are not numerically significant enough for such groupings. A federation was formed in the home service sector in 1996, but it includes all kinds of co-ops regardless of their organizational form. The Fédération des coopératives de services à domicile du Québec thus includes solidarity co-ops, users' co-ops, and even some worker co-ops. In other cases, solidarity co-ops generally belong to the organizations that aided in their development—regional development co-ops (RDCs)—which allows them to be associated with more institutionalized co-ops, networks, or co-ops that are also associated with the RDC.

How do these co-ops keep the interests of the various parties in balance? As in some social co-ops in Italy, isn't there a risk that power will gradually go to the workers? Available information does not allow a definitive answer, although it does indicate that the interests of the different sides have so far been successfully balanced. According to the Direction des coopératives, telephone surveys indicate that positions on the board of directors are usually distributed equally among the member groups. These co-ops do not seem to have had recourse to serious mediation among actors more than others. We should remember, however, that the majority of them still have the founding spirit, which favours compromise. On the whole, they are well grounded in their milieu, providing flexible responses suitable to needs.

Solidarity Co-operatives and Social Cohesion: Parameters of Analysis

From 2000 to 2002, CRISES took part in a variety of research activity concerning social cohesion and financial service co-operatives, which led to the publication of a series of monographs[8] and of a synthesis.[9] Co-operative organizations have been studied in the light of five concepts: *territoriality, accessibility, employability, "democrativity,"* and *networking*. We will define each of these dimensions briefly and then show their relation to the concept of solidarity co-operatives.

Territoriality

As elsewhere in North America, territory is being defined in new ways. In the past, the parish of the local Catholic Church, with a more or less homogeneous population, was central. It is now being replaced by a wider territory corresponding to Municipalités régionales de comté (MRCs)[10] with a heterogeneous population. To what extent do solidarity co-operatives fit into this new division with regard to membership, the structure of the board of directors, and the field of activity? Do the development projects of these co-ops correspond to this new frame of reference?

Accessibility

The level of accessibility of the solidarity co-ops' services is a key element of this research. Starting from Vienney's[11] view that co-operatives are intended to be a response to needs that are not met or not adequately met, and are aimed at actors with relatively little power, the research seeks to describe this accessibility.

As accessibility is directly related to the services provided, one must consider the nature and the effectiveness of these services in direct relation to the urgency of the needs of the population—on the one hand, how well the co-ops meet the need itself (nature), and on the other, how well they are able to meet the demand quantitatively (effectiveness).

It is also worthwhile to see how these organizations develop new services, not from the perspective of doing business with nonmembers, but, as described in the typology of Desforges,[12] to broaden the range of services offered to members, and thus strengthen their ties to the co-op. A good example is the case of personal and home services co-ops, which at the instigation of their members have begun to own and run residential centres. As aging members can no longer remain in their own homes and have to move into group homes, they would have to leave the area if there were no such resources there. The action of the co-operative in this sector allows people to remain in their community, which seems at first sight to have a direct and positive effect on social cohesion.

Correlating it with networking (which will be discussed later), we can analyse accessibility by observing the effect of the introduction of co-ops on already-existing services in the area—the consequences for public health clinics (CLSCs), for example, when co-operative personal and home services appear—in relation to the accessibility of their services. We can also measure the impact of the relations of these co-operatives with the other organizations on the accessibility of the services of the co-op itself, by seeing, for example, how accessibility of the co-op's services is increased or diminished according to whether it is or is not strongly connected to local community organizations. Finally, we can study how accessibility of services is affected by compromises (if there are any) among the individual interests of members, the interests of members as part of the group, and the general interest of the population, in relation to accessibility of services.

Employability

The concept of employability can be interpreted differently depending on the solidarity co-op's sector of activity. In certain cases, this element is secondary—the solidarity co-op offering a number of services to a community that does not have a grocery store, post office, or bank, for example. Here, accessibility is the crucial value. In other cases, employability is central—a co-op working under programs of reintegrating marginal populations into the workforce, for example.

Indicators include the degree to which the jobs created are comparable, in terms of work conditions, to similar jobs in other organizations. The socio-economic characteristics of the people hired could also show the influence of co-ops on social cohesion (employment of people who are poor, unemployed, young or old, men or women, with or without training, etc.). A comparison of these data with other organizations would allow us to measure the co-ops' contribution to social cohesion relative to other organizations of similar kinds.

Democrativity (or simply, Democracy)

The notion of democrativity refers, on the one hand, to the nature of the democratic process in the enterprise (namely the choice of representative, direct, or deliberative democracy) and on the other, to the institutional or composite form of its structure, understood by means of concepts such as "social democracy" and "plural democracy." The distinction between the two, though unclear at first glance, is fundamental. The "nature of the democratic process" refers to the practice of democracy in the operational and dynamic sense of the term, thus to the idea of process. The "institutional or composite form of its structure" refers to the composition of the democratic structure of the enterprise—that is, the composition of its board of directors, the existence of special committees, the socio-economic characteristics of this composition, etc. In this second aspect we find the concepts of plural democracy, which refers to the territorial, institutional (other local organizations), and socio-economic origins of the members of the board, and other instances of the democratic structure of the enterprise; and the concept of social democracy, which refers to the symmetrical representation of local or larger groups in this structure. All these concepts can be studied in light of the development and evolution of co-ops.

Networking

Networking is defined as the links among various individual or collective actors, forming networks, which at the same time use and generate social capital (the values of confidence and reciprocity), which favour co-operation and contribute to the construction of social cohesion. Studying this aspect will allow us to see how the relative networking of actors initiating projects influences their success. We will then be talking of a stock of social capital. We will also study these ties to see whether they constitute what Granovetter refers to as "strong ties" or "weak ties,"[13] and to what extent they influence social cohesion in one or the other case. Then, in an area where networking and degree of democracy overlap, we will look at the influence of the "charismatic personality" on the creation of social ties that increase the potential of success for the project. In other words, we will see how local actors, possessing strong symbolic capital (director general of a financial services co-op, mayor, recognized institution, etc.) are able to form social ties that favour the success of a solidarity co-op's project. At the same time, we will take into account the role of such influence on the process and components of the democratic structure of the enterprise.

As seen above in the discussion of territoriality, this dimension will also allow us to explore the extent to which the networking of the enterprise is favoured by whether or not it adopted the new institutional territory of local development—in this case that of the new municipalités régionales de comté—as the CLSCs in particular have done. In the same way, the correlation between the degree of accessibility of services (quantitatively) and the degree of networking of the enterprise could be analysed (see accessibility). Finally, we will emphasize the presence of various actors who traditionally play an unobtrusive role or only become involved when forced to do so, who have directly and voluntarily contributed to the successful development of solidarity co-ops.

Conclusion

This short article provides a brief overview of solidarity co-operatives and illustrates, by means of five concepts or dimensions, the main themes that will be developed in the CRISES research. In addition to a better knowledge of the modalities and conditions of solidarity co-operatives' activities, this research will describe the composition and evolution of the governance of these organizations. This is interesting for two reasons. First, solidarity co-ops offer a complex model of organization that combines potentially opposing interests. A priori, it may seem more difficult to reconcile the interests of users and workers in a system where both are user-members than, as is the case in a consumer or worker co-op, the interests of consumers or workers alone. This governance model is thus far from the dominant organizational model used in Canada since the beginning of the co-op movement—that is, on both the Francophone and Anglophone sides, an organization with only one category of members. Second, in the past few years, systems of organizational governance, whether public, for-profit, co-operative, or associative, have been the subject of frequent critiques,[14] among other reasons because the power of members' or shareholders' meetings has been weakened; because the way administrators are nominated, elected, or designated is unsatisfactory; or because executives have taken over some functions of the board of directors, including strategic planning. Does the new mode of governance peculiar to co-operatives make it possible to avoid these pitfalls?

A more complete understanding of the development and impact of solidarity co-operatives will aid the study of social cohesion. It will also provide a knowledge base for various uses, such as improving the Québec *Co-operatives Act* or formulating policies for regional or local development. In addition, the concept may be taken up by other provinces to include in their range of models available for the formation of new co-operatives.

Endnotes

1. Québec, *Loi sur les coopératives*, L.R.Q. chapitre C-67.2. Lois refondues du Québec, 1999.
2. Jean-Pierre Girard, E. Pezzini, et I. Faubert-Mailloux, « Les coopératives sociales italiennes: description et éléments de réflexion sur le contexte québécois, » (Montréal : UQAM, Chaire de coopération Guy-Bernier, Cahier de recherche no. 115, 2000).
3. For a detailed description of the context that led to making key actors aware of the concept of multiorganization co-operatives, see Jean-Pierre Girard, « Les coopératives de solidarité au Québec : caractérisation, tendances et perspectives, » titre provisoire, publication à venir (Montréal: UQAM, CRISES, 2004).
4. Commitments made at the Sommet sur l'économie et l'emploi, held October 1996 in Montréal (Girard 2004).
5. Government aid to co-operative or nonprofit organizations that work in this sector and that are accredited has taken the form of a financial support program on request of users who want to receive home aid, either older persons who have lost independence or regular households, under the name of Programme d'exonération financière en services à domicile (PEFSAD, financial relief program for home care services).
6. Not December 2001, as for the other tables.
7. The new legal term for what are traditionally called caisses populaires (credit unions).
8. L. Mager, sous la direction de Marie-Claire Malo et B. Lévesque, « Coopératives financières cohésion sociale et territoire : la Caisse populaire Desjardins Saint-Patrice de Magog issue de fusions de caisses dans la MRC Memphrémagog, »

(Montréal: UQAM, CRISES, *Collection études de cas d'entreprises d'économie sociale*, no. ES0104, 2001); G. Huot, sous la direction de Marie-Claire Malo et B. Lévesque, « Coopératives financières, cohésion sociale et territoire : La Caisse populaire Desjardins de Kildare issue de fusions de caisses dans Lanaudière, » (Montréal: UQAM, CRISES, *Collection études de cas d'entreprises d'économie sociale*, no. ES0105, 2001); A. Camus, sous la direction de Marie-Claire Malo et B. Lévesque, « Coopératives financières, cohésion sociale et territoire : La Caisse populaire Desjardins Allard-St-Paul issue de fusions de caisses dans l'arrondissement Sud-Ouest (Montréal), » (Montréal: UQAM, CRISES, *Collection études de cas d'entreprises d'économie sociale*, no. ES0106, 2001); O. Chouinard, P.-M. Desjardins, É. Forgues, et U. de Montigny, « Coopératives financières, cohésion sociale et territoire : La Caisse populaire Moncton-Beauséjour et la Caisse populaire de Néguac issues de fusions de caisses milieux urbain et rural, » (Montréal: UQAM, CRISES, *Collection études de cas d'entreprises d'économie sociale*, no. ES0107, 2001).

9. M.-C. Malo, B. Lévesque, O. Chouinard, P.-M. Desjardins, et É. Forgues, « Coopératives financières, cohésion sociale et nouveau territoire local à l'ère de la mondialisation, » (Montréal: UQAM, CRISES, *Collection cahier de recherche*, no. 0108, 2002).

10. This is a new territorial division created by the government of Québec in the 1980s, mainly to facilitate regional development.

11. C. Vienney, *L'économie sociale* (Paris: Édition La Découverte, 1994).

12. J.-G. Desforges, « Stratégie et structure de coopérative, » *Coopératives et développement* 12, no. 2 (1979–1980): pp. 32–58.

13. Mark Granovetter, "Economic Action and Social Structure: The Problem of Embeddedness," *American Journal of Sociology* 91, no. 3 (November 1985): pp. 481–510.

14. See, among others, Comité mixte sur la gouvernance d'entreprise, « Au-delà de la conformité, la gouvernance, » rapport final (Toronto : Compables agrées du Canada, TSE, 2001); and Table ronde sur la transparence et la saine gestion dans le secteur bénévole, « Consolider nos acquis : pour une meilleure gestion et transparence au sein du secteur bénévole au Canada, » rapport final (Ottawa : Groupe d'experts sur la saine gestion de la transparence dans le secteur bénévole, 1999).

References Not Appearing in the Endnotes

Direction des coopératives. « Données statistiques sur les coopératives de solidarité (données inédites). » Québec: Gouvernement du Québec, 2001 et 2002.

Girard, Jean-Pierre. "Social Cohesion, Governance and the Development of Health and Social Care Co-operatives." *Review of International Co-operation* 95, no. 1 (2002): pp. 58–64.

Thouin, D., et A. Mercier. « Création de coopératives de solidarité depuis juin 1997 (données inédites). » Québec: Direction des coopératives, Gouvernement du Québec, 2001.

PART THREE

APPLICATION

A scholar offers his reflections on the application of the issues raised in this book to current and future research and practice.

BRETT FAIRBAIRN

SETTING NEW DIRECTIONS

READERS WILL HAVE SEEN BY NOW that this book is a kind of dialogue of multiple voices—a dialogue that so far is tentative and incomplete, but full of hints and fragments of new ways of thinking, new knowledge, new policy, and new action. The voices are those of leaders and professional practitioners from different parts of the co-operative sector, as well as academics and researchers from many disciplines, institutions, areas of concern, and methodologies of inquiry, including both the theoretical and the empirical.

These pages are a transcript of an early stage in this process of discussion and inquiry. Here we have initial questions, off-the-cuff musings and off-the-shelf theories, experimental hypotheses, and plans for how to investigate what we don't know yet.

The preceding chapters have been logically ordered into four sections: general theoretical framing of issues by academics, questions posed by practitioners, more specific essays by specialists attempting to provide answers, and sketches of case studies and methodologies. To sum all this up and synthesize it, I would like to recast this book only a little, by positioning the practitioners' concerns as the true beginning point. Experience and the world are presenting questions here to the research community—questions that will be answered only by returning to the world to study it.

THE WORLD QUESTIONS ACADEMICS

The Canadian Co-operative Association (CCA)—the official apex organization for Canada's thousands of co-operatives and their more than ten million members—offers a number of issues for consideration, helpfully summarized in Karen Philp's paper and based in part on her consultations with others.

Typically, business trade associations (which is partly the function of the CCA) are self-promotional, boosterist, and protectionist of their turf. Anyone not familiar with co-operatives may be surprised, therefore, by the candor, self-questioning, and self-doubt evident in the co-op sector's reflections about itself. This self-questioning is interesting and important, but should not be read as a criticism of co-ops or of the co-op model. It is characteristic of co-operatives, certainly of many Canadian co-operatives, that they are humble—perhaps too much so—in their claims, wary of grandiose assertions (they have suffered in the past from excessive expectations raised by others), and practical in their approach. As Philp puts it, "Co-operators are driven by vision and values, yet are fundamentally pragmatic." People in co-ops seem to spend much more time thinking, What can we do next? How can we do this better? than they spend boasting about what they've done. Undoubtedly this contributes to a widespread underestimation of the movement.

The co-operators writing in this volume offer researchers an exceptionally open, honest, and heartfelt set of questions.

"We need to accept globalization as a fact of life, but we must try to make its effects more fair." The language used by many co-operatives, and accurately reflected and repeated by Philp, demonstrates a lack of enthusiasm for globalization. They "need" to accept it as a "fact"; they "acknowledge" that changes are "irreversible." By contrast, the statement that globalization provides opportunities as well as challenges is made with little passion. But to make globalization more *fair*: that is a large cause, a large concern, a mission for the future, something that co-operatives can actually do by their nature and not just "try" to do.

To observe the defensive or reluctant posture of co-operatives with respect to globalization is not to criticize that posture. It may make perfect sense, and if so, it will be important to understand it. Co-operatives may well discover that globalization is their mission and their future: to do something about it, to embody certain aspects of it, to stand up for fair and equitable forms of it. But the beginning, in 2004, is hesitant.

The CCA's questions are tough ones. *Are* co-ops effective? *Do* they help communities? *Can* they respond to globalization and keep their co-operative identity? *Do* they provide local solutions to globalization? Co-ops are assuming nothing. They are looking for examples, models, directions.

Bill Turner's chapter echoes Philp's questions even more pointedly. Turner, a former CCA president, stresses that "the bottom line for the co-operative is that it must contribute to the enhancement of its members' social and/or economic welfare, and it must do so in competition with other providers of goods and services." Established co-ops have to do this in the face of "rapid change that totally redefines the conditions under which they function."

Philp asks, "How do co-operatives grow to compete in a marketplace of increasing size and diversity, and yet make membership meaningful at the same time?" The question assumes that the pressure to change is in the market-place, and that growth in size is required. Membership is the passive or secondary term, the one that is acted upon and that has to adapt or be adapted to the new reality. It is the term whose meaningfulness is in doubt, whereas competition, the market, and growing size are not. Co-ops want help figuring out how to compete.

The "intuitive perception" of many co-operators is that member identity is weakening, that perhaps society as a whole is fragmenting and social cohesion is declining. The ground beneath their feet has become sand. In all likelihood this, too, is globalization, but whereas the answer to the problem of transnational competition seems obvious—size—the answer to weakening member identity is apparently not.

But how have we ever understood the strength of member identity, anyway? Perhaps in our perceptions, or our memories, we overestimate the homogeneity of co-op people? Perhaps we remember commonalities of a particular generation, which will of course not be shared by new generations who have other experiences? What is fascinating is that co-operatives, which are conceived as member-driven organizations, don't seem to feel their members are driving them anywhere—or perhaps, that different members are going in different directions, and some have driven off altogether.

Based on the sector's own research and its discussions and analysis, Philp writes, "Many co-operatives are perhaps challenged when it comes to articulating their uniqueness in their community." It isn't that co-ops don't do anything for their communities; the problem is that what they do is so taken for granted as to be overlooked even by the members themselves. This is a key problem for mature co-operatives that have been successful: They change their communities, they become part of them, and in so doing, they make their contributions invisible. One of the challenges of an era of societal transformation is to make the old fresh again—if indeed it is still relevant and worth renewing—by explaining it in new ways to new groups of people.

Co-operative Social Responsibility—as a variant on Corporate Social Responsibility (CSR)—is a potential solution that Andrea Harris examines at length in her own piece. Harris describes how she was attracted to co-operatives as a "compelling alternative for conducting business in a more socially just way." Her interest in justice seems similar to the CCA's question about making globalization more fair. Harris wants to know whether co-operatives are the vehicle for doing this. It is worth noting that Harris, who is younger than most senior co-op leaders, is apparently interested in co-operatives *because* of globalization and the potential of co-ops to be alternatives to the new dominant economic models. But like Philp, the tone of her essay is not one of certainty but rather of questioning whether this is true and, in Harris's case, how we can know it is true—how to measure justice, so to speak.

As Harris points out, many companies are working to implement CSR. The SIGMA project, the triple-bottom-line approach, the AA1000 framework she refers to, are models that exist and are being used. Perhaps co-operatives have an advantage in consulting their members and other stakeholders, in measuring, reporting on, and communicating their social, cultural, and economic successes. Where Harris ends up, coming full circle by returning to an original issue of co-operative identity, is with questions of democratic control and of member and employee participation. If co-operatives are indeed to have an advantage, they need to make better use of their democratic framework to achieve it and demonstrate it.

"Perhaps the issue is the divorce between ownership or membership ... and the real control or management of the organization," Philp comments. In today's postmodern context, how *do* large groups of people exert control over anything—a degree of control that they will accept as satisfactory?

Co-operatives that fail to keep their members' genuine support face serious risks. Philp illustrates these in her reference to demutualizations among the large agricultural co-operatives, a theme Turner also explores. According to him, the fate of the Prairie grain co-ops "raises ... fundamental issues" about whether members and their co-operatives can adapt to new circumstances and remain engaged with one another. Perhaps it is not surprising how many co-operators present the troubles and failures of this prominent sector as a backdrop for the questions co-operatives are asking themselves. The questions are not philosophical, or not *just* philosophical; they are a matter of survival.

Turner, from his perspective, stresses the importance of governance, leadership, and volunteerism; of business structure; and of member education and training. His essay makes a strong case for addressing issues of democracy and control by focussing on leadership development and orderly succession, but also on a strategy of avoiding centralization and instead networking "smaller, autonomous or semi-autonomous units" in which members and other stakeholders can be more involved.

From a different angle, Chris McCarville addresses many related, fundamental issues about membership relations and loyalty. Through her profile of Arctic Co-operatives Limited and achievements such as the Co-op Development Fund, and especially through the story of individual co-operative member and leader Annie Goose of Holman Co-op, McCarville illustrates a strongly based organization rooted in the realities of northern and Aboriginal communities. This is a success story, and one that other co-ops might study and learn from.

By introducing us to Annie Goose, McCarville presents a model of community life and service integrated in values, religion, and art.

This co-op story is about business but it is also about the trapline and the residential school, hardship and learning from Elders, the importance of historic rights and land claims, music and dance and crafts, all of this united by respect for the Creator. This story illustrates a model for a new kind of business, an Aboriginal business in a contemporary economy. It is about the past, its inescapable effects and its memory, but it is also about the future: values-based business, business tied to identities that are new/old and hybrid. Here is an example for people who are interested in what the resurgence of Aboriginal peoples may mean for Canada and for Canadian business. It is also an example of the new articulation of identities, one of the facets of globalization.

While Arctic Co-ops and its members constitute an important success story, McCarville nevertheless notes the challenge to "work hard to understand how co-op loyalty will transfer down to the next generation." Young people in the North may take their flourishing co-operatives for granted. Perhaps even Arctic Co-ops needs to study and learn from the difficulties faced by older southern co-operatives in order to prepare itself for future demands.

The practitioners who contributed to this volume raise many other questions. Philp also asks about partnerships, cross-border linkages, and social alliances: What kinds of external connections would help co-ops in this new environment? She wonders why some forms of e-commerce don't seem to be taking off among co-ops, specifically referencing the dot-coop Internet domain and its degree of adoption by Canadian commercial co-operatives. While at first glance it may seem odd for co-operatives to ask someone else why they are not adopting something—Why not ask themselves?—this is in fact a reasonable and significant question. Large co-operatives are complex organizations and their federations are comparatively decentralized and diverse. People in co-operatives may not understand why other co-ops make the decisions they do, or even why other parts of their own systems make certain decisions. Some co-operators are asking for help in understanding themselves and their processes, in this case the adoption of innovations.

Turner proposes that we consider the agenda of a board meeting of any large co-operative, and ask how much time the board spends understanding the larger processes that will help determine the survival and success of the organization. He goes on to discuss factors such as how members are being affected by change, how the co-operative can maintain its linkage to their new needs, and how they will identify with the co-operative under changed conditions. "People interact with the organization through its physical assets, which have given the co-op its identity in people's minds," Turner writes. But he presents the case of Mountain Equipment Co-op (MEC) to show that co-ops can have identities, in the minds of their members, across broad expanses—in MEC's case, most of the country—without having a physical presence in most places. MEC appears able to do this by speaking to a certain lifestyle and values (such as environmental responsibility and social justice) that enable members to feel connected both to each other and to the company regardless of location.

Turner actually begins his piece with a thought that makes a good conclusion to this section: Changes in society require "fresh approaches and … the formation of new co-operatives." There are two important meanings for us in this passage. One message is that sometimes old co-ops don't adapt very well; the co-op sector also adapts to change by the emergence of entirely new co-operatives. We should expect an age of globalization and of evolving processes and mentalities to be reflected in new co-operatives and new kinds of co-operatives, and part of our attention should be directed to where this is happening or can be encouraged.

We can also tease out a second meaning: Older co-ops that succeed will do so by becoming new. Co-operatives need to aim to transform themselves, not by throwing out everything they know, but by making modifications in the right ways to reconnect with changing members and communities.

ACADEMICS QUESTION THE WORLD

The first three essays in this book examine the stresses and tensions among the ideas of globalization, social cohesion, and democracy. Together, these pieces amplify the concerns of the practitioners, contextualize them within some larger issues, and suggest some alternatives for naming and defining what we need to know.

As William Coleman describes it, globalization is a pervasive and multifaceted phenomenon—a change in the nature of society. It is not simply about transnational corporations, business interests, and related international policies and institutions. In fact, the ways that people talk about, protest, and respond to corporate globalization are also forms of globalization. Coleman tells us, in essence, that we have to think for ourselves about globalization and cannot accept uncritically what any person or group tells us it means.

While globalization is often understood simply in popular discourse as a negative force—an emblem of people's powerlessness and of the erosion of established things—it is clearly a tendency that can be neutral, sometimes even good, rather than always bad. Sometimes it may empower. Globalization enables and requires us to engage our neighbours far and wide in the world, even while it sometimes divides us from those close at hand. It forces us to understand our environment and our economy in new ways, and to revisit our understandings of history, of politics, and of social identities, to confront things that were glossed over in more insulated, perhaps even parochial, past times.

The questioning of jobs, identities, and histories can be troubling, particularly for those with a small stake in the way things were, who were perhaps comfortable, but marginally so. For the small and middling in society, change is uncertain and alarming. By contrast, those with larger resources—the wealthy, the educated, the mobile—usually adapt quickly and benefit from times of rapid change. But we also shouldn't forget the excluded and the marginalized, those with little investment in mainstream society. Indigenous peoples see their past plight and present resurgence as a global phenomenon. They likely have little incentive to welcome transnational corporate capitalism, and yet in other respects, globalization may be welcome to people who were dissatisfied with the status quo of the recent past. It is no accident that activists in other social movements—the women's movement, gays and lesbians, and environmentalists, for example—see their causes as international.

To see global as bad is obviously a risky view for co-operatives or other organizations to adopt—not only because of the economic strength of globe-spanning competitors, but also because it disassociates co-operatives from the forces that are reshaping people's lives, and in some cases, motivating their thoughts and actions. In one sense, all organizations have to embrace the global, particularly if they believe in social change or community advancement—but not just anyone's global. As Coleman says, they have to embrace their own idea of it.

Co-operatives are nationally and globally networked; they undertake self-conscious community development and empowerment activities in other countries; they function in global trading systems and bring world products as well as new services and technologies to their members. Perhaps they need to play up and talk about these ways in which they are selective agents of chosen, intentional globalization. Co-operatives can have a public image of being globally aware and networked, while also serving their specific communities.

But there are also reasons why co-operative leaders and officials see globalization as a pressure, a problem, and a worry. Because globalization affects the members of co-operatives, it present co-ops with new realities to which they are compelled to adapt. Globalization is a re-ordering of human relations that cannot fail to pose challenges for existing organizations.

For co-operatives and other community-based organizations, a major issue is to what extent globalization does indeed mean "deterritorialization" of human relations, as some have suggested. Clearly, geographical distances and limits are less important than they once were. It is possible for co-operatives and other organizations today to have a vast geographic extent, within which members affiliate on the basis of nonterritorial identities based on shared values, lifestyle, and culture. But this may not mean locality is unimportant. Geographic communities will be remade in different ways—perhaps even with a "reterritorialization" on some scale. The decline or erosion of some local communities, through population movements and economic restructuring, will be accompanied by new districts and regions.

Note that globalization does not mean "anything goes," that organizations are cut loose from society or history, or that only their size matters. Organizations still have to be well adapted to their circumstances, their owners, and their stakeholders: they do not become disembodied simply because the world is more global. The form of their connection to social conditions, issues, communities, and identities has changed, but not the fact that they must be connected to succeed. Any co-operatives that divest themselves of old forms of member identification, such as the local/territorial bond, will have to replace that connection with some other kind of anchor in some different kind of community.

The speed with which certain large North American co-operatives jettisoned their pasts, and indeed their members, may help explain the difficulties they encountered. The fact that they may be losing their traditional connection to their former members does not mean co-ops can do without members.

Coleman draws our attention to "one of the most important questions of our time: What is the relationship between globalization and autonomy?" How will people have self-determined lives in a world of global forces?

My own chapter emphasizes not so much the word autonomy as related concepts of identities, cohesion, linkage, transparency, and cognition—the attributes and functions that allow a group of members to act autonomously within a co-operative. My purpose in stressing those ideas is to suggest that they are the kinds of things that need to be operationalized in co-operatives today and in the future. All of these words are about members. Linkage is about how the members and the co-operative serve each other economically. Transparency is about how the members understand the co-operative. Cognition refers to how the members and the co-operative can think, act, and change together, rather than growing apart.

Perhaps the key terms are cohesion and identities.

Social cohesion is an increasingly popular way of referring to what co-operatives used to call simply community. The important difference between the two terms is that social cohesion is purely a quality, a form of relationship among people, while the term community has multifaceted meanings and is often used to denote a place, a physical setting, a set of structures, and the people who live within them. It may be fitting that, in an era of globalization and of the remaking of territories and spatial relations, a new term emerges that carries less precise baggage. Would it make a difference to co-operatives—would it shake up their thinking—if they asked not, How do we serve our community? but rather, How do we promote social cohesion? Perhaps it would, but in any case, the new term is here to stay.

Cohesion is certainly something co-operatives need and feel is important. Witness the comments about members growing more heterogeneous, members and co-operatives growing apart from one another, and so on. But what creates cohesion?

One of the best prospects for understanding the dynamics of cohesion is to research member identities. What identities do members see themselves as having—as parent, worker, volunteer, for example, or as a member of a cultural or religious group? What identities do co-operatives have? And how do these interconnect?

People's identities rest on a combination of factors such as experience, memory, values, and choices or commitments. To take any of these things for granted—to assume that people will respond to the same appeal as in the past, for example, or that all people of a certain category are the same despite differing experiences and choices—carries with it a risk of fundamentally misunderstanding members and what is important to them.

Cohesion comes from overlapping or congruent identities, or such is the hypothesis. To the extent that people see themselves reflected in a co-operative, they feel connected to it. Shared values are central to this identification process. Crucially, different members will see things slightly differently. That needn't be a problem, provided they all feel attached and the co-op can maintain the coherence of its different meanings to different groups. We need to move to pluralistic and differentiated ways of thinking about co-op members, rather than stereotyping them.

Understanding members and who they are may, indeed, be the biggest challenge facing co-operatives in an age of social transformation.

Considerations of identities and cohesion are questions of experience, perception, image, and member relations, but Benoît Lévesque and his co-authors Patrick De Bortoli and Jean-Pierre Girard move on to what has often been considered the hard kernel of the co-operative identity: the democratic process. Locating their analysis within history, they see issues of social cohesion as questions made pressing by present-day trends such as social dislocation and the "ideological tidal wave" of neoliberalism. At the same time, they identify concern with social cohesion as a revival of the emancipatory themes of the European Enlightenment. In the modern era, while markets and states can do many things, they fail at the job for which the third sector is most suited: to generate the social bond.

Lévesque and his collaborators argue that co-operatives need all forms of democracy—representative, participatory, social, deliberative, and plural—but that they have been neglecting the deliberative variety. "Democracy consists not only of choosing but of offering the possibility of enlightened choices," they emphasize. To have deliberative democracy, members need to help decide what the questions are before they are asked to vote on the options.

A major issue for Lévesque et al. is that the common good or the general interest can get lost in a postmodern society where individual and collective interests are strongly articulated. We know what one individual wants or a certain group claims, but there is no wholeness. In effect, these writers are pointing out that society itself has the same kind of hollowness that the co-op practitioners were complaining about: What ties people together? Are they committed? Is there anything in particular that is good for the whole, or is it simply an aggregation of individual and collective egos? Is everything just flying apart or drifting away?

The member-involvement and democratic-participation problem of co-operatives is a microcosm of what is happening to society as a whole. This is yet another way in which co-operatives, struggling with their own dilemmas, are confronted with society's difficulties and called upon to address them.

Lévesque, De Bortoli, and Girard emphasize the importance of *deliberation* as a defining characteristic of the kind of democracy that is most lacking. People need to think. In order to think, they need to know about more than their own selves and self- or group interests. They have to know about bigger things, and they have to engage in processes of interaction that are mutually educative.

In the past, deliberation was something that happened in large open meetings, where people listened and took turns speaking. It is an open question whether that form of deliberation is suited to contemporary realities of time, travel, responsibilities, and expectations. At a minimum, what we still need are the intellectual processes of deliberation in the minds of members and leaders, however these processes may be structured or mediated by technology in a present-day setting.

To refer back to Coleman, *autonomy* is what members need—a place where they can participate meaningfully as individuals in questions and decisions that are bigger than the individual, that connect to and help define a common good of society.

The first three chapters in this book raise a number of important issues that co-operatives need to think about in devising their strategies and approaches for a global and postmodern age. Foremost among these is the necessity to understand **globalization** as a multifaceted phenomenon, and to recognize the key challenge of defining what **autonomy** means to people—how to achieve what they value—in a changed social order. Other ideas to consider include **cohesion**, a new and possibly more flexible way of thinking about what co-operatives have often denoted by "community"; **membership** (as a factor in linkage, transparency, and cognition); and **identities** of members. Finally, **democracy** remains a critical term for co-operatives, but one whose meanings and forms have been cast into disarray. Through what processes of **deliberation** will people articulate interests that are larger than themselves?

The most general and most important point that all of the researchers in this section make is that, in times of change, it is important to pay attention to ideas. Things we all think we know and understand turn out to be pitfalls; things we never see coming surprise us. These experiences are typical of eras of rapid social, economic, and cultural change.

Towards Some Answers

The nine authors and seven essays that address theory in part two of this volume provide a number of more specific ideas for investigating the kinds of questions posed by the co-op practitioners. The pieces in that section of the book are not about providing answers—though to some extent they do that—but rather how to go about finding answers.

Compare the contribution by Murray Fulton and Julie Gibbings —one that is strongly influenced by the social sciences and by economics in particular—with that of Isobel Findlay, which stems from the humanities and calls for greater attention to cultural studies. Both conclude (at the risk of oversimplifying) that it is critically important, today, for co-operatives to pay attention to how they think about what they do.

"Paradigm shifts ... have a habit of leaving elite interpretation in control," Findlay tells us. An illustration of her point is the way in which the end of the Cold War and the collapse of Soviet Communism have left the big, corporate version of capitalism as the often-unquestioned norm for economic life. The implication for co-operatives is that co-ops and what they stand for—their values, principles, and goals—will tend to be submerged and forgotten anew. Unless, that is, co-operatives pay renewed attention to how the world is named, in other words, to the culture and discourse that prevail in society. This is a moment for co-operatives to put energy into activities that influence how people think.

The most important thing co-operatives may be in danger of taking for granted is their members. As revealed in the practitioners' comments, people in co-ops are aware of economic competition, global corporatism, and other important trends in the market-place. Of course, co-operators know members are important, but by and large the academics in this volume are telling them they need to think harder and find out more about who their members are, what forces are affecting them, how their experiences are different from one another's, and how a co-operative can speak to their identities, needs, experiences, and differences. The academics appear to be united in stressing that co-ops need a profound understanding of what is going on in their members' lives. This is not simply a superficial question of what member-patrons think of particular, existing products or services.

Michael Gertler provides a reminder that membership needs to be investigated as a social process, not an either/or category; and Lou

Hammond Ketilson raises the idea that, in this investigation, we may need to reconsider the role that traditional understandings of co-operative values and principles play in how we thought about membership in the past. Isobel Findlay argues for the importance of imagination in times of social change, while Murray Fulton and Julie Gibbings stress the impact of cognitive processes in successful adaptation. Findlay as well as Wanda Wuttunee and Warren Weir point out that, particularly in Canada and in western Canada, we need to rethink our past as a colonial era and go beyond the old assumptions and structures, especially if we want to engage Aboriginal peoples respectfully. Leslie Brown writes about marketing and communications, and how co-operatives might more innovatively explain themselves; while Cristine de Clercy focusses on the importance of leadership, above all, on the difficult question of how leadership can represent diversity in an age when diversity is a pressing social reality.

Rather than summarize their points essay by essay, I will attempt to integrate these theoreticians' ideas around four overarching categories that indicate both what co-operatives need to think about and pay attention to, and also what needs to be researched to understand them better. These categories include rethinking membership in *space and time, diversity,* and *connections.*

Space and Time

It is striking how many of the issues raised by academics and co-operators alike are expressed in geographic terms—as questions of locality, globalism, and mapping.

Findlay refers to "the power of naming—of ways of mapping and remapping the world," as something that has disadvantaged co-operatives. She does not have in mind only literal mapping—how geographic communities are defined—though that is certainly one issue.

Globalization can be understood as a transformation in how people experience space and time. It is a process that makes remote things immediate and relevant to people in new ways. This may mean that the role of co-operatives in global processes is more important than before. Co-ops might have to get larger, or might have to position themselves as the alternative to the large size of others, or they might find it advantageous to associate themselves with international causes such as human rights or fair trade. These are all possible meanings of global processes becoming more immediate and more important to co-operative members.

At the same time, globalization changes local attachments, although it doesn't necessarily eliminate them. Co-operatives may become central to new local communities, regional ones perhaps, or may be connected in new and more complex ways. This won't just happen by itself. Regional community identities and attachments won't drop into co-operatives' laps, but will have to be painstakingly built and won.

Some co-operatives, to be sure (thinking back to Turner's example of Mountain Equipment Co-op), will be connected only in symbolic and indirect ways to many local places. We can imagine a member reasoning, the environment of my local place is an important part of my sense of attachment to it; MEC does good things for the environment, so my bond with my place is consistent with my support for MEC. In this way, I can work together with members elsewhere who care about their own locales.

Tying together any group, of course, means excluding or not encouraging others. Gertler comments, "Where belonging to a particular co-op or credit union reflects divisions along political, religious, or ethnic lines, membership may strengthen ties within a particular group, but reinforce separation between social groups and networks." Co-ops may need to be aware of how they divide people and of what implications this has. But this does not seem to be the most common situation. Gertler goes on, "In contemporary communities, co-operative memberships commonly span pre-existing social divides and link together some of the diverse strands that are present. Co-operative memberships thus reinforce and stabilize certain aspects of 'community of place.'"

Gertler also draws our attention to "temporal dimensions of membership," such as the length of membership, mix of new or long-term members, time of joining relative to events in the life of the enterprise, trends of growth or shrinkage over time, the time of joining relative to members' own ages, and the extent to which membership is reproduced between generations. "Achieving membership is a process that does not begin or end with the signing of a membership form," he reminds us. Membership can develop a momentum; it can be a vector, not a place where people park. The implication for co-operatives is to be asking constantly how to move their members on to the next level.

Diversity

Interestingly, Fulton and Gibbings observe that "lack of diversity in views and perspectives" may have contributed to huge failures in certain co-operatives, while de Clercy notes that co-operatives seem to generally lag behind other organizations in how much attention they pay to diversity. Together these observations provide a hint about where some co-operatives need to go.

These authors point out at least two important issues about diversity. The first is a question of representativeness and democracy—that co-ops need to represent their members and look as if they are representing their members. It is a handicap for a co-op that aims for the support of all kinds of people to be operated and governed by one kind of people, whatever that might be. This is one issue de Clercy addresses. Co-ops that are led mainly by middle-aged people, by men, or by white people, will not be completely credible in appealing for loyalty and support from other groups.

Fulton and Gibbings go a step further. Their preliminary results suggest that co-ops that are governed by a single mind-set have deficient cognitive processes. It's not simply that co-ops with insufficient diversity within the staff and leadership won't look good; beyond that, they may also be more prone to make catastrophic mistakes.

In a related point, de Clercy explains that functional diversity is more important than demographic diversity. In other words, it's not simply a matter of having a chart on which we can tick off the categories of people present in a meeting; it isn't enough to look around a room and see diversity, though that may be helpful. What's more important is that participants are able to speak to their individual experiences, to each bring something different to the meeting and feel authorized to present it.

Hammond Ketilson points out that attempts to define co-operative "distinctiveness" in a "purist" form have led to a rigidity and potential loss of supporters. In effect, an inflexible ("rigidity"/"rigid") concern with the co-operative character may have led to less diversity. Her question is whether the co-op principles, as such, are really what attracts people to the model. "What draws members to a co-operative? What holds members' loyalty?" Is it the principles, or are they only "like a secret handshake or whispered password" for the long-initiated?

"It is not enough to value co-ops because they are member-owned and democratic," Hammond Ketilson writes. "If member ownership is to mean anything, a co-operative or credit union must be more responsive than other organizations to the needs of members and consumers in general." She concludes that co-ops need to find some value or values that resonate with their particular community or communities of members. These need not be identical from co-op to co-op nor to the co-op principles.

Different groups of members may be looking for a variety of things. Gertler postulates that some younger, mobile members may be looking for anonymity. It would be easy to pay attention to the lowest common denominator, the least amount of "membership" that any of the members is willing to accept. "Membership issues and co-operative identity may fall below the consciousness threshold for many patrons and other stakeholders. This may be temporarily expedient for managers and may also reduce some of the potential points of conflict among diverse members."

In other words, co-operatives have to decide whether they really care about member commitment and engagement. If they do, they need to allow for different degrees and qualities of membership for different people. If they don't care about member commitment, it is up to them to redefine what it means for their organization to be a co-operative.

Connections

Co-operators and academics agree that the new environment for co-operatives is one in which many old categories and assumptions have been destabilized: co-operatives will experience members as more heterogeneous, communities as more fluid. If they wish to maintain member loyalty, they will have to connect in new ways with different groups of members, to create new common bonds among them.

Multiple contributors point to the general importance of communications, as well as to the need to make them more effective and more supportive of member loyalty.

Commenting that "the world is all but saturated with 'information' and 'communications,'" Brown writes about the many ways in which co-operatives need to use products, marketing, and communications in holistic ways to make connections with members. The implication is that co-operatives need an unusually strong and coherent message if it is going to get through and be heard. She cites examples of "Marketing the Co-operative Advantage," drawing on values, trust, unique ownership structures, and community rootedness; social auditing; and marketing based on character, relationships, or causes, among other possibilities. To make these approaches credible requires that co-operatives co-ordinate their marketing, public relations, human resources, and member relations behind a common message.

"In a postmodern, globalized information age," Findlay writes, "co-operatives have opportunities to press the co-operative advantage in resisting bureaucratic rationality, respecting diverse interests, re-imagining co-operative culture, and rebuilding interrelationships." One of the relationships co-operatives are called upon to rebuild, because of their principles but also because of the businesses many of them are in, is that between Native and non-Native peoples.

Hammond Ketilson, Findlay, Wuttunee, and Weir all address the question of how co-operatives will relate to Aboriginal peoples, a significant group, especially in the West. At least on a Canada-wide scale, Aboriginal peoples and issues do not rate prominently in the remarks of leaders of established co-operatives; and yet, to the extent researchers ever speak with a single voice, the academic research community appears to be saying that this is an area of importance.

The researchers are not thinking only about demographics—about Aboriginal peoples as customers and workers. They are considering the nature of the new Canadian society that is being created, about what will give co-operatives purpose in that society, about how their tasks will have meaning. Connecting with Native peoples is one of the ways in which co-operatives can demonstrate purpose and difference and contribute to a new kind of society in which co-ops are relevant and active on the most important issues of the day.

Are Aboriginal issues more important, in some sense, than environmental matters, global corporate concentration, gender issues, and other considerations of the present and future? Perhaps not, but they are immediate regional and national concerns where co-operatives can show leadership, but so far have not usually done so. This brings to mind Turner's comment that the co-op sector sometimes changes through the creation of new co-operatives rather than through the transformation of old ones. It will be interesting to see how old and new co-operatives learn to address Aboriginal realities in Canada.

Cases

In the context of these many questions and impulses towards answers, we also have three early case studies of co-operative research, all, as it happens, from Québec. What do these cases show about the ability of academics to approach the questions that matter in relation to co-operatives?

The three cases included here—one a finished product of past research and two that are sketches of current research—together address the questions of cohesion between co-operatives and their members, cohesion between co-operatives and geographic communities, and cohesion between social groups.

Daniel Côté examines the way that large dairy co-operative Agropur redefined itself through extensive member involvement and consultation. Even a large co-operative, Côté demonstrates, can renew the bonds of association among widely dispersed members. In this case, the key to success was a multifaceted process that included consulting members, decision making by members, and education and information for members. That this worked so well in Agropur's case may be a little surprising to some, since the dairy industry is a unique environment, a highly regulated setting in which members' pressures and interests are neither easy to judge nor unanimous. If a commercial co-operative of this size, in this setting, can use such techniques, then perhaps many other co-operatives can do so. At the same time, the case as presented here concludes on a note of indeterminacy. Côté presents it in an open-ended way, inviting readers to imagine themselves in Agropur's shoes—and reminding us of the uncertainty of decision making in the real world.

Côté's case illustrates many of the themes identified by other researchers. Clearly, his research bears out Brown's comments on the importance of a co-ordinated approach to marketing, information, and member relations, as well as illustrating Gertler's idea that co-operatives need to see membership as a process with many degrees and types of involvement, not as a given, either/or category. Perhaps most closely of all, Côté's presentation of Agropur shows what both Fulton and Fairbairn were describing as the processes of cognition in membership-based organizations: the formulation of strategy in such a way that members contribute and are brought along as the organization changes directions.

Mario Carrier raises the question of forestry co-operatives and their links to community economic development. Carrier's research sketch basically illustrates a dual conceptualization of innovation in locally based co-operatives. On the one hand, we are used to the idea that business developments, including those of co-operatives, have positive impacts on communities by creating jobs, income, and services. But on the other hand, Carrier opens up the idea that the success of co-operatives depends on inputs from communities and from outside. This includes "multiple institutional bonds" such as connections with regulatory régimes, the state, and large private forestry companies, but also networks and local associations within the community. Carrier proposes to investigate the idea that co-operatives can respond to globalization and contribute to the strengthening of communities by drawing on resources already extant within them, and most importantly on local networks and community identities.

Like Carrier's study of forestry co-ops, Jean-Pierre Girard and Patrick De Bortoli's chapter on social co-operatives is one of few in this collection explicitly to consider policy and regulatory frameworks. In this case, social co-operatives were made possible by a 1997 law that defined the option of multistakeholder coopératives de solidarité. Since then, more than a hundred of these have been created in Québec. Effectively, a statutory provision has facilitated or made possible new forms of partnership and governance in civil society. Such co-operatives are of extraordinary interest as alternative models to mesh volunteer activism and economic activity in an age when both of these are important policy interests.

Girard and De Bortoli also deploy the promising conceptual model of the CRISES (Centre de recherche sur les innovations sociales dans l'économie sociale, les entreprises et les syndicats) network: the concepts of new territorialities among co-operatives; the new roles of co-operatives in ensuring accessibility, employability, and democratization; and the significance of networking for their success. These new concepts, derived from intensive case-study research, are so far unfamiliar to most Anglophone co-operative leaders. In a practical sense, they provide signposts for how co-operatives can turn themselves into "new co-operatives" suited to an age of social and economic transformation.

The practitioners in this volume asked about how to respond to globalization, whether they could retain member support, how to explain the co-op difference, how to govern themselves, and how to make connections with people and communities, among other related questions. The case studies by Côté, Carrier, and Girard and De Bortoli show ways in which researchers can provide some answers. Co-ops can innovate, or new co-operatives can be created. Co-operatives can reconnect with members through multifaceted engagement strategies, and can reconnect with communities through networks and associations. They can adopt new structures, or make the existing ones work better. Though every co-operative and every set of communities may have its own variations, there are models and examples that can be studied to improve the odds of success.

Policy Implications

Together, the worldly-wise co-operators and the academics who share these pages lay out an important agenda for future research. While incomplete and preliminary, there is a foundation here for near-future studies of co-operatives that may answer some of the pressing questions of both co-operative leaders and academic researchers.

The case studies raise an important related question, one that the co-operative practitioners for the most part do not pose: What is the role in all this of government, of policy, of regulation? While it is too soon to present results, let alone recommendations, it is not too soon to speculate about the areas in which research may be desirable.

Existing co-operatives for the most part aspire to be left alone by governments and to be afforded the room and freedom to develop in the directions members authorize. Given their dedication to autonomy, it is clear that the basic stance of existing co-operatives will almost always be to resist legislative and programmatic interventions. Beyond the obvious reason for this—co-operatives work hard to amass resources in the name of the membership and have no desire to share control with officials or politicians—we can speculate that there may be a second element. As alternative enterprises, less well known than other forms of business, representing a minority of the economy and an even smaller percentage of economic lobbying, they may have good reason to expect that policy changes are more likely to disadvantage them than to favour them.

One recalls Findlay's comment that paradigm shifts favour the elites. Policy shifts often do the same. In the face of this, the less powerful often pragmatically favour stability and predictability, reminiscent of the peasants in *Fiddler on the Roof* who wish, God bless and keep the tsar ... *far away from us!*

This hints at a first insight: governments interested in adopting a more interventionist stance with respect to co-operatives had best demonstrate their good intentions tangibly and engage the sector fully in discussions before formulating policy. In many sectors, co-operatives are suspicious partners of government.

Many governments will not be bothered to spend time on sectors that would rather be left alone. Where they choose to, it will probably be because they are interested in what they see as a larger or wider objective, not because they are interested in co-operatives as such. The theory and case studies in this volume provide some good indications as to what these larger or wider objectives could be:

- enabling Canadians and their communities to have a stronger sense of autonomy and control within the context of adapting to globalization
- strengthening the sense of social cohesion within Canadian communities by enabling citizens to work together on common projects
- generating economic activities that are rooted in and support rural, urban, and northern communities that are not participating fully in conventional development
- setting higher standards among businesses for community accountability
- involving communities to provide higher-quality social, health, or other services, better suited to community needs

Governments that are interested in these and similar policy objectives may become interested in co-operatives as a means to these ends. The degree of interest may vary from case to case.

Ann Hoyt of the University of Wisconsin-Madison[1] has suggested that government policies towards co-operatives can be analysed in terms of a spectrum ranging from "destructive" to "controlling":

1. **Destructive policies** towards co-operatives have been carried out where régimes have attempted to restrict, suppress, or outlaw them. In general, such policies are associated with vicious, dictatorial régimes that have, for some reason usually connected to domestic political dynamics, identified co-operatives as enemies. Examples include Fascist Italy, the military dictatorship in Chile in the 1970s and 1980s, or Indonesia before the mid-1960s.

2. **Neutral policies** have been characteristic of many industrialized countries and involve—by intention or through ignorance—avoidance of both punitive and preferential treatment of co-operatives. "In effect," says Hoyt, "cooperative businesses operate in the same climate as all other businesses." This neutral-but-permissive attitude on the part of the state allowed early popular movements to create co-operatives in Britain, France, Sweden, and other countries, based on strong traditions of autonomy, self-help, and voluntarism.

3. **Supportive policies** have been enacted towards co-operatives where governments have recognized them as tools by which citizens can improve their condition. Hoyt describes supportive policies as involving removal of "artificial barriers to cooperative operations," passage of special legislation to make it easier to organize them, provision of education, research, and technical assistance. In this model, governments *encourage* co-operatives while leaving responsibility with the members for *initiating, developing, and operating* them. "Although the government may provide services and incentives, which make the cooperative an attractive form by which to conduct business, the government is not actively involved in the day-to-day affairs of the cooperative." Hoyt's examples include western European countries in the twentieth century, or Egypt since 1980.

4. **Participating policies** lead to direct government involvement in organizing co-operatives and in supplying them with capital and management. This situation is common in developing countries and has led to many recognized examples of excessive state control and failure of authentic co-operative action. Often, such policies result from trying to force a ready-made co-operative model, appropriate to modern industrialized societies, onto nonindustrialized societies, where the fit is poor.

5. **Controlling policies** exist where governments take direct, continuous control of co-operatives as tools to implement state policies. Typically, the régime controls the management and policy of the co-operatives and appoints or dominates the board of directors. Government policy interests dictate operational matters such as production, pricing, and marketing.

The debate for policymakers who are interested in co-operatives is whether governments should be 2. Neutral or 3. Supportive; and if supportive, then in what ways? And how do you ensure this assistance falls short of the excesses that have distorted and devalued co-operative action in many countries?

Hoyt's summary provides some important indications of what kinds of support governments can offer: encouraging co-operatives while not assuming state responsibility for initiating or developing specific co-ops; and removing artificial barriers. This includes special legislation (such as enabled the creation of social co-operatives), and—one would add to Hoyt—ensuring that larger policy frameworks allow room for co-operatives (such as forestry regulation, for example).

As Hoyt suggests, while governments might provide specific services and incentives, *research, education, and technical assistance* are the best areas for supportive state agencies to concentrate upon. As the contributions in this volume make clear, co-operatives require research, rethinking, innovation, and education of many actors. To assist them in these fundamental areas is likely the form of policy or program intervention that is least incompatible with co-operative principles of autonomy.

The degree to which policy and regulatory frameworks should encourage or compel co-operatives to act in community-enhancing ways is an unresolved tension. Several kinds of examples come to mind. The late twentieth-century federal co-operative housing program required housing co-operatives to maintain a certain income mix among residents in exchange for mortgage subsidies. That is one example of constraint. If demutualizations are a major policy concern, legislation could make demutualization more difficult, at the expense of restricting the decision-making power of members and the returns they might make. (Preliminary studies indicate that government policy, together with weak co-op sector institutions, contributed to the rash of demutualizations that occurred in Australia.[2] Some countries (Germany comes to mind) require co-operatives to be members of federations that can provide specialized auditing services, an obligation that both increases one kind of accountability and ensures a membership base for federations. One can imagine futures in which co-operatives might be required to have social audits.

Most of these kinds of interventions would not make sense unless co-operatives were advantaged or subsidized somehow. If the co-op form is given preferential treatment, the state may require in exchange that certain aspects of co-operative behaviour are followed in a mandatory way. Canada's general laissez-faire policy towards co-operatives goes together with the fact that most of them do not seem to be given any discernible preferential treatment.

A special case, from a policy standpoint, is provided by the restructuring of the state itself and of public services—another aspect of globalization. Co-operatives within highly regulated sectors such as health, education, or social services can only exist if government policies are supportive.³

The emergence of *social economy* in recent years—most prominently in Québec—represents an important new departure in the dialogue about policy, society, and development. While unfamiliar still to many Anglophone ears, the discussion of social economy is a renewed attempt to open up conventional categories, understand the role and importance of voluntary action by citizens, and find effective new ways to meet community needs. This discussion is highly relevant to co-operatives.

As one of the first studies on the subject revealed, co-operatives are an integral part of Canada's social economy. In fact, they are likely its most systematically organized and financially strongest component. Social economy may be defined as co-operatives, mutual enterprises, and nonprofits.⁴ Others would define social economy as the sector where enterprises exist to perform social functions, not only to make profits for owners—very much the way in which co-operatives have long seen themselves.

By understanding themselves as part of a social economy, with a resemblance to other social enterprises and some common interests and issues, co-operatives may open up new possibilities for development. What co-operatives may get from social economy is a new injection of purpose, direction, activism, and membership. What they may have to offer the social economy is generations of experience, for example with models of leadership, governance, and federation.

Whether or not all co-operatives come to see themselves as part of a social economy, it seems likely, given the prevailing definitions, that governments will increasingly see them as such, and that the interests of governments will most closely follow those co-operatives whose activities best correspond to social-economy goals.

The easiest policy future to imagine, then, is one in which governmental resources are focussed on research, education, and technical assistance for co-operatives generally; on co-operatives that have clearly evident connections to social-economy goals; and on those types of co-operatives (such as health and social co-ops) that are embedded in state-regulated sectors.

The degree to which co-operatives fulfil larger policy objectives will remain central to the treatment they receive from governments, and, in sectors where government policy is influential, to their survival and success. Social cohesion, as explored by the many authors in this volume, remains one of the promising areas where the activities of co-operatives, the research of academics, and the policy interests of governments overlap in significant ways. The voices represented on the preceding pages provide the beginnings for an exploration of this area of mutual interest.

Endnotes

1. Ann Hoyt, "Cooperatives in Other Countries," in *Cooperatives in Agriculture,* ed. David W. Cobia (Englewood Cliffs, N.J.: Prentice Hall, 1989), pp. 81–97; here, pp. 88–92. This summary of Hoyt's categories first appeared in Brett Fairbairn et al., *Co-operative Development and the State: Case Studies and Analysis,* 2 vols./4 parts (Saskatoon: Centre for the Study of Co-operatives, 2000).

2. See Garry Cronan and Jayo Wickremarachchi, *A Study of Co-operative Development and Government-Sector Relations in Australia,* part 4 of Fairbairn et al., *Co-operative Development and the State.*

3. See John Restakis and Evert Lindquist, eds., *The Co-op Alternative: Civil Society and the Future of Public Services* (Toronto: Institute of Public Administration of Canada, 2001).

4. Jack Quarter, *Canada's Social Economy: Co-operatives, Non-Profits, and Other Community Enterprises* (Toronto: James Lorimer & Co., 1992).

ABOUT THE AUTHORS

Patrick De Bortoli is a research assistant for le Centre de recherche sur les innovations sociales dans l'économie sociale, les entreprises et les syndicats, and also an MA student in sociology at the Université du Québec à Montréal.

Leslie Brown teaches in the Sociology/Anthropology Department at Mount Saint Vincent University in Halifax.

Mario Carrier is the head of L'École supérieure d'aménagement du territoire et de développement régional at Université Laval in Québec.

Cristine de Clercy is an assistant professor in the Department of Political Studies at the University of Saskatchewan as well as a research fellow at the Centre for the Study of Co-operatives.

William D. Coleman holds the Canada Research Chair on Global Governance and Public Policy and is the founding director of the Institute on Globalization and the Human Condition at McMaster University in Hamilton.

Daniel Côté is a professor of business strategy at L'École des Hautes Études Commerciales in Montréal.

Brett Fairbairn is head of the History Department and a research fellow with the Centre for the Study of Co-operatives at the University of Saskatchewan.

Isobel Findlay is an assistant professor in the Department of Management and Marketing, College of Commerce, and a research scholar with the Centre for the Study of Co-operatives at the University of Saskatchewan.

Murray Fulton is a research fellow at the Centre for the Study of Co-operatives, a professor in the Department of Agricultural Economics, and director of the Centre for Studies in Agriculture, Law, and the Environment at the University of Saskatchewan.

Michael Gertler is an assistant professor in the Department of Sociology and a research fellow at the Centre for the Study of Co-operatives at the University of Saskatchewan.

Julie Gibbings is a PhD candidate in the Department of History at the University of

Wisconsin-Madison. She completed her master's degree in history at the University of Saskatchewan in 2004.

Jean-Pierre Girard is associated with le Centre de recherche sur les innovations sociales dans l'économie sociale, les entreprises et les syndicats at the Université du Québec à Montréal co-ordinating that centre's contribution to the research project on which this book is based. He is a former executive director of the Confédération québécoise des coopératives d'habitation.

Lou Hammond Ketilson is acting head of the Centre for the Study of Co-operatives, where she also holds a position as a research fellow. In addition, she is an associate professor in the Department of Management and Marketing in the College of Commerce at the University of Saskatchewan.

Andrea Harris is a program manager with VanCity Credit Union's Sustainability Group, working on environmental and social inclusion initiatives. Prior to working with VanCity, Andrea was part of Mountain Equipment Co-op's Social and Environmental Responsibility team, where she managed MEC's community involvement and granting programs

Benoît Lévesque is a professor in the Sociology Department at the Université du Québec à Montréal and academic member of the Centre de recherche sur les innovations sociales dans l'économie sociale, les entreprises et les syndicats. He is the president of International Scientific Council of CIRIEC international.

Chris McCarville works as a co-operative development specialist with Manitoba Agriculture, Food, and Rural Initiatives. She is the former manager of Member and Public Relations at Arctic Co-operatives Limited in Winnipeg.

Karen Philp is the national director of the Office of Government Relations and Public Policy for the Canadian Diabetes Association. She is the former director of Government Affairs and Public Policy for the Canadian Co-operative Association.

Bill Turner is a farmer, an agrologist, and a co-operator. He is currently a member of the Co-operative Development Initiative Steering Committee for the Government of Canada. He is a past president of both Credit Union Central of Saskatchewan and the Canadian Co-operative Association. He is also a past vice-president of the Americas Region of the International Co-operative Alliance.

Warren Weir is the chair of the MBA Indigenous Management specialization and assistant professor in the Department of Management and Marketing in the College of Commerce at the University of Saskatchewan.

Wanda Wuttunee is an associate professor in the Department of Native Studies at the University of Manitoba. She is Cree and a member of Red Pheasant First Nation, Saskatchewan.